ETHICS OF THE SOUL

Many blessings!

R' Eli Yosser

ETHICS OF THE SOUL

Uplifting and Relevant Commentary on
Ethics of the Fathers פרקי אבות

Rabbi Dr. Eli Yoggev

ISBN: 9798757169651

לעילוי נשמת

ר׳ מרדכי הערשל ז״ל
בן
שמואל דוד וזיסל

Marc Howard Messing
Husband, Father, Brother, Zaide

מקבל את כל האדם בסבר פנים יפות
רצון קונו עשה כרצונו בכל כחו
דרש טוב לעמו ודבר שלום לכל זרעו
כתר שם טוב עלה על ראשו
ישר בכל הליכותיו ומעשיו

העמיד תלמידים הרבה ועמל עמהם באהבה
עמד בנסיונות וקבל יסורים באהבה ובאמונה
רינה ושירה לבורא עולם כשעמד לפניו בתפילה בכונה
שמש תלמידי חכמים ולמד מכל מלמדיו
לב טוב. עין טובה. שכן טוב. חבר טוב.

נלב״ע
י ניסן תשפ״א
June 24, 1953-March 23, 2021
תנצב״ה

Batsheva and Shimmy Messing
and Family

5

INTRODUCTION

The genesis of this book goes back to a 2008–2009 weekly study session on *Ethics of the Fathers* (*Pirkei Avot*—פרקי אבות) with my father, Uri Yoggev. I would email him a source sheet, each week on a different teaching, from my now-defunct Hotmail account, and we would delve deep into the topics together. The learning was very enjoyable, and it was a great way for us to stay connected while I lived in Israel, six thousand miles away from my Philadelphia home. This book is dedicated to you, Dad, for all your love, support, and direction all these years. You teach me "Ethics of the Fathers" on a daily basis. I am grateful to have you as a father and a friend.

The actual composition of this book began in April 2020 as our community went into quarantine in Baltimore, Maryland, because of COVID-19. At the time, there were congregants at my shul, Beth Tfiloh Congregation, who were looking for a way to honor their loved ones, on yahrzeits or over their year of mourning, absent from an in-person kaddish option. In response to this need, I began writing one commentary a day to a mishna (recorded teachings from the oral tradition, third century CE) from *Ethics of the Fathers* (a collection of mishnas on ethical matters) and sent them out in daily emails to these congregants. They learned the mishna and its commentary and dedicated the learning to their loved one's memory. This writing continued for the many weeks we were out of shul. When we finally returned in person, I had written almost half of my commentary to *Ethics of the Fathers*. This pushed me to continue writing whenever I could find time amid a full congregational rabbi schedule: late at night, early in the morning, and on vacations—until I finally, baruch Hashem, completed the book.

A few elements stand out in this commentary. Since this work began as a rabbi writing to his congregants while we all were at home without anywhere to go, I worked hard to offer new interpretations to the mishnas to help keep my congregants' interest and stimulate their minds. As a result, if you read closely, you will find many new directions that have not been offered in the past. Additionally, since we all were struggling in the beginning of the pandemic to find purpose and meaning, I included many personal reflections and stories to offer hope and inspiration, several of which are connected to my own teshuva (repentance) process.

Upon publishing this book, I deliberated on whether to remove them or not. I decided to leave them in because they add a personal touch and help elucidate important ideas in the text. I did, however, aside from one commentary (see 3:9), remove all overt references to COVID-19 (see also 5:11). Another aspect that stands out in this commentary is a clear dialectic between a modern and a spiritual outlook on the world. In my own life, I often toggle between both worlds; this is sharply felt in the commentary. Throughout the book, I map out ways to be both involved in the modern world while also remaining deeply spiritual and religiously connected.

Many of my religious influences can be felt as one reads this work. One such influence is Rabbi Avraham Yitzchak HaKohen Kook (1865–1935). I was first introduced to his writings at the Machon Meir Yeshiva (Jewish seminary) in 1997. His thinking has inspired mine ever since. Another thinker who left his mark on my outlook, and subsequently on this book, is Rabbi Mordechai Leiner (1801–1854). His work, the *Mei Hashiloach*, was the topic of my doctoral dissertation. If you read closely, you will recognize his teachings on cultivating a direct connection with Hashem and ascertaining Hashem's will for us in the present moment reverberating from the text. Rabbi Kenny Cohen, my rabbi, always taught me to be honest, to stay balanced when it comes to spiritual growth, and to work on myself and my relationships. His life guidance and Torah teachings permeate this book. Lastly, my own experiences as a ba'al teshuva (penitent) and God-seeker helped me arrive at understandings which are developed throughout this work.

I owe many thanks to those who assisted with this project. Rabbi Chai Posner, the incoming senior rabbi at Beth Tfiloh Congregation, came up with the idea for writing a commentary a day and pushed me to keep with it for those first months. His support for this project and of me from the beginning of my career as a rabbi has been empowering and edifying. Rabbi Mitchell Wohlberg, our senior rabbi, always put his faith in me and in this project. I am grateful for his support and rabbinic mentoring over the years. I was honored that Dr. Zipora Schorr, director of education at Beth Tfiloh Community Day School, reviewed an early version of this manuscript. Her honest and insightful feedback greatly enhanced the work. Dr. Renee Koplon, Mrs. Sheri Knauth, and Rabbi Dr. Jonathan Rosenbaum offered many wise suggestions and edits, which were incorporated into the text. Thank you to Rabbi Claire Green for her multiple reads and editing of the text, to Elite Authors for the final rounds of editing, and to Mr. Paul Miller for the perfect cover design.

The publication of this book could not have been possible without the generous financial support of Mr. Shimmy and Mrs. Batsheva Messing. Thank you for believing in this project. This book is also dedicated to Shimmy's father of blessed memory, Rabbi Marc Howard Messing. Marc was a seeker of truth according to the words found in *Ethics of the Fathers*, and he dedicated his life to sharing these beliefs with his family and the countless students he taught. May his memory be a blessing for all those he knew and loved.

My good friend Label HaKohen Casden has been at my side every day as I worked on this and other projects throughout my life. Thank you for always being there, *yedidi*. My family has always been supportive and encouraging. I wish you many years of blessing and good health from the bottom of my heart! And a big thank you to all the rabbis and mentors who have offered guidance and taught me Torah over the years, from my early days at yeshiva to my years in rabbinical training. Todah rabbah.

Finally, Hashem has been so kind to me. I remember thinking about passages of this book while sitting in the "Gush" library (at Yeshivat Har Etzion, Alon Shvut), while walking on the streets of Jerusalem, and while teaching the topic over the years. Hashem has so graciously helped me put it all together in this book. It is such a blessing! "מקימי מעפר דל"—He lifts the poor from the dust" (Ps. 113:7). Hashem has lifted me up so many times. Baruch Hashem, may we all merit to lift each other up and bring each other closer to the *Ethics of the Fathers*.

(This is the folder my father has kept on his desk since 2008 with all of the *Ethics of the Fathers* study sheets I forwarded to him for our shared learning.)

(The following introduction to the daily study sheets was sent to our congregants at the beginning of COVID-19 when we were not able to daven together and recite kaddish for our loved ones. The original study sheets included guiding questions for further review.)

Ceremony in Place of Kaddish
(For a yahrzeit and for those in mourning)

Over the generations, our Sages have suggested many ways to help commemorate the memory of our loved ones. One central practice is the recitation of kaddish. However, when one is unable to recite kaddish, other potent options are also available.

It is traditional to learn mishna in honor of the soul. This can be seen in the word "mishna" (משנה) which contains the same letters as נשמה, "the soul." Prayer is also powerful and, of course, giving tzedakah as well. Therefore, each day we will be offering this ceremony, which incorporates all three, to stand in place of kaddish—until our daily minyan resumes. Of course, you should still daven three times a day and are encouraged to join our daily mincha-mariv call-in, which will incorporate a kel maleh (memorial prayer) for the yahrzeits of the day as well as a dvar Torah [a brief Torah lesson].

Open the service with a prayer (listed below) and a chapter of Tehillim. Each day we will provide a different mishna with brief commentary and guiding questions. Read the mishna in either English or Hebrew or both and review the commentary. If it so interests you, answer the guiding questions as well. Then, set aside any amount of money for tzedakah in honor of your loved one.

Innovation and Tradition

מֹשֶׁה קִבֵּל תּוֹרָה מִסִּינַי, וּמְסָרָהּ לִיהוֹשֻׁעַ, וִיהוֹשֻׁעַ לִזְקֵנִים, וּזְקֵנִים לִנְבִיאִים,
וּנְבִיאִים מְסָרוּהָ לְאַנְשֵׁי כְנֶסֶת הַגְּדוֹלָה. הֵם אָמְרוּ שְׁלֹשָׁה דְבָרִים: הֱווּ
מְתוּנִים בַּדִּין, וְהַעֲמִידוּ תַלְמִידִים הַרְבֵּה, וַעֲשׂוּ סְיָג לַתּוֹרָה.

Moshe received the Torah at (lit., from) Sinai and transmitted it to Yehoshua, Yehoshua to the elders, the elders to the prophets, and the prophets to the Men of the Great Assembly. They said three things: Be patient in [the administration of] justice, raise up many disciples, and make a fence around the Torah.

According to the mishna, Moshe received Torah "מסיני," which means "from Sinai." It should have read "בסיני," "at Sinai." Why this unique language? It hints at Moshe's humility, a prerequisite for learning and transmitting Torah (see *Tiferet Yisrael* ad loc.). Moshe received Torah "from a place of Sinai," of humility. The Sages share that Sinai was the lowest of all mountains (*Midrash Tehillim* 68). To truly ensure the proper transmission of our tradition from generation to generation, we must humble ourselves and accept what those before us have shared.

The language used in the continuation of the mishna is "raise up many disciples." Why not just say "teach many disciples?" The reason is that in education it is not enough to simply "teach" or to transfer knowledge. We must encourage our students to stand on their own two feet and implement the teachings independently. The mishna asks us to "raise up many disciples" so that they are able, on their own, to live a full life based on Torah values. This is true at home as well as the workplace.

Why the Mitzvot Didn't Make
It onto the Top Three List

שִׁמְעוֹן הַצַּדִּיק הָיָה מִשְׁיָרֵי כְנֶסֶת הַגְּדוֹלָה. הוּא הָיָה אוֹמֵר: עַל שְׁלשָׁה דְבָרִים
הָעוֹלָם עוֹמֵד: עַל הַתּוֹרָה, וְעַל הָעֲבוֹדָה, וְעַל גְּמִילוּת חֲסָדִים.

Shimon the Righteous was one of the last of the men of the Great Assembly. He used to say: The world stands upon three things: the Torah, the Temple service/prayer, and acts of loving-kindness.

The three forms of service mentioned in the mishna point to three areas in which we serve Hashem: in relation to ourselves, to Hashem, and to others. In Hebrew, this is called "בין אדם לעצמו, בין אדם לה', ובין אדם לחברו." Learning Torah fixes the individual; the Temple service, with all that it entails, is pointed directly to Hashem; and acts of lovingkindness are performed with others. We must be strong on all three fronts.

It's interesting that the mishna does not include "the mitzvot" on this top three list. When I was a young yeshiva student, I had a period where I would ask many different rabbis why this was the case. I must have asked this same question to fifteen or so rabbis. I was interested in the answer, of course, but also found it fascinating to see how each rabbi processed the question. I learned a lot from these answers. A common answer I received was that the concept of mitzvot is a general category. It includes all three of these actions prescribed by the mishna. Therefore, it didn't belong on this list of three specific mitzvot in our mishna.

The answer that I connect to the most, however, is based on a teaching of the Maharal (*Netivot Olam*, Netiv HaTorah 17). The Maharal explains that the Torah is spiritual: its learning is done in one's mind not by engaging all of one's body. The mitzvot, on the other hand, involve the body: eating matzah, putting on tefillin, and lighting candles. When listing things upon which the world stands, Shimon the Righteous discusses primarily spiritual matters. If the topic was "Through which three things is the world corrected and/or elevated?" the mishna instead would have gone into specific details that deal with the body and our physical world.

The Perils of Entitlement

אַנְטִיגְנוֹס אִישׁ סוֹכוֹ קִבֵּל מִשִּׁמְעוֹן הַצַּדִּיק. הוּא הָיָה אוֹמֵר: אַל תִּהְיוּ כַעֲבָדִים הַמְשַׁמְּשִׁין אֶת הָרַב עַל מְנָת לְקַבֵּל פְּרָס, אֶלָּא הֱווּ כַעֲבָדִים הַמְשַׁמְּשִׁין אֶת הָרַב שֶׁלֹּא עַל מְנָת לְקַבֵּל פְּרָס, וִיהִי מוֹרָא שָׁמַיִם עֲלֵיכֶם.

Antigonus, a man of Sokho, received [the oral tradition] from Shimon the Righteous. He used to say: Do not be like servants who serve the master in the expectation of receiving a reward, but be like servants who serve the master without the expectation of receiving a reward, and let the fear of heaven be upon you.

One could read our mishna as discouraging "lower" forms of worship that focus on reward and punishment, instructing us to only serve out of love and deep reverence for Hashem.

However, the language employed in the mishna points to a different message. In describing reward, the word פרס is used instead of the commonly used שכר. The word פרס alludes to a prize. Based on this, it is okay to expect a reward (שכר) for our actions. This is predicated upon our belief in Hashem's faithfulness in rewarding those who live a Torah life.

What is discouraged, however, is the service of Hashem for an *extra* prize—when one expects to receive more than one deserves. This can remove the individual from true fear of Hashem, as one finds oneself never satisfied but always demanding more than one deserves from

Hashem. In place of this attitude, we are instructed to "let the fear of heaven be upon you."

This is an important lesson in life. When we do not feel entitled but instead strive to earn the good we enjoy in life, we are led to contentment. We do not feel let down when our unrealistic expectations from others are not met. And then when we do ultimately benefit from "prizes" the universe sends our way, we receive them with joy and appreciation.

1:4

Rabbis Are Human Too!

יוֹסֵי בֶּן יוֹעֶזֶר אִישׁ צְרֵדָה וְיוֹסֵי בֶּן יוֹחָנָן אִישׁ יְרוּשָׁלַיִם קִבְּלוּ מֵהֶם. יוֹסֵי בֶּן יוֹעֶזֶר אִישׁ צְרֵדָה אוֹמֵר: יְהִי בֵיתְךָ בֵּית וַעַד לַחֲכָמִים, וֶהֱוֵי מִתְאַבֵּק בַּעֲפַר רַגְלֵיהֶם, וֶהֱוֵי שׁוֹתֶה בְצָמָא אֶת דִּבְרֵיהֶם.

Yosi ben Yoezer a man of Tzeredah and Yosi ben Yochanan [a man] of Jerusalem received [the oral tradition] from them [i.e., Shimon the Righteous and Antigonus]. Yosi ben Yoezer used to say: Let your house be a house of meeting for the Sages and sit in the very dust of their feet, and drink in their words with thirst.

In describing our attitude to scholars, the mishna uses the language "והוי מתאבק בעפר רגליהם," which translates to "sit in the very dust of their feet." The text could have relayed the same message by saying: "והוי יושב בעפר רגליהם," replacing the word "מתאבק" with the common "יושב" to connote sitting.

The *Ruach Chaim* commentary on *Ethics of the Fathers* offers a wonderful explanation. The root א-ב-ק means "struggle." (When read as a noun, it means "dust.") Yosi ben Yoezer tells us that with all our welcoming and hosting rabbis, our "drinking in with thirst" their words of Torah, we do not have to blindly accept what they tell us. We should "מתאבק," struggle and grapple, and if things don't make sense, ask, and push back when necessary.

There may be, however, another layer here. The mishna discusses the "dust of the rabbis' feet." This shows us that no matter how holy a rabbi is, they are still human. Maybe they only have a small flaw, represented by the feet here—the lowest part of the body. And perhaps it isn't even that bad; it is only the "dust" of the feet. Nevertheless, we have to recognize that everyone is subject to mistakes and all-too-human reactions. Once we recognize this and are open to sifting through what may not fit for our own spiritual growth ("מתאבק"), we can then appropriately "drink in their holy words in thirst."

1:5

Open Homes and Open Hearts

יוֹסֵי בֶּן יוֹחָנָן אִישׁ יְרוּשָׁלַיִם אוֹמֵר: יְהִי בֵיתְךָ פָתוּחַ לִרְוָחָה, וְיִהְיוּ עֲנִיִּים בְּנֵי בֵיתֶךָ, וְאַל תַּרְבֶּה שִׂיחָה עִם הָאִשָּׁה. בְּאִשְׁתּוֹ אָמְרוּ, קַל וָחֹמֶר בְּאֵשֶׁת חֲבֵרוֹ. מִכָּאן אָמְרוּ חֲכָמִים: כָּל זְמַן שֶׁאָדָם מַרְבֶּה שִׂיחָה עִם הָאִשָּׁה, גּוֹרֵם רָעָה לְעַצְמוֹ, וּבוֹטֵל מִדִּבְרֵי תוֹרָה, וְסוֹפוֹ יוֹרֵשׁ גֵּיהִנֹּם.

Yosi ben Yochanan, a man of Jerusalem, used to say: Let your house be wide open, and let the poor be members of your household. Engage not in too much conversation with women. They said this with regards to one's own wife; how much more [does the rule apply] with regards to another man's wife. From here the Sages said: As long as a man engages in too much conversation with women, he causes evil to himself, he neglects the study of the Torah, and in the end, he will inherit Gehinnom [i.e., Hell].

In the previous mishna, we learned how Yosi ben Yoezer spoke about hosting Torah scholars in one's home. Here, Yosi ben Yochanan speaks more generally, with a focus on the poor. Why the shift in emphasis? Yosi ben Yoezer lived in Jerusalem. This was a center filled with Torah sages. Therefore, he emphasized hosting everyone. Yosi ben Yochanan lived in Tzeredah, an area without as many scholars; therefore, he talked about making one's house a "gathering place" for scholars.

On a deeper level, Yosi ben Yochanan wanted to highlight that amid all of one's Torah learning, one must still make helping others a priority. I once heard a lovely explanation to the blessing we recite on the Haftorah: "אשר בחר בנביאים טובים." It discusses how Hashem "chose good prophets." This is a peculiar statement! Would we expect Hashem to choose anything but "good" prophets?

Rather, the message is that there is a danger when it comes to being involved in high frequencies of spirituality. This can sometimes lead one to become reclusive and disconnected from others (see *Shemonah Kevatzim* 1:75). Our prophets were not like that. They remained "good people" who were kind and welcoming to others. Yosi ben Yoezer was warning those in Jerusalem, a center of Torah, to remember to be kind to others; to let their homes be wide open; and perhaps to use this opportunity to share their Torah with others who need it.

The mishna offers precise guidance on how to properly "open our homes." In discussing hosting those who are in need, the language that is used is "בני ביתך," literally, "children/members of your household." It is one thing to host and welcome those in need. It is another to allow them to feel "at home." Yosi ben Yochanan is telling us to do all we can to make those who are visiting feel at home rather than feel like they are merely "visitors." This translates to finding out which foods they enjoy and the songs they like to sing (if it's a Shabbos meal), showing interest in their lives, and letting them know you care. These are just a few suggestions for making those who you are hosting feel like בני ביתך.

Our mishna continues the discussion on home life by addressing how Torah scholars should properly engage in dialogue with their spouses. Pay close attention: the mishna speaks of "אל תרבה שיחה," engaging in "too much" conversation with one's wife. Nowhere does it say, G-d forbid, that one should not speak with one's spouse! It may be offering guidance to the rabbinic figures of Jerusalem to distribute their time wisely. For them to properly serve the community as Torah leaders, they must find the proper balance between Torah learning and home life.

Yosi ben Yochanan may also be sending a message to anyone looking to enhance and strengthen their spousal relationship at home. Small talk is extremely valuable to the connection. It can be an expression of affection and serve as a springboard to deeper conversations. However, when we engage in too many superficialities with our spouse, we end up zapping the life out of our connection. Our mishna warns against this in saying, "Don't engage in too much superficial conversation ('אל תרבה שיחה')"! Otherwise, we will "cause evil to ourselves, neglect the study of the Torah, and inherit Gehinnom." Instead, we must make the most of our time together and use it for spiritual growth and building a strong home based on Torah values. The sanctity of the home is one of the foundations of a strong religious life. Too much of anything that does not contribute to this lofty goal is worth distancing ourselves from.

Making Space for Others

יְהוֹשֻׁעַ בֶּן פְּרַחְיָה וְנִתַּאי הָאַרְבֵּלִי קִבְּלוּ מֵהֶם. יְהוֹשֻׁעַ בֶּן פְּרַחְיָה אוֹמֵר:
עֲשֵׂה לְךָ רַב, וּקְנֵה לְךָ חָבֵר, וֶהֱוֵי דָן אֶת כָּל הָאָדָם לְכַף זְכוּת.

Yehoshua ben Perachiah and Nittai the Arbelite received [the oral tradition] from them. Yehoshua ben Perachiah used to say: Appoint [lit., make] for yourself a teacher, and acquire for yourself a friend, and judge all people with the scale weighted in their favor.

Our mishna uses the term "make" when it comes to a teacher and "acquire" when it comes to a friend. A possible explanation for this is that when it comes to friends, we must allow space for all their sides, good and bad. It's like going to a store and "acquiring" something. We do not create the items in the store; we accept what is on the shelf and choose to purchase things the way they are.

When it comes to one's rabbi, however, it's not a completely leveled-out relationship. One can expect to take more from the rabbi than one gives. To some extent, one can "make" the connection into what one wants. (Just remember to be gentle with your rabbis!)

Unfortunately, many often get these orientations mixed up. On the one hand, they don't take the initiative to "make" the most out of their connections with their rabbi. And on the other, they forget to respect their friend's space and to allow for all of their sides, turning the relationship into a more of a one-sided connection. Our mishna reminds us to keep the proper order, and when it comes to acquaintances, "all people," to have even less demands—to be kind and to judge everyone favorably.

1:7

Distancing Ourselves from Toxic Relationships

נִתַּאי הָאַרְבֵּלִי אוֹמֵר: הַרְחֵק מִשָּׁכֵן רָע, וְאַל תִּתְחַבֵּר לָרָשָׁע, וְאַל תִּתְיָאֵשׁ מִן הַפֻּרְעָנוּת.

Nittai the Arbelite used to say: Keep a distance from an evil neighbor, do not become attached to the wicked, and do not abandon faith in [divine] retribution.

Some explain the connection between the three suggestions in this mishna as encouragement to distance oneself from an evil influence. It may look like everything is working out in life for an evil neighbor and a wicked person. Nevertheless, don't be drawn after them and their ways. Divine retribution awaits them commensurate with their bad actions.

However, another possible understanding reads the last word about פרענות differently: as not referring to retribution but rather to tough times (פרענות can denote a general calamity or tough situation). Often, it takes a heroic effort to remove oneself from a negative influence (e.g., a tough work environment or a toxic personal relationship). There is often something that just draws us in, and the fear of losing whatever "this" is can make it all the harder to create distance.

The mishna is instructing us to do whatever we can to separate from a bad neighbor or an "evil" influence. We're instructed to not worry about the emptiness and void, the inner פרענות, that will inevitably be experienced upon doing so. Why not? When one makes this step toward positivity, one frees up space that was previously occupied by the negative influence. This space is then open to be filled, God willing, with positive experiences and influences. When one door closes, another more positive door opens.

Divorcing Ourselves from
False Narratives

יְהוּדָה בֶן טַבַּאי וְשִׁמְעוֹן בֶּן שָׁטָח קִבְּלוּ מֵהֶם. יְהוּדָה בֶן טַבַּאי אוֹמֵר: אַל תַּעַשׂ
עַצְמְךָ כְעוֹרְכֵי הַדַּיָּנִין, וּכְשֶׁיִּהְיוּ בַעֲלֵי דִינִין עוֹמְדִים לְפָנֶיךָ, יִהְיוּ בְעֵינֶיךָ כִּרְשָׁעִים,
וּכְשֶׁנִּפְטָרִים מִלְּפָנֶיךָ יִהְיוּ בְעֵינֶיךָ כְזַכָּאִין, כְּשֶׁקִּבְּלוּ עֲלֵיהֶם אֶת הַדִּין.

Yehudah ben Tabbai and Shimon ben Shatach received [the oral tra-
dition] from them. Yehudah ben Tabbai said: Do not [as a judge]
play the part of an advocate; and when the litigants are standing before
you, look upon them as if they were [both] guilty; and when they leave
your presence, look upon them as if they were [both] innocent, when they
have accepted the judgment.

Our mishna teaches us (as judges) not to feed arguments or advice
to the litigating parties: "[D]o not [as a judge] play the part of an advocate." This happens all the time. We, as judges of "cases" in our lives,
want to view them in a certain way, to color them so they will fit into
our own internal narrative. We are told to abstain from doing so and
rather listen *objectively* to the litigants—to assess facts and life situations
for what they really are. This will allow the truth to surface and enable
us to work toward ensuring a greater good emerges.

Rabbi Joseph Dov Soloveitchik has a strong piece in *Kol Dodi Dofek*
where he touches on this point in relation to bad things that befall us:
"Judaism, with its realistic attitude toward man and his position in the

universe, understood that evil cannot be blurred or covered up...Evil is a fact that cannot be denied."

The facts are the facts, and they should not be covered up. We must accept realities for what they are and then work from there to help address or remedy them. This is what Rabbi Soloveitchik instructs us to do in relation to evil. After putting forth his "realistic" attitude, as quoted above, he encourages transforming our current reality, our "fate," into one of "destiny"—a proactive and positive direction of growth. This form of growth is only possible when we judge life objectively with all the pain and discomfort this may entail.

How to Serve Hashem with Both Inclinations

שִׁמְעוֹן בֶּן שָׁטָח אוֹמֵר: הֱוֵי מַרְבֶּה לַחְקֹר אֶת הָעֵדִים, וֶהֱוֵי זָהִיר בִּדְבָרֶיךָ, שֶׁמָּא מִתּוֹכָם יִלְמְדוּ לְשַׁקֵּר.

S himon ben Shatach used to say: Be thorough in the interrogation of witnesses, and be careful with your words, lest from them they learn to lie.

The *Sfat Emet* teaches that we always have two witnesses testifying and pleading their case before us: our good and evil inclinations. Many texts in our tradition explain how despite their distinct titles, neither inclination is completely good or evil.

The "evil" inclination can be good if we channel it toward good. For instance, being angry is usually not a good thing. However, if someone is upset and angry about an injustice they witnessed in the world and this propels them to act, this can be positive. The Sages hinted at this when they said we must serve Hashem with both of our inclinations, the good and evil ones (*Mishna*, Berachot 9:5).

Similarly, the good inclination can at times be detrimental. I had a friend at yeshiva who became very religious in a short amount of time. I remember seeing him learn in the study hall until the very late hours of the night. I was actually a bit envious of this at the time. It turns out he was missing Shacharit (morning prayer services) every day to keep a rigorous study schedule. This may have been a case of too much "good" inclination because it was making him miss daily minyan. Let me share another example. Giving to others is a good thing, but overwhelming someone with giving can at times be bad and not well received.

It's all about balance. This is the message of the mishna. Be careful to scrutinize the "witnesses"—both the evil and good inclinations. See what is good and evil in each of them and choose the correct path. Without this interrogation, our inclinations will be "learning to lie" and deceiving us into thinking they are always correct.

1:10

Why We Must Love Work

שְׁמַעְיָה וְאַבְטַלְיוֹן קִבְּלוּ מֵהֶם. שְׁמַעְיָה אוֹמֵר: אֱהַב אֶת
הַמְּלָאכָה, וּשְׂנָא אֶת הָרַבָּנוּת, וְאַל תִּתְוַדַּע לָרָשׁוּת.

Shemayah and Avtalion received [the oral tradition] from them. Shemayah used to say: Love work, hate acting the superior, and do not attempt to draw near to the ruling authority.

Shemayah and Avtalion promoted working and earning an honest living: "Love work!" Why is it so important to "love" work? There are various answers to this question.

On a practical level, later on in *Ethics of the Fathers* (3:21), we learn that "If there is no flour, there is no Torah." Work is what enables one to live a proper Torah life. When one's basic survival needs aren't met ("flour"), one can't serve Hashem properly ("Torah").

On another level, the more we work, the more mitzvot we can perform with the money we earn. I have a friend who prays to Hashem for extra work so that he can have more money to give to tzedakah. This is a praiseworthy way of approaching one's livelihood. For these reasons and more, we should love work!

Additionally, when one understands that being financially independent is a value, one will come to love work. Hashem is independent. Earning a living, when viewed against this backdrop, can be a way to emulate Hashem. The mishna is perhaps hinting at the idea that we should see work not only as a necessity but as a welcome way to emulate Hashem.

Finally, in his book *The Duties of the Heart* (Gate of Trust, ch. 3), Bachya Ibn Pakudah gives us advice on choosing a profession. We are taught that we must feel connected to what we are doing and be physically fit and inclined to do so (compare *Ha'emek Davar*, Exod. 36:2). This may be hinted at in our mishna in the words "love work." Make sure you choose a profession that you love and are connected to. This "love for work" serves as a sign that you are in line with Hashem's plan for you and your contribution to Hashem's world.

1:11

Be Careful to Inspire the Next Generation!

אַבְטַלְיוֹן אוֹמֵר: חֲכָמִים הִזָּהֲרוּ בְדִבְרֵיכֶם, שֶׁמָּא תָחוּבוּ חוֹבַת גָּלוּת וְתִגְלוּ לִמְקוֹם מַיִם הָרָעִים, וְיִשְׁתּוּ הַתַּלְמִידִים הַבָּאִים אַחֲרֵיכֶם וְיָמוּתוּ, וְנִמְצָא שֵׁם שָׁמַיִם מִתְחַלֵּל.

Avtalion used to say: Sages be careful with your words, lest the penalty of exile be incurred, and you be carried off to a place of evil waters, and the disciples who follow you drink and die, and the name of heaven becomes profaned.

The Torah is eternal. However, its applications and teachings must be adapted to fit each generation's needs and temperament. This is important for rabbis to understand. Unfortunately, I had to learn this the hard way. When I first started out as a rabbi, I thought that I could teach Torah in the same way I delivered presentations in university. Was I wrong! Teaching in an academic setting is very different from a Torah class or a Shabbat sermon.

When I first got going, I would simply read off the material to my audience. People started to fall asleep! Academics and synagogue attendees don't always have the same interests and styles of learning. That's when I realized I must tailor my teachings specifically to my crowd and make the information engaging and accessible. Now, my congregants don't sleep (well, aside from my high schoolers...), and my classes are lively. This is the message of the mishna: rabbis, be careful to adapt your words to your audience! If not, you will lose their interest, "the penalty of exile will be incurred," and they won't grow properly in Torah.

This message is relevant for us as parents, grandparents, and educators. What worked for us when we were younger doesn't always suit today's generation. It's important for us to figure out what our pupils' interests are, even if this takes a bit of time, so we can relate to them on their level. When we do this, we have a better chance of influencing them and keeping them connected to their heritage.

Based on this understanding, we can explain the chain of events in our mishna: 1) not being careful with words, 2) exile, 3) being carried off to a place of evil waters, 4) disciples who follow drinking and dying, 5) and the name of heaven being profaned.

Rabbi Avraham Yitzchak HaKohen Kook witnessed a lot of heresy in his days. Unlike many of his rabbinic colleagues, he wasn't overly critical of these individuals. The opposite was the case: he looked for the inner good in what he saw. One of his famous quotes highlights this: "The truly righteous [lit., the pure righteous ones] do not complain about evil, but rather add justice; they do not complain about heresy, but rather add faith; they do not complain about ignorance, but rather add wisdom" (*Shemonah Kevatzim* 2:99).

Rabbi Kook's way of "adding faith" as a response to heresy was to teach Torah that resonated with the new generation. In particular, he thought that the new generation needed to be inspired by big ideas. Many rabbis in his generation didn't realize that this was one of the causes of heresy. As a result, Rabbi Kook produced some of the more awesome Torah, with an emphasis on national pride, universalism, and so much more. This brought many Jews closer to Torah, and, due to his efforts, a movement was formed in Israel: the National Religious movement.

This is one way to read the mishna. If we do not provide an uplifting presentation of Torah filled with inspirational messages (not being careful with words), our generation will leave the fold (exile) and entertain heretical messages (place of evil waters). This will cause a snowball effect: people will think this is all the Torah has to offer and continue in these heretical ways, suffering spiritually (disciples follow, drink, and die). Instead of adding faith, the opposite will have occurred: they will have moved away from our faith (the name of heaven is profaned).

Rabbi Kook's guidance is still relevant for us today. We must show our generation that there are amazing things and lofty ideals in our sacred religion. When we do so, we will be adding faith, strengthening the youth's connection to our heritage, and sanctifying the name of heaven.

1:12

Drawing Others Close through Love

הֶלֵּל וְשַׁמַּאי קִבְּלוּ מֵהֶם. הֶלֵּל אוֹמֵר: הֱוֵי מִתַּלְמִידָיו שֶׁל אַהֲרֹן, אוֹהֵב שָׁלוֹם וְרוֹדֵף שָׁלוֹם, אוֹהֵב אֶת הַבְּרִיּוֹת וּמְקָרְבָן לַתּוֹרָה.

Hillel and Shammai received [the oral tradition] from them. Hillel used to say: Be of the disciples of Aaron, loving peace and pursuing peace, loving humankind and drawing them close to the Torah.

When it comes to the final guidance in our mishna, "Loving humankind and drawing them close to the Torah," Rabbi Tzvi Yehuda Kook points out that success in outreach lies in our ability to reach out to others from a place of authentic love. Notice, the text does not say that we love others *in order to* bring them close to Torah. Instead, we love others, and as a natural result, they draw closer to Judaism and the Torah.

I see this all the time in my work. People are looking for connection and love—sometimes more than Torah instruction. Once there is a bond and trust, they feel safe and open to instruction I may have to offer. This is relevant for us as parents and educators. It's best to stay away from shortcuts and invest time in relationships! You never know when someone will be ready to connect to Torah. Keep up the connection, if you can, and just show them love. Be there for them. When they are ready to return to Torah, you will then be able to help them through the process.

Another direction to take this teaching is to say that "drawing others close" to Torah can happen as a result of their witnessing observant folk living a life full of love and happiness. This is partially what attracted me to a more observant lifestyle at age eighteen. The love and togeth-erness I experienced in yeshiva and witnessed at Shabbos tables was something I wanted in my life. Those positive experiences propelled me forward in my religious transformation. This is another way to read the mishna. Live a life full of unity and love for humankind, and onlookers will appreciate what they see and naturally draw closer to Torah.

The Detrimental Effects of Improper Torah Usage

הוּא הָיָה אוֹמֵר: נָגֵד שְׁמָא, אָבֵד שְׁמֵהּ. וּדְלֹא מוֹסִיף יָסֵף,
וּדְלֹא יָלֵיף קְטָלָא חַיָּב. וּדְאִשְׁתַּמֵּשׁ בְּתָגָא חֲלַף.

He [Hillel] used to say: One who makes their name great causes their name to be destroyed; one who does not add [to their knowledge] causes [it] to cease; one who does not study [the Torah] deserves death; one who makes [unworthy] use of the crown [of learning] shall pass away.

Our mishna is comprised of four directives that appear to increase in severity as the mishna progresses—both in negative behavior and its accompanying punishment. It begins with someone who makes their name great, who seeks out honor. Their name will be destroyed. It then proceeds to someone who doesn't grow in knowledge. They will lose their knowledge, something more precious than a name. One who doesn't study Torah, our "tree of life," has detached themselves from life and is "deserving of death"—an even more serious outcome.

One who doesn't study Torah is still able to come closer to Torah; they aren't "dead," just "deserving" of death. However, someone who misuses the Torah "shall pass away." Why such a dire fate? When someone uses the Torah for negative purposes, it is much harder for them to come back to Torah and mitzvot. I imagine this referring to a case where someone scorns the Torah or uses the Torah to assert power and control over others. The whole purpose of the Torah is to share good and elevate people. Scorning and abusing the Torah for power is the opposite behavior.

Nobody knew this more than Hillel, the author of our mishna, a truly kind and generous person. The Torah "crowns" us with many spiritual blessings. The purpose of this is for us to share with others. If the outcome of abusing the "crown" is so dire, the inverse, positive effect must be the case for those who use their "crowns" for good. May it come true for all of us.

1:14

The Divinity in Our Whole Being

הוּא הָיָה אוֹמֵר: אִם אֵין אֲנִי לִי, מִי לִי, וּכְשֶׁאֲנִי לְעַצְמִי, מָה אֲנִי. וְאִם לֹא עַכְשָׁיו, אֵימָתָי.

He used to say: If I am not for myself, who will be for me? But if I am only for myself, what am I? And if not now, when?

Why must one be both for oneself and for the other? Isn't the ideal in Judaism to be selfless? On the most basic of levels, if we don't take care of ourselves and our health, there will be no "self" at all to help others. This is pretty straightforward.

On a deeper level, many are familiar with the famous verse: "Love your neighbor as yourself" (Lev. 19:18). From here we learn that love for self—"as yourself"—is a prerequisite for loving one's neighbor. Why so? It's natural to project our feelings toward ourselves onto others. The outside world then reflects back to us what we don't like in ourselves, and we respond to the world based on this reflection. It is therefore crucial to increase love for self. Then the opposite will be the result: we will overlook others' shortcomings and project our inner love outward.

A final answer dismisses the premise of the question altogether, relaying Hillel's endorsement of self-care for its own sake, not just for the sake of others. This is based on the belief that our whole being, both body and soul, is an expression of the divine. Here is a source (*Avot de Rebbe Natan* (second version) 30) that puts forward this idea in the name of Hillel:

When Hillel would go somewhere, they would ask him: "Where are you going?" He would answer, "I am on my way to do a mitzvah." "Which mitzvah, Hillel?" "I am going to the bathroom." "And is this surely a mitzvah?" "Yes. In order to upkeep my body." "Where are you going, Hillel?" "I am on my way to do a mitzvah." "Which mitzvah, Hillel?" "I am on my way to the bathhouse." "And is this surely a mitzvah?" "Yes. In order to wash my body."

"Know that this is true. Just as is the case with statues erected in the courtyards to kings [which are replicas of the kings], where those appointed to wipe and scrub them are annually awarded a *selira* by the king and not this alone but they are also adorned with the grandeur of the kingship—all the more so with us who were created in the *tzelem* [image of Hashem] and the *demut* [likeness of Hashem], as it is written, 'In the *tzelem* of God Adam was created' (Gen. 9:6)!"

There is an important lesson to be learned from the statue analogy: even our bodies are expressions of the divine. It is not enough to see the divinity in others; we must view ourselves as divine beings as well! One of my rebbes once overheard me speaking disparagingly about myself. He immediately interceded and shared that the laws of Lashon Hara (evil speech) apply not only to others but also to ourselves! He knew what Hillel did: We all carry the divine within us. We must in turn honor ourselves and treat ourselves kindly: "If I am not for myself, who will be for me?"

1:15

A Little Smile Goes a Long Way

שַׁמַּאי אוֹמֵר: עֲשֵׂה תוֹרָתְךָ קֶבַע, אֱמֹר מְעַט וַעֲשֵׂה הַרְבֵּה,
וֶהֱוֵי מְקַבֵּל אֶת כָּל הָאָדָם בְּסֵבֶר פָּנִים יָפוֹת.

Shammai used to say: Make your [study of the] Torah a fixed practice; speak little but do much; and receive all people with a pleasant countenance.

One can discern an inner connection undergirding Shammai's three statements. One must learn Torah ("make Torah a fixed practice") and be constantly involved in mitzvot ("speaking little but doing much" in terms of mitzvot). However, this shouldn't lead one to forget to be a nice person. We must always remember the third directive: "Receive all people with a pleasant countenance." We must, amid our frumkeit (deep religiosity), make time to smile at people and let them feel important and wanted.

When I first became more observant at age eighteen, I remember walking so enthused through a very religious Jerusalem neighborhood. I was elated to have found a home in Judaism and in Eretz Yisrael and to be a part of this group. So I decided to just smile and say hello to everyone I saw on the street. True story. Unfortunately, hardly anyone answered me, and this lowered my spirits. From then on, I decided to receive others, especially those who greet me first with hello, with a pleasant countenance.

From my experience, this really makes a difference. You never know what people are going through and how a simple smile can change their day. It's admirable to be very religious, but included in this is giving off good energy to those around us. If you and I do it, and the next person follows suit, we can cause a chain reaction, transforming our world into a happier and kinder place.

Make Yourself into a "Rabbi"

רַבָּן גַּמְלִיאֵל הָיָה אוֹמֵר: עֲשֵׂה לְךָ רַב, וְהִסְתַּלֵּק מִן הַסָּפֵק, וְאַל תַּרְבֶּה לְעַשֵּׂר אֹמָדוֹת.

Rabban Gamaliel used to say: Appoint a rabbi for yourself, avoid doubt, and do not make a habit of tithing by guesswork.

The mishna instructs us to appoint a rabbi for ourselves. One can have rabbis for different purposes. I have a rabbi who I go to for advanced halachic questions. I have another rabbi with whom I discuss personal matters. It is important, as many note, to have consistency with these specialist rabbis and not just "shop around" for answers we want to hear.

The directive "עשה לך רב" ("make for yourself a rabbi") can also be creatively read (this is not the simple reading) as "make *yourself* into a rabbi." No, this doesn't mean you have to go to rabbinical school for five years or that you should decide on all matters of *choshen mishpat* law (and if you don't know what that is, then you *really* shouldn't be deciding on it!). But I once heard that although our main halachic guide, the Shulchan Aruch, consists of only four volumes, a fifth volume can and should be accessed: common sense. Finding a rabbi or rabbis is critical, but we are also allowed to use common sense and decide things for ourselves if we are properly informed.

The term "rabbi" here can at times include an online site. This in no way should take the place of a "live" rabbi. One can pick up on how rabbis think and approach things from spending time around them. They add layers of depth and nuance one can't find online. One also learns about customs and behaviors that cannot be learned in front of a screen. Additionally, rabbis provide much more than data: they are spiritual conduits (see videos of the Lubavitcher Rebbe with his followers, for instance) and great sources of emotional support.

For all these reasons and more, one should appoint themselves a rabbi. Nevertheless, at times, it's fine to find a quick answer to one's question online from a reputable site. This can save time and lead, with the newly acquired knowledge, to better targeted halachic searches in the future, which are positive things.

1:17

Speak Up When Others Are Suffering

שִׁמְעוֹן בְּנוֹ אוֹמֵר: כָּל יָמַי גָּדַלְתִּי בֵין הַחֲכָמִים ,וְלֹא מָצָאתִי לַגּוּף טוֹב אֶלָּא שְׁתִיקָה. וְלֹא הַמִּדְרָשׁ הוּא הָעִקָּר אֶלָּא הַמַּעֲשֶׂה. וְכָל הַמַּרְבֶּה דְבָרִים מֵבִיא חֵטְא.

Shimon, his son, used to say: All my days I grew up among the Sages, and I have found nothing better for a person (lit., for the body, *guf*) than silence. Study is not the most important thing, but actions. Whoever indulges in too many words brings about sin.

Our mishna opens speaking about silence and the body. The simple reading is that one benefits the body by remaining silent. Perhaps this is speaking about a general quieting of the body's drives, such as intermittent fasting, which can prove helpful for the body or maybe it means that staying quiet can keep one out of trouble and out of the public eye, which can protect one's physical body.

The *Tiferet Yisrael*, however, offers an alternative reading. Instead of reading it as "nothing better for the body than silence," he reads it as follows: "I have not found it good for the body to remain exclusively in silence," (placing a comma after *laguf* as in: "לֹא מָצָאתִי טוֹב לַגוּף, כָּאשׁר האדם בשתיקה בלבד"). In other words, remaining silent *is not* beneficial to the body. Based on this explanation, we can highlight a strong message for us as individuals and communities who are witness to physical suffering in our midst. Even if we are among the wisest of people ("among the sages")—in committees or focus groups assigned to tackle a specific social issue—if we see an injustice that is not getting proper attention in our group, we must speak up and try to make a difference. "Remaining silent" in these instances can bring great harm to the "bodies," to the physical welfare of those who being affected. It can be scary and difficult to push back against "sages," experts in a field or just a general groupthink or consensus; however, this must not deter us from speaking our truth.

When we finally do speak up in a group setting, sometimes members of the group, intentionally or unintentionally, shift our practical suggestions into theoretical discussions, distancing us even more from our goal of alleviating suffering. Our mishna reminds us, therefore, to keep the focus on actions: "Study [i.e., theoretical discussions] is not the most important thing, but actions!" The more we shift from the practical to the theoretical and allow ourselves to "indulge in too many words" and theorize instead of acting, the more we "bring about sin"—negative consequences—for all of us as a community.

There is no excuse for remaining silent when others are in danger or being harmed. We must bravely push back against obstacles to proactive change.

Just Courts are the Foundation of Society

רַבָּן שִׁמְעוֹן בֶּן גַּמְלִיאֵל אוֹמֵר: עַל שְׁלשָׁה דְבָרִים הָעוֹלָם עוֹמֵד [נ״א: קַיָּם]: עַל הַדִּין,
וְעַל הָאֱמֶת, וְעַל הַשָּׁלוֹם, שֶׁנֶּאֱמַר (זכריה ח): אֱמֶת וּמִשְׁפַּט שָׁלוֹם שִׁפְטוּ בְּשַׁעֲרֵיכֶם.

Rabban Shimon ben Gamaliel used to say: On three things does the world stand: on justice, on truth, and on peace, as it says: "Execute the judgment of truth and peace in your gates" (Zech. 8:16).

There is a fascinating midrash (*Breishit Rabbah* 8:5) which discusses a dispute between angels upon the creation of humanity. The angels of *chesed* (lovingkindness) and *tzedek* (righteousness) argued that humans should be created: the angel of *chesed* said people will perform acts of lovingkindness, and the angel of *tzedek* argued that people will do righteous deeds. *Emet* (truth) and *shalom* (peace), on the other hand, said that humans should not be created. *Emet* said people are full of falsehood; *shalom* said people are all strife.

It's interesting to note that our mishna lists only two of these four values, and they are the two that argued against the creation of humans: *emet* and *shalom*. And it says that based on these two, along with *din*, the justice system, the world stands! How do we make sense of this?

What perhaps might provide a solution is the third value mentioned in our mishna: *din*, the justice system. With a proper system in place, the concerns of *emet* and *shalom* are mitigated. An ideal justice system is meant to decrease falsehood and strife. This can be understood in the most basic of ways: when the courts pass their judgment, truth is implemented, and strife is diminished as the case approaches some form of a resolution.

This can also be a reminder to members of our court system to not rule based on strife and falsehood. When courts do not liberate themselves from this, the system itself is faulty and doesn't have a leg to "stand" on. For our world to "stand" and progress, we must have just and fair courts who do not plot for benefit, whose rulings do not discriminate or marginalize but rather promote truth and peace for every single person in our society.

Doing the Honorable Thing

רַבִּי אוֹמֵר: אֵיזוֹהִי דֶרֶךְ יְשָׁרָה שֶׁיָּבֹר לוֹ הָאָדָם? כֹּל שֶׁהִיא תִפְאֶרֶת לְעוֹשֶׂיהָ וְתִפְאֶרֶת לוֹ מִן הָאָדָם. וֶהֱוֵי זָהִיר בְּמִצְוָה קַלָּה כְּבַחֲמוּרָה, שֶׁאֵין אַתָּה יוֹדֵעַ מַתַּן שְׂכָרָן שֶׁל מִצְוֹת. וֶהֱוֵי מְחַשֵּׁב הֶפְסֵד מִצְוָה כְּנֶגֶד שְׂכָרָהּ, וּשְׂכַר עֲבֵרָה כְּנֶגֶד הֶפְסֵדָהּ. וְהִסְתַּכֵּל בִּשְׁלֹשָׁה דְבָרִים וְאִי אַתָּה בָא לִידֵי עֲבֵרָה. דַּע מַה לְמַעְלָה מִמְּךָ: עַיִן רוֹאָה, וְאֹזֶן שׁוֹמַעַת, וְכָל מַעֲשֶׂיךָ בַּסֵּפֶר נִכְתָּבִין.

Rabbi [Yehuda Hanasi] said: Which is the straight path that a person should choose for themselves? One which is an honor to the person adopting it and accrues honor to them from others. And be careful with a light commandment as with a grave one, for you do know not the reward for the fulfillment of the commandments. Also, reckon the loss [that may be sustained through the fulfillment] of a commandment against the reward [accruing] thereby, and the gain [that may be obtained through the committing] of a transgression against the loss [entailed] thereby. Apply your mind to three things and you will not come into the clutches of sin. Know what there is above you: an eye that sees, an ear that hears, and all your deeds are written in a book.

The mishna is depicting three levels of worship in descending order. It begins with someone doing the right thing for the right reasons. This person wants to do what is honorable in their own eyes as well as in the eyes of others ("accrues honor to them from others"). The mishna then proceeds to someone who is less motivated by doing the right thing. This individual must remember the effects of their actions: reward and punishment ("be careful with a light commandment"/"reckon the loss").

There is a third person for whom both methods don't work. This individual must remember that God is always watching and hearing ("apply your mind to three things").

All three are valid, but we must strive for the first level: to be motivated by doing the honorable thing in life. In one of my yeshivas, Yeshivat Har Etzion ("The Gush"), this was the general attitude. They did not offer a lot of mussar schmoozes (an often impassioned talk on how to refine our character, highlighting what we are doing wrong and need to fix...). The rabbis encouraged and trusted us to do the honorable thing. I like to think this was effective, although I always do love a good mussar schmooze!

Honestly Assessing Our Needs and Inclinations

רַבָּן גַּמְלִיאֵל בְּנוֹ שֶׁל רַבִּי יְהוּדָה הַנָּשִׂיא אוֹמֵר: יָפֶה תַלְמוּד תּוֹרָה עִם דֶּרֶךְ אֶרֶץ, שֶׁיְּגִיעַת שְׁנֵיהֶם מְשַׁכַּחַת עָוֹן. וְכָל תּוֹרָה שֶׁאֵין עִמָּהּ מְלָאכָה, סוֹפָהּ בְּטֵלָה וְגוֹרֶרֶת עָוֹן. וְכָל הָעֲמֵלִים עִם הַצִּבּוּר, יִהְיוּ עֲמֵלִים עִמָּהֶם לְשֵׁם שָׁמַיִם, שֶׁזְּכוּת אֲבוֹתָם מְסַיַּעְתָּן וְצִדְקָתָם עוֹמֶדֶת לָעַד. וְאַתֶּם, מַעֲלֶה אֲנִי עֲלֵיכֶם שָׂכָר הַרְבֵּה כְּאִלּוּ עֲשִׂיתֶם.

Rabban Gamaliel the son of Rabbi Yehudah Hanasi said: Excellent is the study of the Torah when combined with a worldly occupation (lit., *derech eretz*), for toil in them both keeps sin out of one's mind; but [study of the] Torah which is not combined with a worldly occupation, in the end comes to be neglected and becomes the cause of sin. And all who labor with the community, should labor with them for the sake of heaven, for the merit of their forefathers sustains them (the community), and their (the forefathers') righteousness endures forever. And as for you [God in such case says], I credit you with a rich reward, as if you [yourselves] had [actually] accomplished [it all].

The mishna's term "תורה עם דרך ארץ" (*Torah im derech eretz*) points to a connection between Torah and the ways (*derech*) of the world/earth (*eretz*). Many times, this worldly involvement is depicted as one's livelihood, reminding us to combine Torah learning with a proper means for earning a living. We touched on this topic in an earlier mishna (*Ethics of the Fathers* 1:10).

In his writings, Rabbi Shimshon Raphael Hirsch extends this definition, describing the word *eretz* as referring to our "existence in this world" and all that results from this. For Rabbi Hirsch, *derech eretz* can mean proper social order, etiquette, civil education, and more:

> *Derech eretz* includes everything that results from the fact that man's existence, mission, and social life is conducted on Earth, using earthly means and conditions. Therefore, this term especially describes ways of earning a livelihood and maintaining the social order. It also includes the customs and considerations of etiquette that the social order generates, as well as everything concerning humanistic and civil education. (Commentary on *Ethics of the Fathers* 2:2)

In another place, he expands the definition to include art, science, and culture:

> [Thus] the more the Jew is a Jew, the more universalist will be his views and aspirations [and] the less aloof will he be from...art or science, culture or education... [and] the more joyfully will he applaud whenever he sees truth and justice and peace and the ennoblement of man. (*Religion Allied to Progress*)

If we accept Rabbi Hirsch's broader definition, how might this be an effective way to "keep sin out of one's mind?" For one who has a genuine interest in this world—in culture, art, science, etiquette, and more—engagement in the world plugs them into something that they enjoy and brings them happiness. We must be honest with ourselves and discern our needs. When these needs are met and these inner inclinations find their place in our lives, we can more comfortably and excitedly live a life full of Torah and *yirat shamayim* (fear of heaven).

2:3

Don't Overindulge in the Permitted

הֱווּ זְהִירִין בָּרָשׁוּת, שֶׁאֵין מְקָרְבִין לוֹ לָאָדָם אֶלָּא לְצֹרֶךְ עַצְמָן. נִרְאִין כְּאוֹהֲבִין בִּשְׁעַת הֲנָאָתָן, וְאֵין עוֹמְדִין לוֹ לָאָדָם בִּשְׁעַת דָּחְקוֹ.

Be careful [in your dealings] with the ruling authorities for they do not befriend a person except for their own needs; they seem like friends when it is to their own interest, but they do not stand by a person in their hour of their distress.

An interesting explanation to this mishna, mentioned in *Midrash Shmuel*, suggests the word רשות, which we translated as "ruling authorities," refers to areas in Jewish law which are permitted to us (the word רשות also means "permission"). The mishna instructs us to be careful not to overindulge in permitted areas of Jewish law (eating, watching sports, shopping, etc.) because in our hour of distress, when we need to tap into a spiritual source for strength and inspiration, these endeavors will not be there to help us.

There is something to this. The previous mishna, based on the teachings of Rabbi Hirsch, told us to be involved in the world. We must enjoy what's permitted to us! This mishna instructs us to not lose track and stay connected to Torah. We need these spiritual reservoirs to tap into in our "hour of distress."

Becoming One with Hashem's Will

הוּא הָיָה אוֹמֵר: עֲשֵׂה רְצוֹנוֹ כִרְצוֹנְךָ, כְּדֵי שֶׁיַּעֲשֶׂה רְצוֹנְךָ כִרְצוֹנוֹ. בַּטֵּל
רְצוֹנְךָ מִפְּנֵי רְצוֹנוֹ, כְּדֵי שֶׁיְּבַטֵּל רְצוֹן אֲחֵרִים מִפְּנֵי רְצוֹנֶךָ.

He used to say: Make His will like your will, so that He will make your will like His. Nullify your will in the face of His will, so that he may nullify the will of others for the sake of your will.

The first part of the mishna, about making our will like Hashem's will, teaches that the more we train ourselves in living the Torah and incorporating its values into our worldview, the closer we will be to Hashem. By liking spiritual things, wanting to be a good person, and engaging in spiritual matters ("making our will like Hashem's"), we become godlier, and our inner will and passions are elevated ("will make your will like His").

I have seen this so many times. When I was in a ba'al teshuva yeshiva in Israel, people would come in from trips to India and other Eastern countries completely distanced from Judaism. They then sat, day after day, in yeshiva, and the Torah transformed them. It was a beautiful thing to witness. Perhaps the end of the statement hints as to why this is possible. Hashem helps us in this transformative process: "He will make your will like His." May it come true for all of us.

With this explanation in mind, we can explain the second part of the mishna and its connection to the first. The reward in the second part appears to be even greater: not only does Hashem do one's will, but others' wills are also nullified in front of ours. This is an enhanced level of mastery over this world.

The second part of the mishna describes a nullification of one's will—a submergence of one's will into the divine will. How does one arrive at this high level? Through the direction provided in the first part of the mishna. Through practicing "making God's will like one's own," one draws closer and closer to this divine level until one achieves nullification and merges with the divine.

At this point, we are so united with Hashem that Hashem begins using us to bring forward the divine plan in the world. This means that others' wills are nullified in front of ours because Hashem is now working through us and impacting everything around us. This level of "nullification" helps explain how some of our rabbis over the generations had unique, sometimes magical, abilities to impact the wills and lives of those around them. These rabbis were vessels for Hashem to work in the world and shift the course of history to align with the divine plan that unfolded through them.

Beware of Judging Others Based on Their Public Persona

הִלֵּל אוֹמֵר: אַל תִּפְרשׁ מִן הַצִּבּוּר, וְאַל תַּאֲמִין בְּעַצְמְךָ עַד יוֹם מוֹתְךָ, וְאַל תָּדִין אֶת חֲבֵרְךָ עַד שֶׁתַּגִּיעַ לִמְקוֹמוֹ. וְאַל תֹּאמַר דָּבָר שֶׁאִי אֶפְשָׁר לִשְׁמֹעַ, שֶׁסּוֹפוֹ לְהִשָּׁמַע. וְאַל תֹּאמַר לִכְשֶׁאֶפָּנֶה אֶשְׁנֶה, שֶׁמָּא לֹא תִפָּנֶה.

Hillel said: Do not separate yourself from the community, do not trust in yourself until the day of your death, and do not judge another until you have reached their place. Do not say something that cannot be understood [trusting] that in the end it will be understood. Say not: "When I shall have leisure I shall study;" [because] perhaps you will not have leisure.

The Meiri explains the final part of the first statement in a creative way: don't judge others until you see how they act in their home ("their place") and away from the public eye.

You can never really know someone based on how they present themselves to others in public. For instance, many people can be very stressed out around large groups. Maybe they say silly things or become very quiet in these settings. Or maybe the opposite happens. Refrain from judgment at these and similar times. Get to know people on a personal level. You may find they are completely different from what you originally thought!

Hillel Practices What He Preaches

הוּא הָיָה אוֹמֵר: אֵין בּוּר יְרֵא חֵטְא, וְלֹא עַם הָאָרֶץ חָסִיד, וְלֹא הַבַּיְשָׁן לָמֵד, וְלֹא הַקַּפְּדָן מְלַמֵּד, וְלֹא כָל הַמַּרְבֶּה בִסְחוֹרָה מַחְכִּים. וּבְמָקוֹם שֶׁאֵין אֲנָשִׁים, הִשְׁתַּדֵּל לִהְיוֹת אִישׁ.

He used to say: A brute is not sin-fearing, nor is an ignorant person pious; nor can a timid person learn, nor can an impatient person teach; nor will someone who engages too much in business become wise. In a place where there are no people, strive to be a person.

Hillel lived what he taught. The following story highlights two of his teachings mentioned above: "Nor can a timid person learn" and "Nor will someone who engages too much in business become wise."

> It was reported about Hillel the Elder that every day he used to work and earn one tropaik (small amount), half of which he would give to the guard at the House of Learning, the other half being spent for his food and for that of his family. One day he found nothing to earn, and the guard at the house of learning would not permit him to enter. He climbed up and sat upon the window to hear the words of the living God from the mouths of Shemayah and Avtalion.

RABBI DR. ELI YOGGEV

They say that day was the eve of Sabbath in the winter solstice and snow fell down upon him from heaven. When the dawn rose, Shemayah said to Avtalion: "Brother Avtalion, on every day this house is light and today it is dark. Is it perhaps a cloudy day?" They looked up and saw the figure of a man in the window. They went up and found him covered by three cubits of snow. They removed him, bathed, and anointed him, and placed him opposite the fire, and they said: "This man deserves that the Sabbath be profaned on his behalf." (*Talmud Bavli*, Yoma 35b (Koren translation))

Hillel was careful to not overengage in business and spent a good portion of his days in the house of learning. And when it was time for him to learn, he was not "timid." Instead, he did all he could (maybe too much, as evidenced in this story!) to learn Torah from his teachers

The following story embodies the teaching "nor can an impatient person teach." Pay attention to the silly questions and the multiple attempts to anger Hillel. Despite everything, he remained patient (on Erev Shabbat—a stressful time in itself as everyone is preparing for Shabbat). As a result, Hashem's name was sanctified.

It once happened that two men made a wager with each other, saying, "He who goes and makes Hillel angry shall receive four hundred zuz." One said, "I will go and incense him." That day was the Sabbath eve, and Hillel was washing his head. He went, passed by the door of his house, and called out, "Is Hillel here? Is Hillel here?" Thereupon he robed and went out to him, saying, "My son, what do you require?" "I have a question to ask," he said. "Ask, my son," he prompted. Thereupon he asked: "Why are the heads of the Babylonians round?" "My son, you have asked a great question," he answered. "Because they have no skillful midwives."

He departed, tarried a while, returned, and called out, "Is Hillel here? Is Hillel here?" He robed and went out to him, saying, "My son, what do you require?" "I have a question to ask," he said. "Ask, my son," he prompted. Thereupon he asked: "Why are the eyes of the Palmyreans bleared?" "My son, you have asked a great question," he replied. "Because they live in sandy places."

He departed, tarried a while, returned, and called out, "Is Hillel here; is Hillel here?" He robed and went out to him, saying, "My son, what do you require?" "I have a question to ask," he said. "Ask, my son," he prompted. He asked, "Why are the feet of the Africans wide?" "My son, you have asked a great question," he said. "Because they live in watery marshes."

"I have many questions to ask," he said, "but fear that you may become angry." Thereupon he robed, sat before him and said, "Ask all the questions you have to ask!" (Ibid., Shabbat 30b–31a (Koren translation))

Hillel's recurring words "my son" and "you have asked a great question" point to his patient teaching style: he saw everyone as his child and made space for their questions. This parental love is the foundation of a great teacher.

Step Forward and Break
the Vicious Cycle

אַף הוּא רָאָה גֻלְגֹּלֶת אַחַת שֶׁצָּפָה עַל פְּנֵי הַמַּיִם. אָמַר לָהּ:
עַל דַּאֲטֵפְתְּ, אַטְפוּךְ, וְסוֹף מְטִיפַיִךְ יְטוּפוּן.

Moreover, he saw a skull floating on the face of the water. He said
to it: Because you drowned others, they drowned you. And in the
end, they that drowned you will be drowned.

It is strange to think Hillel would say this to a floating skull. It runs
counter to the sensitive Hillel we know. How do we make sense of this?
Hillel was a balanced individual. With all his selflessness, he reminds
us in another mishna: "If I am not for myself, who will be for me?"
Similarly, we learned on our commentary to the previous mishna in the
story of Hillel climbing on a roof on a frigid winter night to hear his
rabbis, that while Hillel was a kind and patient individual, he also knew
when to assert himself and not be timid. Perhaps here, too, he is teaching
a balanced message: Hashem is kind and patient, but this does not negate
the reality of divine justice.

Another possible direction is to say that Hillel is offering a window into his reflections on the insanity of life, how one person after
another "drowns" the other in an attempt to harm them or rise above
them in status or stature. If we don't step forward and make things better, this chain of events will never stop. Based on this reading, it's less of

a teaching and more of a sad reflection on reality and a call to action. It reminds me of the famous Gandhi quote: "An eye for an eye makes the whole world blind." If we each drown the next person, we all will end up drowning. We must break this vicious cycle and be kind to one another!

Compete with Yourself

הוּא הָיָה אוֹמֵר: מַרְבֶּה בָשָׂר, מַרְבֶּה רִמָּה. מַרְבֶּה נְכָסִים, מַרְבֶּה דְאָגָה. מַרְבֶּה נָשִׁים, מַרְבֶּה כְשָׁפִים. מַרְבֶּה שְׁפָחוֹת, מַרְבֶּה זִמָּה. מַרְבֶּה עֲבָדִים, מַרְבֶּה גָזֵל. מַרְבֶּה תוֹרָה, מַרְבֶּה חַיִּים. מַרְבֶּה יְשִׁיבָה, מַרְבֶּה חָכְמָה. מַרְבֶּה עֵצָה, מַרְבֶּה תְבוּנָה. מַרְבֶּה צְדָקָה, מַרְבֶּה שָׁלוֹם. קָנָה שֵׁם טוֹב, קָנָה לְעַצְמוֹ. קָנָה לוֹ דִבְרֵי תוֹרָה, קָנָה לוֹ חַיֵּי הָעוֹלָם הַבָּא.

He used to say: The more flesh, the more worms; the more property, the more anxiety; the more wives, the more witchcraft; the more female slaves, the more lewdness; the more slaves, the more robbery; the more Torah, the more life; the more sitting, the more wisdom; the more counsel, the more understanding; the more charity, the more peace. If one acquires a good name, one has acquired it for themselves. If one acquires for oneself knowledge of Torah, one has acquired life in the world to come.

The language in the following statement is interesting: "If one acquires a good name, one has acquired it for themselves." If I acquired a good name—that is, a good reputation—clearly, I did so for myself!

This may be hinting at the fact that we can't rely on our parents' or ancestors' good names. They earned them for themselves; they don't automatically transfer to us. I remember when I first came to yeshiva and shared with a rabbi of mine that I come from an important rabbinic family in Israel and that I have *yichus* ("distinguished lineage" is called *yichus* in Hebrew). I was new to Orthodox Judaism at the time and was so proud when I found this out. I wanted my rabbi to be happy and proud along with me. He was, but then he told me that I have big shoes to fill. I had to make my own "name" and not only rely on theirs.

Another possible explanation is to say that when it comes to attaining honor, titles, and accolades, the gaining of "a good name," our intentions should be *for ourselves*, for our own progress and benefit. Instead of striving to gain honor and recognition from others, we should compete with ourselves and strive to be the best version of ourselves that we can be.

Don't Hold on to the Good Solely for Yourself

רַבָּן יוֹחָנָן בֶּן זַכַּאי קִבֵּל מֵהִלֵּל וּמִשַּׁמַּאי. הוּא הָיָה אוֹמֵר: אִם לָמַדְתָּ
תּוֹרָה הַרְבֵּה, אַל תַּחֲזִיק טוֹבָה לְעַצְמְךָ, כִּי לְכָךְ נוֹצָרְתָּ.

Rabban Yochanan ben Zakkai received [the oral tradition] from Hillel
and Shammai. He used to say: If you have learned much Torah, do
not claim credit for yourself [lit., do not hold onto good for yourself],
because for such a purpose were you created.

The first part of our mishna teaches that if one "learned much
Torah," they shouldn't take credit for it. Why not? The mishna's
answer is: "For such a purpose you were created!" Some understand this
as referring to a debt we all owe Hashem. Hashem created, sustains,
and supports us. In return, we demonstrate allegiance through learning
Hashem's Torah.

Our mishna says we shouldn't take credit for learning much Torah
because this is just us paying back our debt to Hashem. It's the equivalent of someone who owes money to a store owner. Upon returning
their debt, they shouldn't take credit because they paid what they owed.
Similarly, we shouldn't take credit for our expanded Torah learning
because we were just doing what we were created to do!

The *Mesillat Yesharim*, in its discussion on humility, takes this in
another direction. The words "אל תחזיק טובה לעצמך," translated above as

"taking credit for oneself," are explained literally as "do not hold (אל
תחזיק) onto good (טובה) solely for yourself (לעצמך)." Based on this reading,
we are being urged to share our blessings with others and to not hold on
to them for ourselves.

> One who possesses an honest intellect, even if they
> have merited to become a great sage and truly
> distinguished, when they look and contemplate, will
> see that there is no room for haughtiness and pride.
> For behold, one who possesses high intelligence, who
> knows more than others, merely does what it is their
> nature to do. They are like a bird which flies upward
> because of its nature or an ox which pulls with its
> might because of its nature. So, too, for one who is
> wise. This is because their nature brings them to this.
> But for another person who is currently not as wise
> if they had possessed natural intelligence would also
> have become just as wise. Hence, there is no room to
> elevate and pride oneself in this.
>
> Rather, if one possesses great wisdom, behold,
> they are under duty to teach it to those in need of
> it, similar to the statement of Rabbi Yochanan ben
> Zakkai: "If you learned much Torah, do not hold
> onto it for yourself since for this you were created!"
> (*Mesillat Yesharim*, ch. 22)

This excerpt from *Mesillat Yesharim* appears to be offering an alternative interpretation to the ending of the statement: "Because for this
you were created." We were each created differently by Hashem, some
with more intellectual capacities than others. Why? So that we can offer
our services to others. This is such a beautiful teaching. There is no
room for haughtiness because our skill level and talents were all decreed
by Hashem. Indeed, we should do the opposite of being haughty! We
must use these blessings to make others' lives better—"since for this
were we created" with this talent!

The Symbiotic Eye-Heart Relationship

חֲמִשָּׁה תַלְמִידִים הָיוּ לוֹ לְרַבָּן יוֹחָנָן בֶּן זַכַּאי. וְאֵלוּ הֵן: רַבִּי אֱלִיעֶזֶר בֶּן הוֹרְקָנוֹס, וְרַבִּי יְהוֹשֻׁעַ בֶּן חֲנַנְיָה, וְרַבִּי יוֹסֵי הַכֹּהֵן, וְרַבִּי שִׁמְעוֹן בֶּן נְתַנְאֵל, וְרַבִּי אֶלְעָזָר בֶּן עֲרָךְ. הוּא הָיָה מוֹנֶה שְׁבָחָן: רַבִּי אֱלִיעֶזֶר בֶּן הוֹרְקָנוֹס, בּוֹר סוּד שֶׁאֵינוֹ מְאַבֵּד טִפָּה; רַבִּי יְהוֹשֻׁעַ בֶּן חֲנַנְיָה, אַשְׁרֵי יוֹלַדְתּוֹ; רַבִּי יוֹסֵי הַכֹּהֵן, חָסִיד; רַבִּי שִׁמְעוֹן בֶּן נְתַנְאֵל, יְרֵא חֵטְא; וְרַבִּי אֶלְעָזָר בֶּן עֲרָךְ, מַעְיָן הַמִּתְגַּבֵּר. הוּא הָיָה אוֹמֵר: אִם יִהְיוּ כָל חַכְמֵי יִשְׂרָאֵל בְּכַף מֹאזְנַיִם, וֶאֱלִיעֶזֶר בֶּן הוֹרְקָנוֹס בְּכַף שְׁנִיָה, מַכְרִיעַ אֶת כֻּלָּם. אַבָּא שָׁאוּל אוֹמֵר מִשְּׁמוֹ: אִם יִהְיוּ כָל חַכְמֵי יִשְׂרָאֵל בְּכַף מֹאזְנַיִם וְרַבִּי אֱלִיעֶזֶר בֶּן הוֹרְקָנוֹס אַף עִמָּהֶם, וְרַבִּי אֶלְעָזָר בֶּן עֲרָךְ בְּכַף שְׁנִיָה, מַכְרִיעַ אֶת כֻּלָּם. אָמַר לָהֶם: צְאוּ וּרְאוּ אֵיזוֹהִי דֶרֶךְ יְשָׁרָה שֶׁיִּדְבַּק בָּהּ הָאָדָם. רַבִּי אֱלִיעֶזֶר אוֹמֵר: עַיִן טוֹבָה. רַבִּי יְהוֹשֻׁעַ אוֹמֵר: חָבֵר טוֹב. רַבִּי יוֹסֵי אוֹמֵר: שָׁכֵן טוֹב. רַבִּי שִׁמְעוֹן אוֹמֵר: הָרוֹאֶה אֶת הַנּוֹלָד. רַבִּי אֶלְעָזָר אוֹמֵר: לֵב טוֹב. אָמַר לָהֶם: רוֹאֶה אֲנִי אֶת דִּבְרֵי אֶלְעָזָר בֶּן עֲרָךְ מִדִּבְרֵיכֶם, שֶׁבִּכְלָל דְּבָרָיו דִּבְרֵיכֶם. אָמַר לָהֶם: צְאוּ וּרְאוּ אֵיזוֹהִי דֶרֶךְ רָעָה שֶׁיִּתְרַחֵק מִמֶּנָּה הָאָדָם. רַבִּי אֱלִיעֶזֶר אוֹמֵר: עַיִן רָעָה. רַבִּי יְהוֹשֻׁעַ אוֹמֵר: חָבֵר רָע. רַבִּי יוֹסֵי אוֹמֵר: שָׁכֵן רָע. רַבִּי שִׁמְעוֹן אוֹמֵר: הַלֹּוֶה וְאֵינוֹ מְשַׁלֵּם. אֶחָד הַלֹּוֶה מִן הָאָדָם, כְּלֹוֶה מִן הַמָּקוֹם בָּרוּךְ הוּא, שֶׁנֶּאֱמַר (תהלים לז): לֹוֶה רָשָׁע וְלֹא יְשַׁלֵּם, וְצַדִּיק חוֹנֵן וְנוֹתֵן. רַבִּי אֶלְעָזָר אוֹמֵר: לֵב רָע. אָמַר לָהֶם: רוֹאֶה אֲנִי אֶת דִּבְרֵי אֶלְעָזָר בֶּן עֲרָךְ מִדִּבְרֵיכֶם, שֶׁבִּכְלָל דְּבָרָיו דִּבְרֵיכֶם.

Rabban Yochanan ben Zakkai had five disciples: Rabbi Eliezer ben Hyrcanus, Rabbi Yehoshua ben Chananiah, Rabbi Yosi, the priest, Rabbi Shimon ben Netanel and Rabbi Eleazar ben Arach. He [Rabbi Yochanan] used to list their outstanding virtues. Rabbi Eliezer ben Hyrcanus is a plastered cistern which loses not a drop. Rabbi Yehoshua ben Chananiah, happy is the woman that gave birth to him. Rabbi Yosi, the priest, is a pious man. Rabbi Shimon ben Netanel is one that fears sin. And Rabbi Eleazar ben Arach is like a spring that [ever] gathers force. He [Rabbi Yochanan] used to say: If all the Sages of Israel were on one scale of the balance and Rabbi Eliezer ben Hyrcanus on the other scale, he would outweigh them all. Abba Shaul said in his name: If all the Sages of Israel were on one scale of the balance, and Rabbi Eliezer ben Hyrcanus also with them, and Rabbi Eleazar ben Arach on the other scale, he would outweigh them all.

He [Rabban Yochanan] said unto them: Go forth and observe which is the right way to which a person should cleave. Rabbi Eliezer said: a good eye. Rabbi Yehoshua said: a good companion. Rabbi Yosi said: a good neighbor. Rabbi Shimon said: foresight. Rabbi Elazar said: a good heart. He [Rabban Yochanan] said to them: I prefer the words of Elazar ben Arach, for in his words your words are included. He [Rabban Yochanan] said unto them: Go forth and observe which is the evil way which a person should shun? Rabbi Eliezer said: an evil eye. Rabbi Yehoshua said: an evil companion. Rabbi Yosi said: an evil neighbor. Rabbi Shimon said: one who borrows and does not repay for he that borrows from man is as one who borrows from God, blessed be He, as it is said, "The wicked borrow and do not repay, but the righteous deal graciously and give" (Ps. 37:21). Rabbi Elazar said: an evil heart. He [Rabban Yochanan] said to them: I prefer the words of Elazar ben Arach, for in his words your words are included.

Rashi teaches (Num. 15:39) that the eyes influence the heart: "The eyes see, the heart covets, and the body performs the act." This is a well-known statement. Our mishna, however, seems to say otherwise: that a good eye (Rabbi Eliezer) is "included in" ("affected by") a good heart (Elazar ben Arach).

I don't see these as contradictory because the heart and eyes affect one another in a symbiotic manner. Therefore, when we embark on overcoming a powerful lust or a negative trait, we must approach them in terms of both our heart and our eyes. Here is an example. You are at work, and you see a colleague get promoted. This makes you jealous. By seeing their success (eyes), you feel jealousy in your heart. And vice versa: through your jealous thoughts, you begin to look at the individual in a different light. Now, each comment your colleague makes stands out as boasting and "rubbing it in."

One must tackle negative traits both in terms of one's heart and one's eyes. When it comes to jealousy, think good thoughts in your heart about the other and do your best not to look at what they are doing. Instead, shift the focus to your life and your own blessings.

2:15

Avoiding Spiritual Burnout

הֵם אָמְרוּ שְׁלֹשָׁה דְבָרִים. רַבִּי אֱלִיעֶזֶר אוֹמֵר: יְהִי כְבוֹד חֲבֵרְךָ חָבִיב עָלֶיךָ כְּשֶׁלָּךְ, וְאַל תְּהִי נוֹחַ לִכְעֹס. וְשׁוּב יוֹם אֶחָד לִפְנֵי מִיתָתְךָ. וֶהֱוֵי מִתְחַמֵּם כְּנֶגֶד אוּרָן שֶׁל חֲכָמִים, וֶהֱוֵי זָהִיר בְּגַחַלְתָּן שֶׁלֹּא תִכָּוֶה, שֶׁנְּשִׁיכָתָן נְשִׁיכַת שׁוּעָל, וַעֲקִיצָתָן עֲקִיצַת עַקְרָב, וּלְחִישָׁתָן לְחִישַׁת שָׂרָף, וְכָל דִּבְרֵיהֶם כְּגַחֲלֵי אֵשׁ.

They [each] said three things. Rabbi Eliezer said: Let the honor of your friend be as dear to you as your own, be not easily provoked to anger, and repent one day before your death. And warm yourself before the fire of the Sages, but beware of being singed by their glowing coals, for their bite is the bite of a fox, and their sting is the sting of a scorpion, and their hiss is the hiss of a serpent, and all their words are like coals of fire.

Rabbi Eliezer teaches that one must "repent one day" before their death. How can one know when this is? That is exactly the point! We can't ever know. That is why it's important to always be engaged in repentance. This is true when it comes to relationships as well. You never know how long they will last. I can't count the number of funerals at which I officiated where the family shared that they "just spoke with their loved one yesterday." Every day we have with those we love is a blessing. Let them know this today!

In the continuation of the mishna, Rabbi Eliezer shares some tough words in relation to rabbis, comparing them to hot coals, a fox, a scorpion, and a serpent. This may ironically allude to the elevated spiritual level of the rabbis.

71

Let me bring you an example from a love of mine: the NBA. True greats work very hard to master their craft. They take thousands of shots, spend hours upon hours in the weight room, and maintain meticulous diets (well, some of them). If a beginner were to take on (even a part of) this work regimen, they would burn out very quickly. One must take small steps and only later larger ones.

This is the mishna's message: "warm yourself" up by the rabbis' words, follow in their ways the best you can, but don't burn out by attempting to mimic their high levels of spirituality. If one does this, one will feel the bite, the sting, and the burn. The Torah is supposed to be a candle that lights our way and illuminates our lives. When we take on too much, it can become a stressful burden—"like coals of fire."

2:16

Living in the Present

רַבִּי יְהוֹשֻׁעַ אוֹמֵר: עַיִן הָרָע, וְיֵצֶר הָרָע, וְשִׂנְאַת הַבְּרִיּוֹת מוֹצִיאִין אֶת הָאָדָם מִן הָעוֹלָם.

Rabbi Yehoshua said: An evil eye, the evil inclination, and hatred for humankind remove a person from the world.

There is so much truth in this short mishna! We all enjoy blessings in our lives. Even the fact that you are reading this right now means that you have merited to learn Torah. That's a blessing! However, when we are caught up in distractions such as the evil eye, the evil inclination, and hatred for others, we struggle to recognize and access these blessings. We see this from Haman (Esther ch. 5). The whole kingdom was his, but "all this meant nothing to him" as long as Mordechai wouldn't bow to him. His evil eye, evil inclination, and hatred toward Mordechai literally "removed him from the world." These traits are what ultimately led to his death and unraveling.

The "punishment" or negative effect of these traits, removal from the world, doesn't have to equate to a physical removal. This removal can simply be a general disconnect from what is happening around us: not being present in the moment. Your spouse is discussing something with you at the table, and you are thinking about something else you want to do or purchase. You may want to pay a compliment to someone, but you can't open your mouth because you are plagued with hatred or jealousy (evil eye) toward them. The more we remove these three impediments, the greater we will be able to live in the present, "in the world," readily available for others.

2:17

Tzedakah as Spiritual Savings

רַבִּי יוֹסֵי אוֹמֵר: יְהִי מָמוֹן חֲבֵרָךְ חָבִיב עָלֶיךָ כְּשֶׁלָּךְ, וְהַתְקֵן עַצְמְךָ לִלְמֹד
תּוֹרָה, שֶׁאֵינָהּ יְרֻשָּׁה לָךְ. וְכָל מַעֲשֶׂיךָ יִהְיוּ לְשֵׁם שָׁמָיִם.

Rabbi Yosi said: Let the property of your fellow be as precious unto you as your own, make yourself fit to study Torah for it will not be yours by inheritance, and let all your actions be for [the sake of] the name of heaven.

The mishna relays a simple yet pertinent message: be careful with everyone's money like it was your own! It's very tempting, for instance, for government officials to treat government funds differently than their own. We hear this often on the news: this senator spent this amount of taxpayer money on an extravagant event or that government official lavishly spent thousands of dollars on food for a seemingly small affair. We even see this in our own lives. How much easier is it to spend our company's money on something rather than our own? We must try to be mindful of all property, including that of large corporations!

Jewish law is specific when it comes to treatment of others' finances. I have even learned of laws which ask us to first obtain permission from our company prior to printing out personal documents on their printer. Some get frustrated upon hearing these minutiae of Jewish law; I find this deep concern for the other beautiful.

Another possible way to read this directive is to view it as referring to tzedakah that one bequeathed to another: "Let the property of your fellow (that you gave to them as tzedakah) be as precious unto you as your own." Giving tzedakah to others is precious, like the money we own in our savings account. Our savings consists of our financial earnings; tzedakah is similar in that it is a form of spiritual savings.

Tzedakah is one of the greater mitzvahs. Therefore, the more we give, the more we spiritually receive. With this in mind, we must ensure others benefit from our tzedakah with the same zeal with which we put money into our own savings or retirement account. Through this we will accrue for ourselves immense spiritual savings.

Tips for Intentional Davening

רַבִּי שִׁמְעוֹן אוֹמֵר: הֱוֵי זָהִיר בִּקְרִיאַת שְׁמַע וּבַתְּפִלָּה. וּכְשֶׁאַתָּה מִתְפַּלֵּל, אַל תַּעַשׂ תְּפִלָּתְךָ קֶבַע, אֶלָּא רַחֲמִים וְתַחֲנוּנִים לִפְנֵי הַמָּקוֹם בָּרוּךְ הוּא, שֶׁנֶּאֱמַר (יואל ב): כִּי חַנּוּן וְרַחוּם הוּא אֶרֶךְ אַפַּיִם וְרַב חֶסֶד וְנִחָם עַל הָרָעָה. וְאַל תְּהִי רָשָׁע בִּפְנֵי עַצְמֶךָ.

Rabbi Shimon said: Be careful with the reading of Shema and with prayer, and when you pray, do not make your prayer something automatic, but a plea for compassion before God, for it is said: "For He is gracious and compassionate, slow to anger, abounding in kindness, and renouncing punishment" (Joel 2:13). And be not wicked in your own esteem.

How are the three directives connected? Davening on time and at a minyan is important, as is following the other *halachot* (laws) of prayer. This is alluded to in the opening words of the mishna: "Be careful with the reading of Shema and with prayer." However, if one only abides by the "letter of the law," to some extent, one has missed the point of davening. It should not be "automatic" but rather "a plea of compassion"—a deeper, more spontaneous experience.

It's not always easy to daven with proper *kavanah* (intention). I struggle with this as well. Many a time I have been "that person" who calls out to remind everyone to insert a certain prayer into the amidah (the silent devotional prayer) and then, due to my lack of concentration, forget to insert it myself! There are other times when I can't muster up the proper emotions to "plea for compassion." Our mishna recognizes this and reminds us just to do our best and not be hard on ourselves: "And be not wicked in your own esteem." We aren't always going to get it right, but we can still try!

This brings me to the following davening tips that have worked for me over the years:

- Choose parts to focus on: Nobody has full intention on all parts of *tefilla* (well, aside from very pious people…). Oftentimes, especially during Shacharit, we have trouble internalizing the messages while reading all of the required words. A friend's young daughter performs this funny skit where she moves her lips really quickly, pretending to "daven like a rabbi." It's very funny, but unfortunately, this happens a lot. So here's a tip: focus on one or two things each day. It may be the first part of Shema, or it may be one blessing in the amidah. It's not an all-or-nothing experience. Find a piece that works for you on that day and hone-in on it.
- Try English every once in a while (or any other language you are comfortable with): I do this sometimes just to keep it fresh. I will read a Psalm in Psukei D'Zimra (verses of praise recited during the morning service) in English. I will then go back over it in Hebrew. When one prays in the same language each time, one can lose track of its meaning.
- Bodily motions: Shuckling is a Jewish thing. What is shuckling? That swaying back and forth you sometimes see as people learn or pray. This bodily movement is predicated upon the interconnectedness of one's whole being. When we move our bodies, we stir up our insides, and that's our goal when offering a "plea of compassion" as we pray. I once thought of making a YouTube comedy skit with all the rabbinic bodily motions: from the beard stroke to the back-and-forth pace on the bema and the different forms of shuckling. Some of them look funny to outsiders. That's okay because we are more focused on our insides! Try out different movements. Some might work for you and arouse your heart to a better davening experience.
- Insert personal prayers: One can insert personal prayers into the Shema Koleinu part of the amida. I remember doing this

a lot while in yeshiva. It's a bit harder now as a rabbi because people are waiting for me to finish to start the amidah repetition. But when I get the chance, this is an awesome way to express one's emotions and add spontaneity to one's davening.

- Learn about the prayers: The more informed you are, the better you will be able to connect. It's as simple as that. Even just reading through the Siddur alone at home can enhance one's davening experience.

These are just a few ways to go about davening. The most important thing is to care. When we care about something, we put effort into making it better. Prayer is one of the "pillars" upon which one's spiritual growth stands (see *Ethics of the Fathers* 1:2). So, it's worth putting in our efforts on this front, always remembering that if our prayer is not perfect, it's okay: "Be not wicked in your own esteem."

2:19

Knowing "What" to
Respond to a Heretic

רַבִּי אֶלְעָזָר אוֹמֵר: הֱוֵי שָׁקוּד לִלְמֹד תּוֹרָה. וְדַע מַה שֶׁתָּשִׁיב לְאֶפִּיקוֹרוֹס. וְדַע לִפְנֵי מִי אַתָּה עָמֵל, וְנֶאֱמָן הוּא בַעַל מְלַאכְתְּךָ שֶׁיְשַׁלֶּם לְךָ שְׂכַר פְּעֻלָּתֶךָ.

R abbi Elazar said: Be diligent in the study of the Torah. And know how to answer a heretic. And know before whom you toil, and that your employer is faithful to pay you the reward of your labor.

In the mishna's words, "know how to respond to a heretic," there may be a tip for engaging "heretics"—those distanced from our tradition. The language used in the mishna is "מה" ("what"), as in "know to respond with the word 'what' to a heretic." When speaking to someone distanced from religion, it's pertinent to first see what may be underlying their heresy. We must ask the other "What?" prior to offering our answer.

Many times, people deny pillars of our faith for reasons that aren't ideological. I once had someone say, "Rabbi, I don't believe in God." Instead of pushing him away, I asked, "What do you mean by 'belief in God'?" He explained his belief system. Then, I answered, "Guess what? I don't believe in that God either!" Sometimes just asking "What?" can help clarify things.

Another example: I was helping run a minyan one Rosh Hashanah in a New York City jail. After hearing my sermon on repentance, a young inmate in his twenties approached me and said, "Rabbi, I hear what you

81

are saying, but I will never be able to return to God." I am happy I didn't accept his words at face value. Instead, I asked "What?": I inquired and didn't dismiss his ostensibly heretical statement. I found out he held much guilt for things he had done. He truly believed in God; he just didn't believe in himself! I tried to uplift his spirits and make space for his pain and remorse. I think it helped!

When others express heretical views, first ask "what" they are really saying and investigate their motives. You may just find the source of heresy isn't what you originally thought!

2:20–21

Hashem as a Supportive Coach

רַבִּי טַרְפוֹן אוֹמֵר: הַיּוֹם קָצָר וְהַמְּלָאכָה מְרֻבָּה, וְהַפּוֹעֲלִים עֲצֵלִים, וְהַשָּׂכָר הַרְבֵּה,
וּבַעַל הַבַּיִת דּוֹחֵק. הוּא הָיָה אוֹמֵר: לֹא עָלֶיךָ הַמְּלָאכָה לִגְמֹר, וְלֹא אַתָּה בֶן חוֹרִין
לִבָּטֵל מִמֶּנָּה. אִם לָמַדְתָּ תוֹרָה הַרְבֵּה, נוֹתְנִים לְךָ שָׂכָר הַרְבֵּה. וְנֶאֱמָן הוּא בַעַל
מְלַאכְתְּךָ שֶׁיְּשַׁלֶּם לְךָ שְׂכַר פְּעֻלָּתֶךָ. וְדַע מַתַּן שְׂכָרָן שֶׁל צַדִּיקִים לֶעָתִיד לָבֹא.

Rabbi Tarfon said: The day is short, and the work is plentiful, and
the laborers are indolent, and the reward is great, and the master of
the house is insistent. He [Rabbi Tarfon] used to say: It is not your duty
to finish the work, but neither are you at liberty to neglect it. If you have
studied much Torah, you shall be given much reward. Faithful is your
employer to pay you the reward of your labor. And know that the grant
of reward unto the righteous is in the world to come.

These are two mishnas which I combined. If one reads the first
mishna by itself, one will come out with an unbalanced view of Rabbi
Tarfon's understanding of Hashem. In the first mishna, he depicts
Hashem as an "insistent master" who is prodding "laborers" to complete
their required chores. The second mishna mitigates this, reminding us
that Hashem just wants us to do our best: "It is not your duty to finish
the work, but neither are you at liberty to neglect it."

For me, the second mishna has always been a helpful addition to
the first teaching. When I first became more observant at the age of
eighteen, I remember feeling very stressed out. Judaism seemed like a
religion of never-ending laws. (It didn't help that I was at a seminary

where everyone was newly religious and ever so eager to "show me the light" and teach me each and every one of these laws…). I experienced Hashem originally as more of an insistent lawgiver. As the years passed, I came to realize that Hashem is like any good coach or guide I have had throughout my life. Hashem does not want me to neglect everything I need to do ("neither are you at liberty to neglect"), but also: "It is not my duty to finish the work."

Remain Humble!

עֲקַבְיָא בֶּן מַהֲלַלְאֵל אוֹמֵר: הִסְתַּכֵּל בִּשְׁלֹשָׁה דְבָרִים וְאִי אַתָּה בָא לִידֵי עֲבֵרָה.
דַּע מֵאַיִן בָּאתָ, וּלְאָן אַתָּה הוֹלֵךְ, וְלִפְנֵי מִי אַתָּה עָתִיד לִתֵּן דִּין וְחֶשְׁבּוֹן. מֵאַיִן
בָּאתָ: מִטִּפָּה סְרוּחָה. וּלְאָן אַתָּה הוֹלֵךְ: לִמְקוֹם עָפָר רִמָּה וְתוֹלֵעָה. וְלִפְנֵי מִי
אַתָּה עָתִיד לִתֵּן דִּין וְחֶשְׁבּוֹן: לִפְנֵי מֶלֶךְ מַלְכֵי הַמְּלָכִים הַקָּדוֹשׁ בָּרוּךְ הוּא.

Akavyah ben Mahalalel said: Look at three things and you will not come into the power of sin: Know from where you come, and where you are going, and before whom you are destined to give an account and reckoning. From where do you come? From a putrid drop. Where are you going? To a place of dust, of worms, and of maggots. Before whom you are destined to give an account and reckoning? Before the King of the kings of kings, the Holy One, blessed be He.

This mishna encourages us (to put it lightly) to remain humble. Three things can lead to haughtiness. The first is one's spiritual state when one sees oneself as spiritually superior to another. I would include here people who were born into a well-respected family, who view themselves as loftier due to their "pedigree" (*yichus*). A second is one's financial status. We see this all the time. Someone strikes it rich and no longer has time for the "simple folk" anymore. But it can also be subtler: someone gains more wealth and forgets to be nice to people as they now view themselves on a higher level.

Finally, some may see themselves as more important because of their achievements. Titles, honors, and life successes can lead to a false and "bloated" sense of self in relation to others. There is a joke I love which demonstrates this.

> It's Yom Kippur and the venerated senior rabbi of a large congregation in New York stops in the middle of the Mussaf prayer service, prostrates himself next to the holy Ark, and cries out, "O God. Before You, I am nothing!"
>
> The cantor of many years is so moved by this demonstration of piety that he immediately follows suit, throwing himself to the floor beside the rabbi and crying, "O God! Before you, I am nothing!"
>
> In the ensuing silence, the new assistant rabbi immediately jumps up from his seat, prostrates himself and cries, "O God! Before You, I am nothing!"
>
> Seeing this, the cantor nudges the senior rabbi and whispers, "So look who thinks he's nothing!"

This is a funny joke, but it points to a real issue: titles and achievements can lead, even rabbis and cantors, to haughtiness.

In our mishna, Akavyah ben Mahalalel teaches that "looking" at three things can help us with all of this. In relation to our spiritual pursuits and "yichus," he reminds us that our life and spirituality started from a single drop of life; we are all equal in this sense. With regards to our financial status, we aren't going to leave the world with any of it. We are all destined to enter "a place of dust." This thought also encourages us to feel a sense of equality and shared humanity with others.

Finally, even our accomplishments are judged not in relation to others but in relation to ourselves ("before whom you are destined"). This is the idea of God's account and reckoning. We each stand as individuals in front of Hashem and give a reckoning in relation to what we achieved with our own unique skill set and talents. This protects us from comparing ourselves to others and, in turn, leads to humility.

3:2

Judaism as a Universalist Religion

רַבִּי חֲנִינָא סְגַן הַכֹּהֲנִים אוֹמֵר: הֱוֵי מִתְפַּלֵּל בִּשְׁלוֹמָהּ שֶׁל מַלְכוּת,
שֶׁאִלְמָלֵא מוֹרָאָהּ, אִישׁ אֶת רֵעֵהוּ חַיִּים בְּלָעוֹ.

R abbi Chanina, the vice-high priest, said: Pray for the welfare of the government, for were it not for the fear it inspires, every person would swallow their neighbor alive.

We recite a prayer in shul each week called Prayer for the Welfare of the Government (Koren Sacks Siddur, p. 521). It may have been instituted based on Rabbi Chanina's teaching. As for the content of the mishna, Rabbeinu Yonah (thirteenth century) has an awesome teaching:

> This matter is wanting to say that a person should pray for the peace of the whole world and be in pain about the pain of others. And this is the way of the righteous ones, as David, peace be upon him, stated (Ps. 35:13), "As for me, when they were ill, my dress was sackcloth, I afflicted myself in fasting." A person should not make their supplications and requests for their needs alone, but rather pray for all people that they be at peace. When the government is in good welfare, there is peace in the world.

Judaism has always been a universalist religion with its vision to improve the world. True, there are many texts which indicate otherwise, with a more exclusionary tilt, but Professor Alan Brill points out that this is only one of four strands in our tradition when it comes to our attitude toward other nations (see *Judaism and Other Religions: Models of Understanding*).

We have access to Rabbi Kook's (1865–1935) personal journal entries. They were compiled in a short book called *Hadarav*. Several passages are dedicated to his overflowing love for the whole world. This is the message of this mishna according to Rabbeinu Yonah. We should care about and pray for the peace of the world, not just for our personal community. Here are two of Rabbi Kook's entries on the topic (my translation):

- I love everything! I cannot but love all people, all nations. In the depths of my soul, I wish for the splendor of everything, the rectification of all. My love for Israel burns more greatly and is deeper, but the inner desire, in its overpowering love, truly extends to everything. I feel no need to force this loving feeling; it emanates directly from the holy depths of the wisdom of the divine soul" (p. 167)
- I love all of creation! Under no circumstances will I change this internal trait of mine. And I find meritorious aspects and positive sides in everything—truly in everything! (p. 163)

All of us, "all of creation," are in this together. We should not only be concerned about our community's welfare but also with those suffering in other parts of the country and the world. Of course, there is a hierarchy, as Rabbi Kook notes, delineated in our tradition: "The poor of your own community take precedence" (*Talmud Bavli*, Bava Metzia 71a). This goes for the Jewish community as a whole in relation to other global "communities." Nevertheless, when it comes to helping others and giving charity, we should keep the "welfare of the world" in mind and take proactive measures toward helping those outside of our immediate Jewish circle as well. We are all children of one God as is taught in Malachi: "Have we not all one Father? Has not one God created us?" (Mal. 2:10) We must pray for each other's welfare so we can all flourish together as a global community.

Don't Forget Your Vitamin G!

רַבִּי חֲנִינָא בֶּן תְּרַדְיוֹן אוֹמֵר: שְׁנַיִם שֶׁיּוֹשְׁבִין וְאֵין בֵּינֵיהֶן דִּבְרֵי תוֹרָה, הֲרֵי זֶה מוֹשַׁב לֵצִים, שֶׁנֶּאֱמַר (תהלים א): וּבְמוֹשַׁב לֵצִים לֹא יָשָׁב. אֲבָל שְׁנַיִם שֶׁיּוֹשְׁבִין וְיֵשׁ בֵּינֵיהֶם דִּבְרֵי תוֹרָה, שְׁכִינָה שְׁרוּיָה בֵינֵיהֶם, שֶׁנֶּאֱמַר (מלאכי ג): אָז נִדְבְּרוּ יִרְאֵי ה' אִישׁ אֶל רֵעֵהוּ וַיַּקְשֵׁב ה' וַיִּשְׁמָע וַיִּכָּתֵב סֵפֶר זִכָּרוֹן לְפָנָיו לְיִרְאֵי ה' וּלְחֹשְׁבֵי שְׁמוֹ. אֵין לִי אֶלָּא שְׁנַיִם, מִנַּיִן שֶׁאֲפִלּוּ אֶחָד שֶׁיּוֹשֵׁב וְעוֹסֵק בַּתּוֹרָה, שֶׁהַקָּדוֹשׁ בָּרוּךְ הוּא קוֹבֵעַ לוֹ שָׂכָר? שֶׁנֶּאֱמַר (איכה ג): יֵשֵׁב בָּדָד וְיִדֹּם כִּי נָטַל עָלָיו.

Rabbi Chananiah ben Teradion said: If two sit together and there are no words of Torah [spoken] between them, then this is a session of scorners, as it is said: "Nor sat he in the seat of the scornful…[rather, the teaching of the Lord is his delight]" (Ps. 1:1); but if two sit together and there are words of Torah [spoken] between them, then the Shechinah abides among them, as it is said: "Then they that feared the Lord spoke one with another; and the Lord hearkened and heard, and a book of remembrance was written before Him, for them that feared the Lord and that thought upon His name" (Mal. 3:16). Now I have no [scriptural proof for the presence of the Shechinah] except [among] two, how [do we know] that even one who sits and studies Torah the Holy One, blessed be He, fixes their reward? As it is said: "Though one sits alone and [meditates] in stillness, yet one takes [a reward] unto themself" (Lam. 3:28).

The mishna is careful to note that the two individuals in our mishna are sitting together but are not exchanging words of Torah. What is so wrong with not exchanging words of Torah? Perhaps they were both learning on their own, but there was no exchange of ideas. Nothing is wrong with learning on one's own. However, without feedback from others, one can easily miss details and err in judgment. This is the secret to yeshiva system of *chevruta* learning: learning in pairs.

I am very careful to have people review my sermons prior to their delivery. I always gain important tips and pick up on errors through this peer review. This may be why the verse, while referencing two who learn together, mentions their words being written in a "book of remembrance before Hashem." Only after one's words have been shared with another, reviewed, and scrutinized are they worthy of being "published" in Hashem's book of remembrance.

Another way to understand the first part of the mishna is to see the two who are sitting together as two people "hanging out" but not engaged in spiritual pursuits (even on their own). "Hanging out" and enjoying each other's company is fine. The mishna is reminding us, however, that it's also important to find ways to grow spiritually, to add vitality and life to the discussion through a connection to Torah. This is the origin of the custom to deliver a dvar Torah at a meal.

I was chatting with someone the other day about all the vitamins she takes each morning. She shared about her vitamin C and B12 intake, among others. I asked if she took her vitamin G that morning. She looked at me with a puzzled look until I explained: "That stands for God. Did you find a moment to consume, among all your other important vitamins, the one that can give you spiritual nourishment and energy?" She glanced at me with a smile and laughed at my joke, but I was serious!

3:4

Jewish Mindful Eating

רַבִּי שִׁמְעוֹן אוֹמֵר: שְׁלֹשָׁה שֶׁאָכְלוּ עַל שֻׁלְחָן אֶחָד וְלֹא אָמְרוּ עָלָיו דִּבְרֵי תוֹרָה, כְּאִלּוּ אָכְלוּ מִזִּבְחֵי מֵתִים, שֶׁנֶּאֱמַר (ישעיה כח): כִּי כָּל שֻׁלְחָנוֹת מָלְאוּ קִיא צֹאָה בְּלִי מָקוֹם. אֲבָל שְׁלֹשָׁה שֶׁאָכְלוּ עַל שֻׁלְחָן אֶחָד וְאָמְרוּ עָלָיו דִּבְרֵי תוֹרָה, כְּאִלּוּ אָכְלוּ מִשֻּׁלְחָנוֹ שֶׁל מָקוֹם בָּרוּךְ הוּא, שֶׁנֶּאֱמַר (יחזקאל מא): וַיְדַבֵּר אֵלַי זֶה הַשֻּׁלְחָן אֲשֶׁר לִפְנֵי ה'.

Rabbi Shimon said: If three have eaten at one table and have not spoken words of Torah, [it is] as if they had eaten sacrifices [offered] to the dead, as it is said, "For all tables are full of filthy vomit, when the All-Present is absent" (Isa. 28:8). But, if three have eaten at one table, and have spoken words of Torah, [it is] as if they had eaten at the table of the All-Present, blessed be He, as it is said, "And He said unto me, 'This is the table before the Lord'" (Ezek. 41:22).

This mishna is like the previous one which discussed, according to our second interpretation, sanctifying the mundane in a group setting. I'd like to take a moment to focus on the topic of the mishna: Jewish food. In Judaism, food carries with it a lot of symbolism. For instance, we eat two challahs on Shabbat to symbolize the double portion of manna in the desert, and we consume matzah, maror, and charoset at the Passover Seder to remind us of our exile and redemption. One explanation for the centrality of food is that it helps recall important concepts and historical events.

What I'd like to focus on is a form of eating that is discussed less in Jewish texts: mindful eating. I was introduced to mindful eating in recent years. It's nothing more than living in the moment and paying attention to the eating process from start to finish. I spent time practicing mindful eating with a piece of dark chocolate. I put the food in my mouth and paid attention to its texture, its bittersweet taste, its slow-melting sensation in my mouth, and any other elements that presented themselves to me in the moment. It's very rare that we have opportunities to do this. Usually, we eat while doing something else: watching a show, checking our phone, or chatting with a friend. I know that if you place certain foods in my hands, they will be gone quicker than you can even say "mindful eating" (including Chex Mix and certain pastries). Nonetheless, if you can try this method, even for a bit, it can be very powerful and offer a deep appreciation for the food we consume and the blessing of food that Hashem has bestowed upon us.

There are many ways to elevate our table from "sacrifices [offered] to the dead" to a table before the Lord. One way is to learn Torah, as is mentioned in our mishna. Another is to reflect on the food's Jewish symbolism. But it doesn't stop there! Taking time to appreciate the eating process itself, to eat mindfully, can "enliven" our meals and draw us closer to Hashem.

3:5

Making the Most of Alone Time

רַבִּי חֲנִינָא בֶּן חֲכִינַאי אוֹמֵר: הַנֵּעוֹר בַּלַּיְלָה, וְהַמְהַלֵּךְ בַּדֶּרֶךְ
יְחִידִי, וְהַמְפַנֶּה לִבּוֹ לְבַטָּלָה, הֲרֵי זֶה מִתְחַיֵּב בְּנַפְשׁוֹ.

Rabbi Chananiah ben Chakinai said: One who wakes up at night, walks on the way alone, and turns their heart to idle matters, behold, this person is mortally guilty.

Some read the final statement as qualifying the first two: one who is awake or walks on the way alone, while turning their heart to idle matters, is mortally guilty. On this reading, what is the issue with the first two actions? One way to explain this is to say that being awake late at night and travelling on the way can be lonely experiences. At night, no one is around, and it's dark and quiet. Similarly, when we visit new locations and travel far away from our hometown, it can feel lonely and scary. One way to mitigate these feelings is to keep oneself busy. This is the final piece of the mishna: do not turn your heart to idle matters.

Another possible direction is to assert that the first two activities are positive when done properly. It's praiseworthy to find alone times to connect with Hashem and reflect on life. One can do this late at night or by going out walking alone. Rebbe Nachman of Breslov speaks a lot about *hitbodedut*, personal prayer, alone, preferably in the woods. The end of the mishna warns us, however, that we mustn't be idle during these alone moments. We should cherish them and make the most of them.

3:6

When the Spirit Shines,
Everything Is More Pleasant

רַבִּי נְחוּנְיָא בֶּן הַקָּנָה אוֹמֵר: כָּל הַמְקַבֵּל עָלָיו עֹל תּוֹרָה, מַעֲבִירִין מִמֶּנּוּ עֹל מַלְכוּת וְעֹל
דֶּרֶךְ אֶרֶץ. וְכָל הַפּוֹרֵק מִמֶּנּוּ עֹל תּוֹרָה, נוֹתְנִין עָלָיו עֹל מַלְכוּת וְעֹל דֶּרֶךְ אֶרֶץ.

Rabbi Nechunia ben Hakkanah said: Whoever takes upon themselves
the yoke of the Torah, has removed from themselves the yoke of
government and the yoke of worldly concerns. And whoever breaks off
from themselves the yoke of the Torah, the yoke of government and the
yoke of worldly concerns is placed upon them.

Many read this mishna in the following manner: When one completely devotes themselves to Torah learning, Hashem will in turn
remove from them the burden of government and the need to work and
earn a living (see *Ohr LeTzion, Zichron Hadassah: Chochmah U'mussar*, pp.
11–12 for a discussion on the mechanics behind this understanding). In
other words, Hashem will provide for all their needs, as was the case with
Eliyahu Hanavi and the tribes of Issachar and Levi, who were involved in
Torah and spiritual matters and supported by others.

Another interpretation reads the mishna through a psychological
prism. Let me explain by means of an interesting halacha. The *Shulchan
Aruch* requires that all synagogues be built with windows (*Shulchan
Aruch* OH 90:4). Many explanations are offered for this. Rabbeinu
Yonah teaches us that it is to ensure there is always light and air in the

synagogue. This can be understood figuratively, hinting at the idea that prayer should be both inspiring ("air") and enlightening ("light"). I think our mishna is alluding to this in a more general sense: in relation to the positive effects on our overall spiritual connection.

When we truly accept upon ourselves the "yoke of Torah," when we experience a deep connection to Yiddishkeit and its spiritual experiences, we will feel uplifted, inspired, and enlightened. While in this enlightened state, everything is rosier and brighter. We have energy for all our pursuits, both on a communal ("yoke of government") and professional ("yoke of worldly concerns") level. Rabbi Kook alludes to this in the following quote: "When the spirit shines, even foggy skies make pleasant light" (*Meged Yerechim*, Cheshvan).

I have seen this many times. When I come back from shul on Shabbat, I am filled with renewed energy, which I can then share with others. This is just one example among many. According to this explanation, the mishna is not asking us to remove ourselves from our daily pursuits; it is reminding us that the greater our spiritual connection, the easier our other pursuits will be.

Power in Numbers

רַבִּי חֲלַפְתָּא בֶּן דּוֹסָא אִישׁ כְּפַר חֲנַנְיָה אוֹמֵר: עֲשָׂרָה שֶׁיּוֹשְׁבִין וְעוֹסְקִין בַּתּוֹרָה, שְׁכִינָה שְׁרוּיָה בֵּינֵיהֶם, שֶׁנֶּאֱמַר (תהלים פב): אֱלֹהִים נִצָּב בַּעֲדַת אֵל. וּמִנַּיִן אֲפִלּוּ חֲמִשָּׁה? שֶׁנֶּאֱמַר (עמוס ט): וַאֲגֻדָתוֹ עַל אֶרֶץ יְסָדָהּ. וּמִנַּיִן אֲפִלּוּ שְׁלֹשָׁה? שֶׁנֶּאֱמַר (תהלים פב): בְּקֶרֶב אֱלֹהִים יִשְׁפֹּט. וּמִנַּיִן אֲפִלּוּ שְׁנַיִם? שֶׁנֶּאֱמַר (מלאכי ג): אָז נִדְבְּרוּ יִרְאֵי ה' אִישׁ אֶל רֵעֵהוּ וַיַּקְשֵׁב ה' וַיִּשְׁמָע וְגוֹ'. וּמִנַּיִן אֲפִלּוּ אֶחָד? שֶׁנֶּאֱמַר (שמות כ): בְּכָל הַמָּקוֹם אֲשֶׁר אַזְכִּיר אֶת שְׁמִי אָבֹא אֵלֶיךָ וּבֵרַכְתִּיךָ.

Rabbi Chalafta of Kefar Chananiah said: When ten sit together and occupy themselves with Torah, the Divine presence abides among them, as it is said: "God stands in the congregation of God" (Ps. 82:1). How do we know that the same is true even of five? As it is said: "This band of His He has established on earth" (Amos 9:6). How do we know that the same is true even of three? As it is said: "In the midst of the judges He judges" (Ps. 82:1). How do we know that the same is true even of two? As it is said: "Then they that fear the Lord spoke one with another, and the Lord hearkened, and heard" (Mal. 3:16). How do we know that the same is true even of one? As it is said: "In every place where I cause my name to be mentioned I will come unto you and bless you" (Exod. 20:20).

Rabbi Chalafta lived in the time of the Roman persecution during which it was dangerous for Jews to congregate and learn Torah. Therefore, he wanted to encourage them to learn, nevertheless, even in smaller groups of ten, five, three, two, or even on one's own. Notwithstanding, a close reading of his words hints at an order of preference, in regular times when we aren't under imminent threat, in which the larger groups achieve greater closeness to Hashem.

When it comes to ten people learning together, we are told that Hashem "stands" among them. This is the optimal reality, where Hashem is an active part of the group learning. The group of five is "held in Hashem's hand," so to say. The mishna arrives at the number five from the verse's description of a band that is often bound together with five fingers. Hashem is not standing among the group but is on the outside "holding on to" the Torah learners. This is a bit more distanced.

We then have the group of three in relation to which Hashem is "in their midst." The root of "in the midst" is ק-ר-ב, which signifies that Hashem is close (קרוב, *karov*). Hashem is not standing among or holding them but is a separate entity that is albeit close.

The final learning engagement, solitary learning, presents Hashem as coming in from the "outside": "I will come unto you and bless you." Hashem is not only a separate entity but comes in from the outside to bless individual Torah learners.

The message is clear, but the question remains: what is so special about learning in a larger group? For me, it's the spiritual energy and momentum that I find in a group setting. Each member brings a special energy. When these energies combine, a more robust spirituality is generated; it's as simple as that. Being a part of a community of learners allows one to tap into this collective energy and achieve even greater heights than possible on one's own.

How to Strike it Rich

רַבִּי אֶלְעָזָר אִישׁ בַּרְתּוֹתָא אוֹמֵר: תֶּן לוֹ מִשֶּׁלּוֹ, שֶׁאַתָּה וְשֶׁלְּךָ שֶׁלּוֹ. וְכֵן בְּדָוִד
הוּא אוֹמֵר (דברי הימים א כט): כִּי מִמְּךָ הַכֹּל וּמִיָּדְךָ נָתַנּוּ לָךְ.

Rabbi Elazar of Bartota said: Give to Him of that which is His, for you and that which is yours is His; and so it says with regards to David: "For everything comes from You, and from Your own hand have we given you" (I Chron. 29:14).

There is a teaching in our tradition: "Give tithes so that you will become rich" (*Talmud Bavli*, Shabbat 119a). This is based on a verse which states: "עשר תעשר" (Deut. 14:22). From the repetition of the same root ע-ש-ר, which means "tithes," the Sages learned "עשר בשביל שתתעשר— tithe so you will become rich." They read the first word with the Hebrew letter "sin" as referring to ma'aser and the second with a "shin" as referring to riches.

What is ma'aser, and how does this process work? Ma'aser, literally, means "a tenth" ("עשר," ten). In the Torah, we are commanded to remove a tenth of our crop and donate it to the Temple. Our tradition extends this to our overall earnings: we are asked to donate a tenth of our income to those in need. But how does this make us rich? Giving away money usually doesn't add to our bank accounts; the opposite is often the case!

One way to answer this is to simply disagree with this premise, not from logic per se but from scripture. There is a verse in Malachi (3:10) that encourages us to "test" Hashem when it comes to ma'aser, promising us riches in return: "Bring the whole of the tithes into the treasury… and test Me now therewith, says the Lord of Hosts, [to see] if I will not open for you the sluices of heaven and pour down for you blessing until there be no room to suffice for it." It is very rare that we are offered the option to test Hashem. It may be because of the difficulty mentioned above. Logic and experience teach us that giving away money depletes our funds. The verse promises us that the opposite will happen.

Another way to explain this promised blessing of riches is connected to our mishna. Our mishna teaches that not all our money is really our own. I know this may sound foreign to some, but the idea is that Hashem places money in our hands that is intended for others. Our role is to disburse these entrusted funds to those who need it.

Our mishna is reminding us of this by asking us to "give to Him of that which is His, for you and that which is yours is His." The mishna is teaching that our money isn't ours, and therefore, Hashem's will should be done with it. It may also be warning us to not go overboard with this by instructing us to give of that which "is His" and no more. Our Sages tell us that unless one is very wealthy, one should designate no more than 20 percent of their earnings to tzedakah.

This is how ma'aser can make us rich. When Hashem sees that we consistently give a percentage of our earnings to those in need, Hashem will then proceed to apportion more money to us in the hopes that we will then give an even higher amount to charity. For example, if one used to give $100 from their $1,000 earnings, when allotted $1,200, one will hopefully give $120. This is similar to someone who was employed to handle several real estate projects. Upon seeing that this individual took good care of the projects, the owner then assigned even more projects, in turn increasing the overall wealth of the employee.

Giving Hashem what "is His" is not only the right thing to do in terms of our debt of gratitude to Hashem, it also brings with it great spiritual and material blessing.

Finding Hashem amid Social Distancing

רַבִּי יַעֲקֹב אוֹמֵר: הַמְהַלֵּךְ בַּדֶּרֶךְ וְשׁוֹנֶה, וּמַפְסִיק מִמִּשְׁנָתוֹ וְאוֹמֵר, מַה נָּאֶה אִילָן זֶה וּמַה נָּאֶה נִיר זֶה, מַעֲלֶה עָלָיו הַכָּתוּב כְּאִלּוּ מִתְחַיֵּב בְּנַפְשׁוֹ.

Rabbi Yakov said: If one is studying while walking on the road and interrupts their study and says, "How fine is this tree!" [or] "How fine is this newly ploughed field!" scripture accounts it to them as if they were mortally guilty.

I wrote the following commentary on March 23, 2020, just a week into our social distancing due to COVID-19, in Pikesville, Maryland. In this entry, I was trying to make sense of our new socially distanced reality and to offer meaning and support to my congregants during this fearful time. The following commentary reminds us, in every generation, to seek out Hashem in all we do.

> For many years I struggled with the following teaching in *Pirkei Avot* (*Ethics of the Fathers* 3:9): "Rabbi Yakov said: If one is studying while walking on the road and interrupts their study and says, 'How fine is this tree!' [or] 'How fine is this newly ploughed field!' scripture accounts it to them as if they are worthy of death." Yikes! As someone who grew up spending many hours in nature, this

statement always bothered me. What's wrong with appreciating God's works?

It wasn't until I heard Rabbi Tzvi Yehuda Kook's explanation that I was put at ease. He places the emphasis on the "interrupts their study" part of the statement. It's only an issue when one fails to recognize nature as part of one's study. God can be found not only in the study halls but in nature and our everyday activities. When one sees the outside world as an "interruption" to one's Torah, they've missed the mark—they are "worthy of death."

I was standing outside this past Shabbat morning at the hour when our congregation usually meets in shul. I was a bit down because I was missing the voice of our cantor, my congregants' beautiful smiles, the Torah reading, and so much more. But I remembered this saying, and it lifted my spirits. I looked at a tree in blossom and said, "How fine is this tree!" I smelled the air, took in the sun's rays, and remembered that God can be found everywhere.

We are used to rooms with aisles and armrests, but Rabbi Tzvi Yehuda reminds us to broaden our vision and not see where we are and what we are doing right now as devoid of Torah and Godliness. It may be a brief conversation with a spouse, a moment of inner calm and serenity (if you can find one!), or a fun experience with your children. This is where we can find God today. These endeavors are not interruptions to Torah. They are unique opportunities for growth and spiritual connection. May we merit to seize them and find God amid our social distancing.

3:10

The Need for Review in the Google Age

רַבִּי דּוֹסְתַּאי בְּרַבִּי יַנַּאי מִשּׁוּם רַבִּי מֵאִיר אוֹמֵר: כָּל הַשּׁוֹכֵחַ דָּבָר אֶחָד מִמִּשְׁנָתוֹ, מַעֲלֶה עָלָיו הַכָּתוּב כְּאִלּוּ מִתְחַיֵּב בְּנַפְשׁוֹ, שֶׁנֶּאֱמַר (דברים ד): רַק הִשָּׁמֶר לְךָ וּשְׁמֹר נַפְשְׁךָ מְאֹד פֶּן תִּשְׁכַּח אֶת הַדְּבָרִים אֲשֶׁר רָאוּ עֵינֶיךָ. יָכוֹל אֲפִלּוּ תָּקְפָה עָלָיו מִשְׁנָתוֹ, תַּלְמוּד לוֹמַר (שם): וּפֶן יָסוּרוּ מִלְּבָבְךָ כֹּל יְמֵי חַיֶּיךָ. הָא אֵינוֹ מִתְחַיֵּב בְּנַפְשׁוֹ עַד שֶׁיֵּשֵׁב וִיסִירֵם מִלִּבּוֹ.

Rabbi Dostai ben Rabbi Yannai said in the name of Rabbi Meir: Whoever forgets one word of their study, scripture accounts it as if they were mortally guilty, as it is said, "But take utmost care and watch yourselves scrupulously, so that you do not forget the things that you saw with your own eyes" (Deut. 4:9). One could [have inferred that this is the case] even when their study proved [too] hard for them, therefore scripture says, "that they do not fade from your mind as long as you live" (ibid.). Therefore, one is not mortally guilty unless one deliberately removes them from their heart.

When I was in yeshiva, we learned three *sedarim* (learning sessions) a day. In the morning, we learned Talmud in depth (*iyyun* learning); in the afternoon, we moved quicker through the rest of the Talmudic tractate in less depth in an attempt to get through a page or two a day (*bekiyut* learning); and in the evening, we would *mechazer*, review the material from earlier in the day (*chazara* learning).

The final part of the day was always the hardest. In addition to being fatigued, I was also less excited to revisit the material I had already learned earlier in the day. In time, I found this repetition to be very beneficial for me. Today I can recite, from memory, pages I reviewed in those late hours, even from about twenty years ago. It's pretty amazing what we can remember when we put in the effort to do so.

Why is it important for our mishna, and my rabbis in yeshiva, that we remember our learning? One simple explanation for the mishna's directive is that there was no Google during Talmudic times! For the Torah to not be forgotten, much review was needed on each scholar's part. At a certain time, it was even forbidden to write down oral traditions: "One is forbidden to transcribe oral teachings" (*Talmud Bavli*, Gittin 60b), so constant repetition was needed.

Today, in the age of Google, why is it important to review? Reviewing our learning forges a connection to the material. The more someone reviews and remembers their learning, the more they become a "walking Torah," a source of accessible Torah knowledge. There is holiness to be found in review in the sense that the more one has Torah in one's mind and heart, the higher level of connection they experience to Torah and Hashem. This is important in itself, even in today's world where online Torah knowledge is ubiquitous.

In general, remembrance is of huge importance in Judaism. The nation of Israel has been around for thousands of years. One reason for this longevity is that we never forget the past; we are always learning from it and expressing gratitude for all the good it granted us. This may also be another reason the mishna warns us to not forget the messages of the Torah. It's one thing to attend a good class or listen to a soundbite from a rabbi on YouTube or other social media; it's another to carry that Torah with us in our lives and internalize its messages and mission.

This may be what the mishna is relaying with the following verse: "But take utmost care and watch yourselves scrupulously, so that you do not forget the things that you saw with your own eyes." The Torah has important lessons for us. It's so easy to forget them in the course of our day as we are bombarded with messages from the outside world or are just busy with the daily grind. This is why we must "watch ourselves scrupulously"—so we won't forget its powerful and uplifting messages.

3:11–12

Learning from a Place of Simplicity

רַבִּי חֲנִינָא בֶּן דּוֹסָא אוֹמֵר: כָּל שֶׁיִּרְאַת חֶטְאוֹ קוֹדֶמֶת לְחָכְמָתוֹ, חָכְמָתוֹ מִתְקַיֶּמֶת. וְכָל שֶׁחָכְמָתוֹ קוֹדֶמֶת לְיִרְאַת חֶטְאוֹ, אֵין חָכְמָתוֹ מִתְקַיֶּמֶת. הוּא הָיָה אוֹמֵר: כָּל שֶׁמַּעֲשָׂיו מְרֻבִּין מֵחָכְמָתוֹ, חָכְמָתוֹ מִתְקַיֶּמֶת. וְכָל שֶׁחָכְמָתוֹ מְרֻבָּה מִמַּעֲשָׂיו, אֵין חָכְמָתוֹ מִתְקַיֶּמֶת.

Rabbi Chanina ben Dosa said: Anyone whose fear of sin precedes their wisdom, their wisdom is enduring, but anyone whose wisdom precedes their fear of sin, their wisdom is not enduring. He [also] used to say: Anyone whose deeds exceed their wisdom, their wisdom is enduring, but anyone whose wisdom exceeds their deeds, their wisdom is not enduring.

What is the connection between enduring wisdom and fear of sin? One way to understand this is to read the Hebrew "חכמתו מתקיימת" not as "enduring wisdom" but as "applied knowledge" ("לקיים" also means "to apply"). When one is afraid of sin, one will seek to apply one's knowledge.

In my earlier years (1997–2000) in the Machon Meir Yeshiva, I learned alongside ba'alei teshuva (individuals who had recently become observant). There is a certain passion and openness that marks the newly observant's attitude. They (I am including myself as a ba'al teshuva in all of these descriptions—at least in those years) come to the text from a place of "fear of sin." They want to know what to do to steer clear of sin and fulfill Hashem's will, oftentimes because they didn't grow up with a lot of exposure to our tradition. When one learns from this place of fear of sin, one's learning will surely be applied in one's life.

Another story connected to my ba'al teshuva yeshiva experience can help elucidate the other translation: "fear of sin" that leads to *enduring* wisdom. At Machon Meir, they encouraged us to learn emunah. There was a whole curriculum dedicated to *limmudei emunah*. Emunah translates as "faith." They urged us to strengthen our faith in Hashem through learning works of mussar (Jewish ethics), mysticism, chassidism, and Jewish philosophy, but they were careful not to call it philosophy. For them, the term *philosophy* indicated a more internally detached orientation to the material being learned. We were to approach the texts with a certain "fear" or reverence, seek out the truth, and focus on how the text animates our lives. For me, this was extremely impactful. The wisdom I learned there endures to this day because it penetrated my whole being and transformed me. I learned from a place of simplicity and reverence, based on their guidance, and it changed me. This is how the "fear of sin," or a general reverence toward Torah, can lead to enduring wisdom.

Admittedly, this isn't as simple nowadays, as we are all sophisticated and trained to question and dissect phenomena through a critical and scientific lens. Nevertheless, this shouldn't prevent us from benefitting from a simple and reverent read of the text. Paul Ricoeur, the French philosopher, speaks about three stages of relation to texts: precritical, critical, and postcritical. In this final stage, one accepts that things aren't so simple but moves beyond one's critical analysis to find meaning and purpose in the text. He defines this as a "second naivete."

I have always found this three-part model instructive, especially during my academic years. If my academic training taught me anything, it was to read texts critically. I do not need to return to my less-informed precritical childhood perspective. But Ricouer stresses the need, even from this critical place, to allow for awe, innocence, and reverence to accompany our reading of the text. Ricoeur's second naivete is informed by critical thinking, an informed naivete, if you will. Our mishna frames this as "fear of sin" preceding one's wisdom. When we open ourselves up to the text, we can be inspired for many years to come.

Making Hashem Look
Favorable in the World

הוּא הָיָה אוֹמֵר: כָּל שֶׁרוּחַ הַבְּרִיּוֹת נוֹחָה הֵימֶנּוּ, רוּחַ הַמָּקוֹם נוֹחָה הֵימֶנּוּ.
וְכָל שֶׁאֵין רוּחַ הַבְּרִיּוֹת נוֹחָה הֵימֶנּוּ, אֵין רוּחַ הַמָּקוֹם נוֹחָה הֵימֶנּוּ.

He used to say: One with whom people find favor (lit., their spirit is at ease), Hashem also finds favor. One with whom people do not find favor, Hashem does not find favor.

I love this mishna. Its message is simple and potent. Act kindly with others, find favor in the eyes of those around you and your community, and, as a result, you will find favor in the eyes of Hashem. On a most basic level, Hashem is interested in peaceful and positive relationships in the world. The more we promote this goal by getting along with others and maintaining our good name, the more "favorable" we will be in Hashem's eyes.

Another way to read the words "Hashem will find favor" is to point to Hashem finding favor in others' eyes due to our positive behavior with others. In our tradition this is called *kiddush Hashem* (sanctification of God's name). There is a law that rabbis must not walk around with stains on their clothing (*Talmud Bavli*, Shabbat 114a). It is explained that because they are representatives of Hashem, walking around in this fashion would "make Hashem look bad." Therefore, they are discouraged from doing so.

We can extend this to all Jews and to all "stains," not just those on our clothing. If our actions appear "off" to those watching, we will be relaying the wrong message. The good thing is: the opposite is the case as well. When people see how nice we are, how careful we are in caring for others, they will be drawn more to Hashem and Torah, making Hashem more favorable in the world.

3:14

Embracing Our Current Stage in Life

רַבִּי דּוֹסָא בֶּן הַרְכִּינַס אוֹמֵר: שֵׁנָה שֶׁל שַׁחֲרִית, וְיַיִן שֶׁל צָהֳרַיִם, וְשִׂיחַת הַיְלָדִים,
וִישִׁיבַת בָּתֵּי כְנֵסִיּוֹת שֶׁל עַמֵּי הָאָרֶץ מוֹצִיאִין אֶת הָאָדָם מִן הָעוֹלָם.

Rabbi Dosa ben Harkinas said: Morning sleep, midday wine, children's talk, and sitting in the assemblies of the ignorant remove an individual from the world.

Some commentators to this mishna tap into the idea of embracing one's current stage in life. It's good to remain young at heart, but when one is stuck in the stage of childhood without "growing up," one misses out on so much good to be found in the present. It's funny when you think about it. When we are young, we want to be older. And then when we get older, we often want to be young again.

Embracing ourselves now, where we are, at our current age, is not simple to do. If you pay attention, the behaviors mentioned in the mishna resemble what many of us might have been doing while in high school and/or college: sleeping, drinking, engaging in immature discussions, attending parties ("assemblies"). This may have been fine back then, but when we continue this behavior on a recurring basis into adulthood, we are missing out on all the good there is to receive at this stage.

Kohelet (chapter 3) teaches us that, "There is a time for everything and a season for every activity under the heavens." It then goes on to list those times: "A time to be born and a time to die, a time to plant and a time to uproot, a time to kill and a time to heal, a time to tear down and a time to build…" (This may bring to mind a famous song by The Byrds based on these verses.) I would add to this: there is a time to be older and a time to be younger. Each stage in life brings with it unique challenges and blessings.

This is highlighted in an upcoming mishna that lists the specific good that comes with each decade: "At thirty, the peak of strength. At forty, wisdom. At fifty, able to give counsel. At sixty, old age. At seventy, fullness of years" (*Ethics of the Fathers* 5:25). It's okay to sleep, drink, chatter, etc., but when these are done as a form of escapism from our current reality, then we are simply missing out.

We are good where we are, each of us. There is a time for our age under the heavens. Let's embrace it, find out what our calling is at this stage in life, and make the most out of the skills and opportunities it affords us.

3:15

Seeing the Inner Dimension

רַבִּי אֶלְעָזָר הַמּוֹדָעִי אוֹמֵר: הַמְחַלֵּל אֶת הַקֳּדָשִׁים, וְהַמְבַזֶּה אֶת הַמּוֹעֲדוֹת, וְהַמַּלְבִּין פְּנֵי חֲבֵרוֹ בָרַבִּים, וְהַמֵּפֵר בְּרִיתוֹ שֶׁל אַבְרָהָם אָבִינוּ עָלָיו הַשָּׁלוֹם, וְהַמְגַלֶּה פָנִים בַּתּוֹרָה שֶׁלֹּא כַהֲלָכָה, אַף עַל פִּי שֶׁיֵּשׁ בְּיָדוֹ תוֹרָה וּמַעֲשִׂים טוֹבִים, אֵין לוֹ חֵלֶק לָעוֹלָם הַבָּא.

Rabbi Elazar of Modi'in said: One who profanes sacred things, one who scorns the festivals, one who causes another's face to blush in public, one who annuls the covenant of our father Avraham, may he rest in peace, and one who is contemptuous toward the Torah, even though they have to their credit [knowledge of the] Torah and good deeds, they do not have a share in the world to come.

Our mishna lists five actions that lead one to "not have a share in the world to come." What is the common denominator? These directives share a similar concern for an inner dimension. One who views sacred objects (in this case, sacrifices) as nonsacred, as mere "things," is not picking up on this inner dimension. The same goes for one who scorns the festivals. The commentators explain that this refers to one who doesn't respect the intermediary days, the days of *chol hamo'ed*, between the first and last days of Sukkot and Pesach. The main idea is that sacrificial meat could simply be seen as "meat" and the days in-between the first and last days of the holiday could be seen as "not as special" as the other days, but this is a mistake. The mishna is reminding us that we can't always see the inner dimension of things, but that doesn't discount its importance.

I'd like to focus on the mishna's third statement, one who causes one's fellow's cheeks to blush in embarrassment also ignores this inner dimension. When one embarrasses another in public, they forget the foundation of Jewish ethics: that each one of us was created in the image of Hashem. This is one of the most important "inner dimensions."

One of my favorite stories from the Talmud shares the following:

> Rabbi Yehuda HaNasi was sitting and teaching, and he smelled the odor of garlic. Rabbi Yehuda HaNasi was very sensitive and could not tolerate this odor. He said: Whoever ate garlic should leave.
>
> Rabbi Chiyya stood up and left. Out of respect for Rabbi Chiyya, all of those in attendance stood up and left as well.
>
> The next day, in the morning, Rabbi Shimon, son of Rabbi Yehuda HaNasi, found Rabbi Chiyya, and he said to him: Are you the one who disturbed my father by coming to the lecture with the foul smell of garlic?
>
> Rabbi Chiyya said to him: There should not be such behavior among the Jewish people! I would not do such a thing, but I assumed the blame and left so that the one who did so would not be embarrassed (*Talmud Bavli*, Sanhedrin 11a (Koren translation)).

Rabbi Chiyya did all he could to not embarrass another Jew. He didn't even know who ate the garlic, but that didn't matter. His love and respect for each person in that class led him to walk out of the lesson. He even led everyone to think that he, himself, had the garlicky breath. This is the lesson of our mishna. All humans are created in the divine image (see Gen. 1:26, which refers to all of humanity). Once we truly internalize this, we will be careful, like Rabbi Chiyya, to treat this inner dimension with the care, respect, and dignity it deserves.

3:16

Everyone Is Equal before Hashem

רַבִּי יִשְׁמָעֵאל אוֹמֵר: הֱוֵי קַל לְרֹאשׁ, וְנוֹחַ לְתִשְׁחֹרֶת, וֶהֱוֵי מְקַבֵּל אֶת כָּל הָאָדָם בְּשִׂמְחָה.

Rabbi Yishmael said: Be suppliant to a superior, submissive under compulsory service, and receive every person happily.

Our mishna contains three directives. What do they mean, and how are they interconnected? The mishna opens by saying we must be "easy" or "light" (*kal*, קל) to the head (*rosh*, ראש). It then asks us to be amenable or kind/soft (*noach*, נוח) to the *tishchoret* (תשחורת). It's not clear exactly what this last word means. It concludes by stressing how we should receive everyone in a joyous manner.

Here is one way to tie the directives together: our mishna is talking about one's perceived status in relation to others. Most of the time, we will find others above or below us. This person could be someone earning more or less at work or a superior or someone one supervises. Our mishna could also be referencing where we stand in relation to others in terms of popularity, with some more popular and others less. In all these cases, we are taught to return to Ramban's guidance in his famous letter to his son:

> Why should one feel proud? Is it because of wealth? Hashem makes one poor or rich (I Sam. 2:7). Is it because of honor? It belongs to Hashem, as we read (I Chron. 29:12), "Wealth and honor come from You." So how could one adorn oneself with Hashem's

honor? And one who is proud of his wisdom surely knows that Hashem "takes away the speech of assured men and reasoning from the Sages" (Job. 12:20)?! So we see that everyone is equal before Hashem, since with His anger He lowers the proud and when He wishes He raises the low. So, lower yourself and Hashem will lift you up!

We are all equal in the eyes of Hashem because all we have or don't have is because of Hashem. This is an equalizing factor. We must keep this in mind when it comes to others to whom we might compare ourselves—at school, at home, at work, or wherever we are.

Our mishna may be hinting at this attitude. It opens by talking about those "above us." This is the ראש, or head, referred to in the first directive. We are asked to be "light" (קל) when it comes to them because there is a tendency to go overboard in seeing oneself as lowly and unworthy around them or, alternatively, to hold resentment against or be jealous of those "above us."

The second directive refers to *tishchoret*, תשחורת. This word contains within it the word *shachar* (שחר), which means dawn or early morning. This may be referring to those who are perceived as "lower on the totem pole" (as in, the beginning of the day). With regards to these individuals, we are asked to be "נוח," meaning "kind" or "amenable." Remember that you, too, were once "working your way up." Or just be grateful for the privileges you have been afforded in life and be sensitive (נוח) to those who are still "moving up" or are perceived in a less favorable light in your circle. This may be an assistant at work, someone who maintains one's institution, or a vice president in relation to the president of a company. Be nice to everyone because everyone is "equal in the eyes of Hashem!" Such a powerful statement.

The mishna concludes by asking us to not adopt this attitude only as a form of duty but to do so in a joyful manner: "And receive every person happily." When we are filled with love and care for others, we accept them happily and allow them to feel comfortable around us, whether their station in life is above or below ours. With this attitude, we will thrive on a personal level, as we won't be overly swayed by what happens around us. It will also lift others and allow them to feel genuinely accepted and valued as we joyfully accept them as equals.

3:17

Innovation from within Tradition

רַבִּי עֲקִיבָא אוֹמֵר: שְׂחוֹק וְקַלּוּת רֹאשׁ מַרְגִּילִין לְעֶרְוָה, מָסֹרֶת סְיָג לַתּוֹרָה, מַעַשְׂרוֹת סְיָג לָעֹשֶׁר, נְדָרִים סְיָג לַפְּרִישׁוּת, סְיָג לַחָכְמָה שְׁתִיקָה.

Rabbi Akiva said: Merriment and frivolity accustom one to sexual licentiousness, tradition is a fence to the Torah, tithes are a fence to wealth, vows are a fence to abstinence, a fence to wisdom is silence.

This is the first of four mishnas that contain Rabbi Akiva's teachings. Our mishna lists five statements; I'd like to focus on the second: "Tradition is a fence to the Torah." The simple understanding of this statement is that the masoretic text and the traditions handed down from generation to generation about the accurate way to read it allow for the Torah to be read in the proper way and to not be forgotten. This is the greatest protective fence around the Torah.

Another way to explain the mishna is to shift the focus to innovation in Torah. Rabbi Akiva started his career outside of the rabbinic world. He was a shepherd. He didn't grow up with a clear tradition. At age forty, he accepted for himself a more observant lifestyle. He is known for his innovation in Torah learning. This trait may have emerged precisely from the fact that he didn't grow up in a set tradition. He was more fluid; his perspective had not been fixed.

His innovation is evidenced in this fascinating Talmudic story that discusses time travel:

When Moshe ascended on High, he found the Holy One, blessed be He, engaged in attaching crowns to the letters [of the Torah]. Moshe said, "Lord of the Universe, Who stays Your hand?" [lit., Who is holding you back?/Why can't you give the Torah as is?]

God answered, "There will arise a man, at the end of many generations, Akiva son of Yosef, who will expound upon each dot and mark heaps and heaps of laws."

"Lord of the Universe," said Moshe; "permit me to see him."

God replied, "Turn around"/"Go backward."

Moshe went and sat down behind eight rows [and listened to the discourses upon the law]. Not being able to follow their arguments, his strength was deflated.

However, when they came to a certain subject and the disciples said to Rabbi Akiva, "From where do you know this?" and Rabbi Akiva replied, "It is a law given unto Moshe at Sinai," Moshe was comforted. (*Talmud Bavli*, Menachot 29b)

Several components of this story are worth highlighting. Rabbi Akiva is portrayed as the innovator extraordinaire in that he extrapolated specific laws—even from crowns on the letters of the Torah. The crowns we are referring to look like this:

ואלה שמות בני ישראל הבאים מצרימה את
יעקב איש וביתו באו ראובן שמעון לוי ויהודה
יששכר זבולן ובנימן דן ונפתלי גד ואשר ויהי
כל נפש יצאי ירך יעקב שבעים נפש ויוסף היה
במצרים וימת יוסף וכל אחיו וכל הדור ההוא
ובני ישראל פרו וישרצו וירבו ויעצמו במאד
מאד ותמלא הארץ אתם

Second, Rabbi Akiva was so innovative that Moshe, the giver of the Torah, didn't even recognize what he was teaching. This is accentuated by the fact that Moshe was seated way back in the eighth row, from which it is often hard to follow the lesson.

The last element worth noting is Moshe's shift from being "deflated" to "comforted." How did Rabbi Akiva's statement that it is the "law given to Moshe at Sinai" bring Moshe comfort? Think about it: If Moshe didn't recognize the laws, how could the message that this was taught to none other than "Moshe at Sinai" comfort him? One way this was explained to me is that, indeed, Moshe didn't recognize these innovative teachings. What brought him comfort was that Akiva understood that he must innovate from within tradition. The fact that he was continuing the Torah of Moshe brought Moshe comfort. Moshe laid down the general principles of Torah. It is up to the rabbis of every generation to extend these principles to current realities and reinterpret texts based on the values taught to us by Moshe. When Moshe understood this was Rabbi Akiva's intention, he was at ease.

This may be what Rabbi Akiva is teaching in our mishna when he says, "Tradition is a fence to the Torah." We are allowed, even encouraged, to innovate in Torah learning. The Torah was never meant to remain static. Moshe knew this, as is evidenced in this Talmudic story. If innovation was not an integral part of our tradition, he would have remained uneasy with Rabbi Akiva's teachings, even at the conclusion of this entry. Notwithstanding, innovation must extend from tradition, and the innovations need to be developed using traditional tools.

People install fences in their yards to mark how far their territory extends. They also do so for protection. When it comes to creative interpretations and applications of Torah principles, there is a lot of flexibility, but that flexibility isn't infinite. This must be done in a way that protects tradition, extending from within the "territory" of Torah. This is the recipe for Judaism to remain relevant and authentic today and for years to come.

Universalism, Nationalism, and Religiosity

הוּא הָיָה אוֹמֵר: חָבִיב אָדָם שֶׁנִּבְרָא בְצֶלֶם. חִבָּה יְתֵרָה נוֹדַעַת לוֹ שֶׁנִּבְרָא בְצֶלֶם, שֶׁנֶּאֱמַר (בראשית ט): כִּי בְּצֶלֶם אֱלֹהִים עָשָׂה אֶת הָאָדָם. חֲבִיבִין יִשְׂרָאֵל שֶׁנִּקְרְאוּ בָנִים לַמָּקוֹם. חִבָּה יְתֵרָה נוֹדַעַת לָהֶם שֶׁנִּקְרְאוּ בָנִים לַמָּקוֹם, שֶׁנֶּאֱמַר (דברים יד): בָּנִים אַתֶּם לַה' אֱלֹהֵיכֶם. חֲבִיבִין יִשְׂרָאֵל שֶׁנִּתַּן לָהֶם כְּלִי חֶמְדָּה. חִבָּה יְתֵרָה נוֹדַעַת לָהֶם שֶׁנִּתַּן לָהֶם כְּלִי חֶמְדָּה שֶׁבּוֹ נִבְרָא הָעוֹלָם, שֶׁנֶּאֱמַר (משלי ד): כִּי לֶקַח טוֹב נָתַתִּי לָכֶם, תּוֹרָתִי אַל תַּעֲזֹבוּ.

He used to say: Beloved are humans for they were created in the image [of God]. Especially beloved are those to whom it was made known that they have been created in the image [of God], as it is said: "For in the image of God He created humanity" (Gen. 9:6).

Beloved are Israel in that they were called children to the All-Present. Especially beloved are those to whom it was made known that they are called children of the All-Present, as it is said: "You are children to the Lord your God" (Deut. 14:1).

Beloved are Israel in that a precious vessel, the Torah, was given to them. Especially beloved are those to whom it was made known that the desirable instrument, with which the world had been created, was given to them, as it is said: "For I give you good instruction; forsake not my teaching" (Prov. 4:2).

A few questions arise upon reading this mishna. What is the significance of something "being made known" to us? What is the difference

119

between the three layers mentioned in the mishna: humanity, Israel, and the reception of the Torah? And how are these three interconnected?

In this fascinating entry, Rabbi Kook appears to be discussing the three elements mentioned in our mishna:

> Three forces are wrestling now in our camp... The Holy, the Nation, and Humanity—these are the three major demands of which all life, our own and every person's, is composed...[I]t is impossible to find a permanent form of human life that is not composed of these three elements. This goes for both the individual and the community. (*Shemonah Kevatzim* 3:1)

This text is a bit difficult. The bottom line is that the nation of Israel, and our own communities, as well, consist of three "forces" that are constantly at odds with one another. The first is a religious drive, "the Holy." The second, a national drive, "the Nation." The third is a more universal drive, "humanity."

Examine any point of public debate, and you will find people advocating from these three vantage points. Take the immigration debate in the US. Some see it as a religious issue; others as a national one; and others stress the universal aspects. Those seeing the issue through a religious lens will quote scripture or discuss ethics and divine mandates. Those approaching the issue from a national perspective may discuss stronger borders. The universalist approach may highlight the humanitarian plight of the individual who crossed or is trying to cross over the border. Many combine these different approaches, advocating for a national approach expressed in the Torah, for example, or for a more universal Torah perspective.

I am not getting into politics here. I am simply highlighting the fact that the three perspectives listed above are present in most debates. (An interesting exercise is seeing which political parties in Israel promote which of these three agendas or a combination thereof.) Later in this source, Rabbi Kook recommends that upon personally developing our own approach, we should take all three into consideration, even if in our final assessment one takes precedence over the other.

This may be what Rabbi Akiva is telling us. Our mishna lines up well with these three "forces." It opens by talking about the universalist force: all of humanity is created in the image of God. It then speaks of the national: all of Am Yisrael are children of Hashem. It concludes with the religious force: the Torah given to Am Yisrael.

It's important that all three of these "become known to us." Perhaps it is so that we consider the other sides of an argument even as we hold on tightly to our own. Oftentimes, when we look really hard, we will find the other side is speaking from a certain value. When we see that, we can have more respect for the other and perhaps even find a way to incorporate their values into our own approach. We have much to gain through understanding another side, even if we completely disagree. This is the secret of us being "especially beloved" when all three elements are "made known" to us.

Hashem Judges with Goodness

הַכֹּל צָפוּי, וְהָרְשׁוּת נְתוּנָה. וּבְטוֹב הָעוֹלָם נִדּוֹן. וְהַכֹּל לְפִי רֹב הַמַּעֲשֶׂה.

Everything is foreseen yet freedom of choice is granted. And the world is judged with goodness. And everything is in accordance with the preponderance of works.

People often ask me: "Rabbi, if Hashem knows everything, can do everything, and is good, why is there evil in the world?" In philosophical circles, this is called *the problem of evil*. Many times, this question will be asked in a less explicit manner, but this is often the basis of what is being asked.

The most well-known response is coined the *freedom of choice defense*. One could read Rabbi Akiva's opening words as addressing the issue from this perspective: even though Hashem knows everything ("everything is foreseen"), freedom of choice is granted. What is this line of argument? The ultimate good God can grant to us is to allow us to earn the good on our own. Hashem is autonomous. For us to be like Hashem, the ultimate Good, we must choose good on our own. This requires that there be evil in the world so that we can choose on our own to steer clear of this evil and choose good. This at times can lead to many choosing evil and, in turn, horrible outcomes, but for our choice to be free, this must be the case. When we choose good, we have earned the good autonomously. This is understood to be a far superior experience than Hashem forcing us to do good without free choice.

The mishna goes on to teach: "And the world is judged with goodness. And everything is in accordance with the preponderance of works." One may despair in thinking that if Hashem allows for evil, perhaps evil will overcome good, and our world will turn into utter chaos. Rabbi Akiva therefore adds that the world is judged favorably. Hashem intervenes, when necessary, to ensure the world is judged favorably and that the scales are tipped toward good and blessing.

One way this favorable judgment plays out is that Hashem judges us on the majority of our deeds. Even if we do choose evil, when Hashem sees we are predominantly on the path toward good, Hashem will help us advance more and more toward good (see *Mei Marom: Ori Ve'Yishi*, p. 204). This is what is meant by "everything (is judged) by the preponderance (or majority) of (one's) deeds." This is just one aspect of divine intervention tipping the scales toward good, even though free choice is granted.

Rabbi Akiva is known for saying, "Everything Hashem does is for the good" (*Talmud Bavli*, Berachot 60b–61a). Our mishna, based on the above explanation, adds another layer to this. When we choose good, Hashem judges us for the good. May this come true for all of us!

Share with Your Siblings!

הוּא הָיָה אוֹמֵר: הַכּל נָתוּן בְּעֵרָבוֹן, וּמְצוּדָה פְרוּסָה עַל כָּל הַחַיִּים. הַחֲנוּת פְּתוּחָה, וְהַחֶנְוָנִי מֵקִיף, וְהַפִּנְקָס פָּתוּחַ, וְהַיָּד כּוֹתֶבֶת, וְכָל הָרוֹצֶה לִלְווֹת יָבֹא וְיִלְוֶה. וְהַגַּבָּאִים מַחֲזִירִים תָּדִיר בְּכָל יוֹם, וְנִפְרָעִין מִן הָאָדָם מִדַּעְתּוֹ וְשֶׁלֹּא מִדַּעְתּוֹ, וְיֵשׁ לָהֶם עַל מַה שֶׁיִּסְמֹכוּ, וְהַדִּין דִּין אֱמֶת, וְהַכּל מְתֻקָּן לַסְעוּדָה.

He used to say: Everything is given against a pledge, and a net is spread out over all the living; the store is open and the storekeeper allows credit, but the ledger is open and the hand writes, and whoever wishes to borrow may come and borrow. The collectors go round regularly every day and exact dues from the individual, either with their consent or without their consent, and they have that on which they [can] rely [in their claims], seeing that the judgment is a righteous judgment, and everything is prepared for the banquet.

This is the last of Rabbi Akiva's four consecutive teachings. The imagery in this mishna is taken from a store and its storekeeper. In another of Rabbi Akiva's statements (*Mishna*, Yoma 8:9), Hashem is referred to as a parent: "Rabbi Akiva said: Happy are you, Israel! Who is it before whom you become pure? And who is it that purifies you? Your Father who is in heaven."

These two forms of imagery portray an ostensibly different experience of the divine. Hashem as Father performs kindnesses for us, oftentimes unconditionally. Hashem as Father expresses kindness through purifying us on Yom Kippur. A storekeeper, on the other hand, is much more demanding. Everything we benefit from in the store is only given to us against a pledge on collateral. If we do take items home for our own use, without payment or collateral, it's always on credit. There are no unconditional handouts (at least not in this store!). We must pay back what we took, and if we don't, creditors will make sure we return our debt, whether we consent or not. And they are in the right because "the judgment is a righteous judgment."

What is all this about? Why all the pressure? What is this debt the mishna is referring to? I like to read this mishna as relaying the underlying purpose of the skills and privileges we each have and benefit from in our lives. We enter this world and enjoy many pleasures and blessings. This is like going into a store and seeing enticing items on the shelves; however, the items are not free. Similarly, we should understand that our blessings are also not "free." We owe a debt when it comes to our benefit from them—to Hashem and to others. We should use our skills and privileges in the service of Hashem and share our blessings with others. Hashem is very much interested in this, to the point that we will be "hounded" by Hashem and Hashem's collectors until we use these skills in Hashem's service.

The storekeeper and the Father imagery are not in conflict. Hashem, as our beloved Father, loves all of us like children. This is why Hashem, like any good parent, wants us to share. We must share with our siblings! The purpose of it all is so that we can enjoy life together, as those do at a banquet that is prepared and arranged for everyone's enjoyment: "And everything is prepared for the banquet."

3:21

What Modern Orthodoxy
Can Learn from Chabad

רַבִּי אֶלְעָזָר בֶּן עֲזַרְיָה אוֹמֵר: אִם אֵין תּוֹרָה, אֵין דֶּרֶךְ אֶרֶץ. אִם אֵין דֶּרֶךְ אֶרֶץ, אֵין תּוֹרָה. אִם אֵין חָכְמָה, אֵין יִרְאָה. אִם אֵין יִרְאָה, אֵין חָכְמָה. אִם אֵין בִּינָה, אֵין דַּעַת. אִם אֵין דַּעַת, אֵין בִּינָה. אִם אֵין קֶמַח, אֵין תּוֹרָה. אִם אֵין תּוֹרָה, אֵין קֶמַח.

Rabbi Elazar ben Azariah says: If there is no Torah, there is no worldly occupation; if there is no worldly occupation, there is no Torah. If there is no wisdom, there is no fear of God; if there is no fear of God, there is no wisdom. If there is no understanding, there is no knowledge; if there is no knowledge, there is no understanding. If there is no flour, there is no Torah; if there is no Torah, there is no flour.

Whenever I read this mishna, I am reminded of a statement of a later authority, Rava (fourth century CE), that discusses what happens when we pass on to the next world. It lists questions we are asked by the Heavenly Tribunal:

> Rava said: After departing from this world, when a person is brought to judgment for the life they lived in this world, it is said: Did you conduct business faithfully? Did you designate times for Torah study? Did you engage in procreation? Did you yearn for salvation? Did you engage in the dialectics of

wisdomor understand one matter from another?
(*Talmud Bavli*, Shabbat 31a (Koren translation)).

All the traits mentioned in our mishna appear in Rava's teaching in one form or another. This points to their ultimate importance, as these are *the* topics addressed during one's judgment.

Let's go through the parallels. Our mishna opens mentioning Torah and derech eretz. Above, derech eretz is translated to "worldly occupation." However, this term also refers to conjugal relations (in the *maggid* section of the Haggadah we mention *prishut derech eretz*, which translates to "separating from conjugal relations"). Here we have two questions: "Did you designate times for Torah study?"; "Did you engage in procreation?"

Wisdom, understanding, and knowledge from our mishna correspond to: "Did you engage in the dialectics of wisdom or understand one matter from another?" Fear of God is connected to: "Did you yearn for salvation?" Believing that there is a purpose and a divine hand who will bring salvation is based on fear of heaven. And the first question, "Did you conduct business faithfully?" is related to the "flour" mentioned at the end of our mishna which refers to earning a livelihood.

In sum, between the two sources, this is what's important to focus on:

- Torah
- Wisdom in its various forms
- Yearning for salvation
- Procreation
- Honest business dealings

I once gave a sermon on what Modern Orthodoxy can learn from Chabad. There is much to learn, especially when it comes to their outreach. However, one item on this list that stands out is yearning for salvation. Modern Orthodoxy is filled with Torah and secular knowledge. People earn a good living, and families include many children. This checks off four out of the five boxes, which is commendable. However, when it comes to an active faith and yearning for Mashiach (the messiah) and the redemptive era, there is much to learn from Chabad. This is more of a central focus in Chabad circles.

Rava's statement reveals how important these values are. Our mishna reminds us that all these traits are interdependent. I am adding that as a nation we must be careful to steer away from denominational politics and come together, so each group can strengthen the other through their stronger values. In the language of our mishna: if there is no Modern Orthodoxy, there is no Chabad; if there is no Chabad, there is no Modern Orthodoxy. And this can be said for other streams as well. To be sure, I am not speaking existentially: these movements are self-sufficient. I am speaking in terms of each being open to being its best by looking around and taking the good that is accentuated in other groups. Each movement can benefit by being inspired by the others. This is my dream for the Jewish world. If we do so, we will live in harmony with each other and enjoy many blessings—in this world and the next.

3:22

The Power of Jewish Experiences

רַבִּי אֶלְעָזָר בֶּן עֲזַרְיָה אוֹמֵר: כָּל שֶׁחָכְמָתוֹ מְרֻבָּה מִמַּעֲשָׂיו, לְמָה הוּא דוֹמֶה? לְאִילָן שֶׁעֲנָפָיו מְרֻבִּין וְשָׁרָשָׁיו מֻעָטִין, וְהָרוּחַ בָּאָה וְעוֹקַרְתּוֹ וְהוֹפַכְתּוֹ עַל פָּנָיו, שֶׁנֶּאֱמַר (ירמיה יז): וְהָיָה כְּעַרְעָר בָּעֲרָבָה וְלֹא יִרְאֶה כִּי יָבוֹא טוֹב וְשָׁכַן חֲרֵרִים בַּמִּדְבָּר אֶרֶץ מְלֵחָה וְלֹא תֵשֵׁב. אֲבָל כָּל שֶׁמַּעֲשָׂיו מְרֻבִּין מֵחָכְמָתוֹ, לְמָה הוּא דוֹמֶה? לְאִילָן שֶׁעֲנָפָיו מֻעָטִין וְשָׁרָשָׁיו מְרֻבִּין, שֶׁאֲפִלּוּ כָל הָרוּחוֹת שֶׁבָּעוֹלָם בָּאוֹת וְנוֹשְׁבוֹת בּוֹ אֵין מְזִיזִין אוֹתוֹ מִמְּקוֹמוֹ, שֶׁנֶּאֱמַר (שם): וְהָיָה כְּעֵץ שָׁתוּל עַל מַיִם וְעַל יוּבַל יְשַׁלַּח שָׁרָשָׁיו וְלֹא יִרְאֶה כִּי יָבֹא חֹם, וְהָיָה עָלֵהוּ רַעֲנָן, וּבִשְׁנַת בַּצֹּרֶת לֹא יִדְאָג, וְלֹא יָמִישׁ מֵעֲשׂוֹת פֶּרִי.

Rabbi Elazar ben Azariah used to say: Anyone whose wisdom exceeds their deeds, to what are they compared? To a tree whose branches are many but whose roots are few; then the wind comes and uproots it and turns it upside down; as it is said: "And he shall be like a lonely juniper tree in the wasteland and shall not see when good comes, but shall inhabit the parched places of the wilderness, a salt filled land which is uninhabitable" (Jer. 17:6).

But one whose deeds exceed one's wisdom, what is that person like? Like a tree whose branches are few, but whose roots are many; even if all the winds of the world were to come and blow upon it, they would not move it from its place, as it is said: "He shall be like a tree planted by the waters, which spreads out its roots by the river, and shall not perceive when heat comes, but its leaf shall remain fresh; and it will not be troubled in the year of drought, nor will it cease to bear fruit" (ibid., 17:8).

From a Jewish perspective, understanding what we are doing is critical. Many times, actions can help us understand even more than what we glean from book knowledge. This may be what Am Yisrael meant when they said, "We will do and we will listen," on Mount Sinai (Exod. 24:7). We will do, and through this we will come to listen and understand even more.

This is true for all Yiddishkeit. When I first became more observant, I had a stage where I held that until someone could prove to me, in my head, that Judaism was correct, I wouldn't commit to an observant lifestyle. My Orthodox cousin invited me over for Shabbos to talk about this and other issues. He didn't answer everything, but he did provide a warm Shabbos table experience, and that in itself drew me in. This is the way that whole period was for me. My yeshiva experience and Shabbos table attendance throughout those impressionable years left a large mark on how my religious life is led today. I studied a lot in those years; however, my Jewish experiences during those years played a large part in "grounding" me in our tradition.

This is the message of our mishna. Someone whose wisdom exceeds their actions can find themselves at times less "rooted" than one whose actions exceed their wisdom. One who has fully experienced Judaism, through actions and involvement, stands a better chance to be connected to the extent that even if "all the winds of the world were to come and blow upon them, they would not move them from their place."

3:23

Inside While Outside

רַבִּי אֱלִיעֶזֶר בֶּן חִסְמָא אוֹמֵר: קִנִּין וּפִתְחֵי נִדָּה, הֵן הֵן גּוּפֵי
הֲלָכוֹת. תְּקוּפוֹת וְגִימַטְרִיָאוֹת, פַּרְפְּרָאוֹת לַחָכְמָה.

Rabbi Eliezer ben Chisma said: The laws of mixed bird offerings and the laws regarding the beginning of menstrual periods—these are the body of the halacha. Astronomy and mathematics are the seasonings of wisdom.

Being involved in the world can be challenging. It's often easier just to focus on spiritual matters and to not be engaged at all. However, not everyone has that luxury as most of us need to work and be involved in the world for various reasons. And many of us simply don't want to be set apart, intuitively sensing that Torah and the modern world should work together. Our mishna provides two reminders to us on how to remain "inside" Judaism while actively engaged in the "outside" world.

The first lesson is to stay on track with one's Torah learning and to not forget to learn details of Jewish law. The mishna opens by listing two complicated areas of Torah law, composed of many details. The laws of niddah, calculations of menstrual cycles, are very detailed, as are the laws of mixed-bird offerings. The latter deal with doubts that arise when one bird gets mixed with another bird and one must decide which can be accepted as a sacrifice.

When one is heavily involved in *olam hazeh*, "this world," there is a tendency to learn Torah in a superficial manner due to a lack of time, energy, and focus. These are real challenges. The mishna guides us, nev-

133

ertheless, to work on overcoming them. We must find time to learn these details as well, even the difficult ones mentioned in our mishna, because this is the "body" of halacha. I like to see this "body" reference as hinting at the fact that without digging into the details and minutiae of Jewish law, all we are left with are abstract ideas. We need to ground these ideas in tangible and applied details. These details improve our lives and keep us "grounded" in Torah.

Being involved in the world can also lead one to lose perspective regarding the proper hierarchy of values. This happened to me when I was heavily engrossed in real estate while living in Israel. I had a two-year stretch where I worked as a real estate agent. During this time, I found it hard to stay plugged in to Torah and Yiddishkeit, no doubt due to all the competing influences around me.

Our mishna teaches us that secular studies such as math and astronomy, along with other engagements of the world, are worthy pursuits. However, if we can find a way to bring them into the world of Torah, this is even better. This is the second lesson of the mishna: "Astronomy and mathematics are the seasonings of wisdom." If we can use our engagement in the world to "season" our Jewish lives, to help us better understand Torah or enhance our Jewish experience, this is the ideal form of engagement.

These two directives of the mishna are not easy. I admit that I myself did not live up to the mishna's direction while trying my hand at real estate. There was a period when I learned with a study partner, but over time, regrettably, I became lax in my studies. And, as I mentioned, I struggled to maintain perspective and "season" my Yiddishkeit with the good I gleaned from the world. I ended up going back to yeshiva and rededicating myself to Torah and, in time, becoming a rabbi. I like to hope, though, that if given another chance, I would be smarter than I was fifteen years ago and heed Rabbi Eliezer ben Chisma's guidance. Remaining grounded "inside" Judaism while involved in the "outside" world is a huge challenge. If one can do this, as per our mishna's suggestion, one will enjoy the best that both worlds have to offer.

Every Person Has a Lesson to Teach

בֶּן זוֹמָא אוֹמֵר: אֵיזֶהוּ חָכָם? הַלּוֹמֵד מִכָּל אָדָם, שֶׁנֶּאֱמַר (תהלים קיט): מִכָּל מְלַמְּדַי
הִשְׂכַּלְתִּי כִּי עֵדְוֹתֶיךָ שִׂיחָה לִי. אֵיזֶהוּ גִבּוֹר? הַכּוֹבֵשׁ אֶת יִצְרוֹ, שֶׁנֶּאֱמַר (משלי טז): טוֹב
אֶרֶךְ אַפַּיִם מִגִּבּוֹר וּמֹשֵׁל בְּרוּחוֹ מִלֹּכֵד עִיר. אֵיזֶהוּ עָשִׁיר? הַשָּׂמֵחַ בְּחֶלְקוֹ, שֶׁנֶּאֱמַר (תהלים
קכח): יְגִיעַ כַּפֶּיךָ כִּי תֹאכֵל אַשְׁרֶיךָ וְטוֹב לָךְ. אַשְׁרֶיךָ בָּעוֹלָם הַזֶּה וְטוֹב לָךְ לָעוֹלָם הַבָּא.
אֵיזֶהוּ מְכֻבָּד? הַמְכַבֵּד אֶת הַבְּרִיּוֹת, שֶׁנֶּאֱמַר (שמואל א ב): כִּי מְכַבְּדַי אֲכַבֵּד וּבֹזַי יֵקָלּוּ.

Ben Zoma said: Who is wise? The one who learns from every person, as it is said: "From all who taught me have I gained understanding" (Ps. 119:99). Who is mighty? One who subdues their [evil] inclination, as it is said: "One that is slow to anger is better than the mighty; and one that rules their spirit than one that takes a city" (Prov. 16:32). Who is rich? One who rejoices in their lot, as it is said: "You shall enjoy the fruit of your labors, you shall be happy and you shall prosper" (Ps. 128:2) "You shall be happy" in this world, "and you shall prosper" in the world to come. Who is one that is honored? One who honors their fellow human beings as it is said: "For I honor those that honor Me, but those who spurn Me shall be dishonored" (I Sam. 2:30).

I'd like to discuss the idea of the title "wise" being bestowed upon one who learns from others. One could make an argument that this is not always the case. When I started out in yeshiva, my rebbes asked me to attend class every day. As I progressed and became more comfortable with the texts, they encouraged the opposite: more individual learning.

They believed I would gain more at that stage from grappling with the text on my own. They were correct.

Therefore, I'd like to suggest that the mishna is not talking about amassed knowledge. Sometimes (of course, not all the time!) one can amass more knowledge on one's own. Instead, it is speaking about our *orientation* toward others. The mishna guides us to see the positive sides in others—what we can learn from each and every person.

The mishna refers to this as a "wise" direction because it is the truth. We often live in the bubble of delusional thinking, especially when we are younger. As we mature, we realize things aren't so simple, and we really don't "know it all." We realize the truth: we have a lot to learn from everyone. It could be simplicity from a three-year-old, patience from an elder, or diligence from a younger person embarking on their career. The Sages even extend this to animals (*Talmud Bavli*, Eruvin 100b).

The more we are aware of the truth, the wiser we will be, and the more we will, in the end, come to learn from others. "Who is wise? The one who (is willing to) learn from every person."

A Bit of Light Can Banish
a Lot of Darkness

בֶּן עַזַּאי אוֹמֵר: הֱוֵי רָץ לְמִצְוָה קַלָּה כְּבַחֲמוּרָה, וּבוֹרֵחַ מִן הָעֲבֵרָה. שֶׁמִּצְוָה גּוֹרֶרֶת
מִצְוָה, וַעֲבֵרָה גּוֹרֶרֶת עֲבֵרָה. שֶׁשְּׂכַר מִצְוָה מִצְוָה, וּשְׂכַר עֲבֵרָה עֲבֵרָה.

Ben Azzai said: Be quick in performing a minor commandment as in the case of a major one and flee from transgression [lit., the transgression]. For one commandment leads to another commandment, and one transgression leads to another transgression. For the reward for performing a commandment is another commandment and the reward for committing a transgression is another transgression.

In discussing positive commandments, Ben Azzai speaks of running even to minor commandments. However, when it comes to sin, from a literal reading, it appears that he is referring to a single transgression: "Flee from *the* transgression," מן העבירה (see *Sfat Emet* ad loc., s.v. ve-chen uvoreach). A possible way to explain this is to say that, indeed, our mishna's whole focus is on one transgression: the transgression we are struggling with most at this moment. Everyone has their vices: it could be stealing, lying, gossiping, or even cheating on your diet. All of us have that "thing" that we are working on. This is "*the* transgression" mentioned in our mishna.

One way to deal with negativity is to face it head-on, by assessing the problem and then overcoming it through willpower or some other tactic. Our mishna offers another model: staying connected to positivity. It opens by telling us to run after a minor mitzvah. We must run without hesitation to do good. On some level it doesn't matter how "major" a mitzvah it is: just grab onto good and don't let go. There is a principle discussed a lot in chassidic works: "A little bit of light banishes a lot of darkness." This is the message relayed when reading the opening of the mishna in sequential order: even a minor positive deed (a little bit of light) can help one with one's major transgression (a lot of darkness).

The continuation of our mishna fleshes out this idea a bit more. It speaks of the downward spiraling effect of being steeped in sin. We cheat that one time on our diet, and then you know the rest. You are right back where you started, hiding for cover as you scarf down cookie after cookie. This is the concept of "one transgression leads to another transgression…and the reward for committing a transgression is another transgression." It's not so much a reward, but a direct result of being connected to a negative trait or reality.

Our mishna shares that the inverse is true as well: "one commandment leads to another commandment." This is why it's imperative to constantly be involved in good acts, running to perform even a small deed. One small deed leads to another, and after a while we have gained momentum and garnered enough strength to fight off negative influences and even "flee from *the* transgression."

4:3

Shortcomings as Misplaced Attributes

הוּא הָיָה אוֹמֵר: אַל תְּהִי בָז לְכָל אָדָם, וְאַל תְּהִי מַפְלִיג לְכָל דָּבָר. שֶׁאֵין לְךָ אָדָם שֶׁאֵין לוֹ שָׁעָה וְאֵין לְךָ דָבָר שֶׁאֵין לוֹ מָקוֹם.

He used to say: Do not despise any person, and do not discriminate against anything, for there is no person that has not their hour, and there is no thing that has not its place.

This mishna teaches the idea that many times shortcomings are simply misplaced attributes. When I was in high school, I attended many self-help seminars. I wasn't religiously observant at the time and was looking for direction in life. At the time, these workshops helped fill that need. They forced me to focus on myself and to make lists of what I needed to work on. I would list my attributes and my shortcomings and then commit to strengthening the former and correcting the latter. Even at a young age, albeit without the language to define it, I felt something was off with this binary outlook on good versus bad traits, attributes versus shortcomings. It wasn't until I came across kabbalistic works, and more precisely Rabbi Kook's thought, that I realized what didn't sit well with me.

In many places, Rabbi Kook discusses the idea that failure in one area is due to a lack of proper channeling of one's positive traits (see *Shemonah Kevatzim* 2:168). I had a friend who just couldn't sit down in yeshiva. Based on yeshiva standards, perhaps he wasn't a success story. He went on, however, to be a great cantor in a prominent synagogue. You see this all the time. Someone is skilled at one thing, but when asked to do another, they don't have the proper skill set to succeed. When they apply their skills properly, they see themselves flourish.

Our mishna teaches us that we should be very careful before we despise or discriminate against anyone or anything. A shortcoming in one area may be an improperly channeled attribute. This is the idea that there is "no thing that has not its place." On the surface, something may seem completely bad, but when we look a bit deeper, we discover that it may just be in the "wrong place"!

Humility Versus Lowliness

רַבִּי לְוִיטָס אִישׁ יַבְנֶה אוֹמֵר: מְאֹד מְאֹד הֱוֵי שְׁפַל רוּחַ, שֶׁתִּקְוַת אֱנוֹשׁ רִמָּה.

R abbi Levitas a man of Yavneh said: Be very, very lowly in spirit, for
the end of the individual is the worm.

In his commentary to this mishna, Maimonides lists a group of three
traits: arrogance (גאוה), humility (ענוה), and lowliness of spirit (שפל רוח),
with humility stationed as the middle path between these two extremes.
Our mishna discusses the third trait: lowliness of spirit. Maimonides
says that when it comes to most character traits, we should choose the
middle path. For instance, in relation to spending, we should be neither overly frugal nor overly lavish. However, regarding arrogance, he
says we should lean toward lowliness even though humility is the middle
path. This is what the mishna means when it tells us to be "very, very"
("מאד מאד") lowly in spirit: we should always lean to the side of lowliness
even though it is not the middle path.

Rabbeinu Yonah, in his commentary to our mishna, brings a debate
in relation to the need to distance ourselves all the way toward lowliness.
He begins by listing the opposing view to that expressed in our mishna:

> And the Sages of the Talmud have already argued
> about this thing in *Talmud Bavli*, Sotah 5a: "One
> said, 'In excommunication is the one that has it and
> in excommunication is the one that does not have

it at all,'" that is to say that a person should not be humble in spirit to the final extreme and not to be so lowly that people disparage him. Rather, they should be moderate in when it comes to haughtiness—not to (beautify themselves), but not to lower their spirit to the utmost lowliness, that they not come to disgrace.

As we see, this is a debate in the Talmud. In our mishna, Rabbi Levitas foreshadows the Talmudic approach that prefers lowliness over humility.

We should make room for both approaches in our service of Hashem. Rabbi Levitas's direction can greatly aid us in our overall orientation toward life. We should realize we are no better than others because we are all destined to arrive at the same destination: the grave (with its "worms"). This doesn't have to be a depressing thought. It can lead to deep humility ("very, very lowly") as we realize that no matter how important we think we are, our ultimate destiny, at least when it comes to our bodies, is shared with everyone else.

However, in terms of functioning in the world, the alternative view can be very useful. The middle path of humility (ענוה) recognizes objective truths such as the talents and skills we all uniquely possess. This outlook enhances our daily performance and engenders a positive perspective of ourselves and life. When done correctly, a healthy combination of lowliness and humility can propel us to great heights in our spiritual work.

There are No Shortcuts When
it Comes to Self-Correction

רַבִּי יוֹחָנָן בֶּן בְּרוֹקָא אוֹמֵר: כָּל הַמְחַלֵּל שֵׁם שָׁמַיִם בַּסֵּתֶר, נִפְרָעִין
מִמֶּנּוּ בְגָלוּי. אֶחָד שׁוֹגֵג וְאֶחָד מֵזִיד בְּחִלּוּל הַשֵּׁם.

Rabbi Yochanan ben Berokah said: Whoever desecrates the name of heaven in secret, shall be punished in the open. Unwittingly or wittingly, it is all one in desecrating God's name.

When it comes to mitzvah performance, Judaism isn't against a "fake it till you make it" attitude. *Sefer HaChinuch* famously teaches that "the hearts are drawn after the actions." Performing actions, even if one isn't on the fitting "level" to perform them, can prove beneficial in that it influences one to desire achieving that higher level. Similarly, Rebbe Nachman of Breslov teaches that happiness is so important that at times we should force ourselves to act silly in the hopes that through this we will stir up inner joy (see *Likutei Moharan* 2:24).

However, when we end up settling for these forced behaviors instead of correcting our insides, things veer from the right path. Rabbi Moshe Chaim Luzzato discusses a case in which someone pretends to be humble on the outside without truly cultivating an attitude of humility on the inside. In the end, this inner arrogance surfaces on the outside:

One may find another arrogant person who wants to be very renowned for his qualities...that he wants that they praise him...for being the humblest of the humble...This arrogant person will set his place among those of much lower status than himself or among the disgraceful men thinking that through this he displays absolute humility. He does not wish for any titles of greatness and refuses all praise, all the while saying to himself: "There is no wiser and humbler person than me in the whole world!" Such arrogant people, although they may appear to be humble, nevertheless there are no lack of stumbling blocks which, without their knowledge, reveal their arrogance like the flame which bursts forth between shards. Our sages of blessed memory have already made an analogy on this: "This is like a house full of straw. The walls had cracks through which the straw entered. After some days, the straw inside the cracks began to emerge outside. Thus, everyone realized that the house was full of straw." (*Mesillat Yesharim*, ch. 11)

This is what our mishna is saying when it proclaims, "Whoever desecrates the name of heaven in secret, shall be punished in the open." These things done in secret end up manifesting themselves in one way or another on the outside and come back to haunt (punish) us. There are no shortcuts when it comes to self-correction. It's about being honest and assessing what needs correction, then diligently working toward improvement. When we do so, the opposite fate awaits us: we sanctify Hashem's name in public as our inner goodness shines for all to see.

4:6

Translating Learning into Social Action

רַבִּי יִשְׁמָעֵאל בְּנוֹ אוֹמֵר: הַלּוֹמֵד תּוֹרָה עַל מְנָת לְלַמֵּד, מַסְפִּיקִין בְּיָדוֹ לִלְמֹד וּלְלַמֵּד.
וְהַלּוֹמֵד עַל מְנָת לַעֲשׂוֹת, מַסְפִּיקִין בְּיָדוֹ לִלְמֹד וּלְלַמֵּד, לִשְׁמֹר וְלַעֲשׂוֹת.

Rabbi Yishmael his son said: One who learns in order to teach, it is granted to them to study and to teach; but one who learns in order to practice, it is granted to them to learn and to teach and to practice.

I had a rabbi who used to criticize traditional yeshiva learning. In yeshiva, we would spend months learning Talmudic discussions that were theoretical and impractical. Sometimes our rebbes even searched out these impractical discussions, following the tradition adopted in seminaries of "learning for the sake of learning." There is a mitzvah to toil in learning. This brings us close to Hashem because through this we attain *sechel shel Torah* (the intellect of Torah). This is how it was explained to me.

Based on this agenda, it matters less if the learning is practical. Sometimes the practicality of the learning makes it less difficult and esoteric, leading to less "toil" in Torah. This is one of the ideas behind choosing theoretical topics.

As I mentioned, this rabbi wasn't pleased with this. In discussions on this topic, he directed our attention to our mishna and asked which of the following *does not* appear as an ideal to strive for:

a)   Learning for the sake of learning

b) Learning for the sake of teaching

c) Learning for the sake of practicing

The answer, of course, is A. He encouraged us to focus more on the latter two, which are more practical in nature.

While I don't completely ascribe to this view, I do see the truth underlying his guidance. While it's important to know, think, and analyze, it's also imperative to translate these teachings into action. This is especially true these days.

Our mishna reminds us that our Torah learning must not remain theoretical. When applied to current events, we are reminded to find ways to teach others of the wrongs of racism and injustice (learn for the sake of teaching) and to act in our lives on behalf of changing things for the better (learn for the sake of practice). We all must fight the right fight against injustice in our world.

We, as Jews, are citizens of the larger world. If we only learn about caring for the stranger and the divine image in all humans but aren't moved to manifest these positive ideals on the ground, we are missing something in our learning. Our Torah is a *Torat Chaim*, a Torah of life, which deals with real-life matters. Our Torah, as is evidenced in this mishna, urges us to not only theorize about the right thing to do but to work toward improving our world through education and action.

4:7

The Torah is Meant to be Enjoyed

רַבִּי צָדוֹק אוֹמֵר: אַל תַּעֲשֵׂם עֲטָרָה לְהִתְגַּדֵּל בָּהֶם, וְלֹא קַרְדֹּם לַחְפֹּר בָּהֶם. וְכָךְ הָיָה הֵלֵּל אוֹמֵר: וּדְאִשְׁתַּמֵּשׁ בְּתַגָא, חָלָף. הָא לָמַדְתָּ, כָּל הַנֶּהֱנֶה מִדִּבְרֵי תוֹרָה נוֹטֵל חַיָּיו מִן הָעוֹלָם.

Rabbi Tzadok said: Do not make them a crown for self-exaltation, nor a spade with which to dig. So, too, Hillel used to say, "One that puts the crown to their own use shall perish." Thus, you have learned, anyone who derives benefit from the words of the Torah removes their life from the world.

The straightforward understanding of this mishna reminds us of the great reverence due to the Torah. Due to its holiness, we must not derive unfitting benefit from the Torah, such as using it for self-exaltation (as a crown) or for financial benefit (as a spade). This is so severe that one who does so "removes their life from the world."

A possible alternative reading of the mishna highlights another required element of Torah learning: enjoyment and happiness. Some believe that we must not enjoy our learning of the Torah because this would equate to us engaging in Torah learning for ulterior motives. Rabbi Avraham Borenstein, the Socochover Rebbe, in his introduction to his seminal work on the laws of Shabbat, *Iglei Tal*, says the opposite. He argues that this is the ideal way to learn Torah. The more one enjoys one's learning, the more optimal it is. In his words: "This is the essence of the mitzvah of learning Torah—to be able to rejoice,

147

delight, and enjoy in his learning, and then the words of Torah are absorbed into his blood."

Our mishna, when read a bit out of its original context, relays this same message. Above, we translated נהנה as "benefit." However, this Hebrew word can also mean enjoyment. With this in mind, we can read the final line in the positive: one who truly enjoys their Torah learning (כל הנהנה מדברי תורה) *merits* to be removed (נוטל חייו) from the world (מן העולם). In other words, we must "remove" ourselves from secondary reasons for learning Torah that are related to "the world" and learn solely from a spiritual place—due to enjoyment of the Torah.

Our mishna alludes to the need to distance oneself from worldly motives by bringing examples reflective of the full range of secondary reasons for learning. Earlier in the mishna we hear about one who uses the Torah as a crown or as a spade for digging. Many interpretations are offered for these two engagements; I would like to bring attention to the reason why these specific examples were chosen. A crown is used on the top of one's body, on one's head, while a spade is used near the bottom, at one's feet. Perhaps this is hinting at the full spectrum of secondary reasons: from head to toe! It's always praiseworthy to learn Torah. However, the highest level is true enjoyment and excitement from learning. "This," according to the Socochover Rebbe, "is the essence of the mitzvah of learning Torah."

Respect Yourself and You'll be Respected by Others

רַבִּי יוֹסֵי אוֹמֵר: כָּל הַמְכַבֵּד אֶת הַתּוֹרָה, גּוּפוֹ מְכֻבָּד עַל הַבְּרִיּוֹת.
וְכָל הַמְחַלֵּל אֶת הַתּוֹרָה, גּוּפוֹ מְחֻלָּל עַל הַבְּרִיּוֹת.

Rabbi Yosi said: Whoever honors the Torah is themselves honored by others, and whoever dishonors the Torah is themselves dishonored by others.

Observant Jews sometimes think that if they change the way they behave and just "fit in" with those around them, this will lead to them enjoying greater acceptance among these groups. To be sure, this sometimes works. I grew up nonobservant, so I know that when I am around my nonobservant friends from childhood, it's best if I don't say "baruch Hashem" (thank God) every other sentence. These omissions and other similar gestures foster a better connection between us and allow them to feel more comfortable around me.

However, on a more fundamental level, people tend to respect those who are authentic and true to themselves. True acceptance from others often results from us respecting ourselves (see *Chelek Yakov* ad loc.). This is what our mishna relays when it teaches, "Whoever honors the Torah is themselves honored by others." When we honor our own Torah lifestyle—not hiding or diminishing in shame but instead projecting a message of passion and authenticity—we engender respect from those around us. Conversely, when we attempt to hide who we are, seeking to fit in with others, the opposite result may ensue: "Whoever dishonors the Torah is themselves dishonored by others."

Holding Our Public Officials
Accountable

רַבִּי יִשְׁמָעֵאל בְּנוֹ אוֹמֵר: הַחוֹשֵׂךְ עַצְמוֹ מִן הַדִּין, פּוֹרֵק מִמֶּנּוּ אֵיבָה, וְגָזֵל, וּשְׁבוּעַת שָׁוְא. וְהַגַּס לִבּוֹ בַהוֹרָאָה, שׁוֹטֶה, רָשָׁע, וְגַס רוּחַ.

Rabbi Yishmael his son said: One who refrains from judgment, rids themselves of enmity, robbery, and false swearing; but one whose heart is presumptuous in giving a judicial decision, is foolish, wicked, and arrogant.

Our mishna discusses the great responsibility of serving as a community leader. This is quite a relevant lesson for us today against the backdrop of our heated political climate. Our mishna describes the challenges and dangers of serving as a judge, but similar lessons can be applied to serving in the police force as well.

It's definitely not easy being a judge. One often is hated (enmity) by at least one of the sides. And one constantly runs the risk of making the wrong legal decisions. This can unwittingly lead to a perversion of justice, allowing one side to "rob" the other or force one side to offer an unnecessary oath.

These pitfalls are not always the fault of the judge. One will inevitably let one side down and end up being the object of enmity; this is part of the job. And one is bound to make mistakes. Nobody is perfect. This is why the mishna recommends seeking out a compromise, a reconciliation, if possible, and "refraining from judgment."

The continuation of the mishna lists three obstacles that are more directly under one's control: foolishness, wickedness, and arrogance. All three lead one to be presumptuous in deciding cases, which is defined by the commentators as a hastiness to decide without proper research or a placing of oneself in the center instead of the needs of those who appear in court.

As mentioned, this is a very relevant mishna in today's political climate. Just replace the title "judge" with "police officer" and you realize they face similar obstacles. Police face the inevitable fate of being hated by a large swath of the community. This is just the nature of their job as enforcers of the law. Cops make mistakes. Some are due to foolishness, wickedness, and arrogance. This needs to be called out and condemned, especially when the wickedness manifests as racism and blatant discrimination. Other times, however, it is due to them being human, as we mentioned in relation to the judge and the robbery and false oaths which may ensue from their decisions.

Our mishna provides a balanced view when it comes to our authorities. We should hold them accountable when they are acting foolish, evil, or arrogant. However, we must also recognize that many are trying their best and are under constant pressure from many directions. Rabbi Chanina already taught us in an earlier mishna (*Ethics of the Fathers* 3:2): "Pray for the welfare of the government, for were it not for the fear it inspires, every person would swallow their neighbor alive." We must pray for the law enforcers that they will not judge presumptuously but instead improve the quality of life, ensuring daily that our community members don't "swallow each other alive."

4:10

Making Space for Opposing Views

הוּא הָיָה אוֹמֵר: אַל תְּהִי דָן יְחִידִי, שֶׁאֵין דָּן יְחִידִי אֶלָּא אֶחָד.
וְאַל תֹּאמַר: קַבְּלוּ דַעְתִּי, שֶׁהֵן רַשָּׁאִין וְלֹא אָתָּה.

He used to say: Do not judge alone, for none may judge alone except for one. And do not say, "Accept my view," for they are free but not you.

Our mishna urges us to make space for others' views during the decision-making process. It starts off by warning judges to not judge alone. In Jewish law, it is generally forbidden to judge a case without companions. Only one person is allowed to do so ("for none may judge alone except for one"): a *dayan mumcheh*, a judge with expertise. All others must refrain from judging alone. Another explanation is that even this judge, although technically allowed to judge alone, shouldn't do so, because only One—Hashem—can truly judge alone. Hashem knows all sides of the case; we must consult with others.

The mishna goes on to warn that when we finally do bring others into the mix, we should actually listen to their input. Do not enforce your view on them ("accept my view"). Instead, give them the freedom and space to disagree. Hold yourself back to make space for their views ("they are free but not you").

Why is it so important to listen to other voices? One obvious answer, which I alluded to above, is that unlike Hashem, we as limited mortals can't see all sides of the picture. The more input we receive from others, the more educated and balanced a judgment we can pass on any given topic.

The previous answer assumes that our own approach is partial and needs to be bolstered and/or adapted to some extent through the aid of an outside voice. Another direction to go with this is to say the opposite: sometimes we don't know what we really think until we hear an opposing view. The opposing view helps us strengthen our own convictions and realize what we truly feel.

Additionally, hearing an outside voice can help us sharpen and better articulate our own approach. I sometimes will start out a class teaching a topic in a certain way. Upon hearing questions and feedback from participants, I emerge from my lecture better able to articulate my approach and understand it in a more nuanced manner.

There is a verse in the Bible which encapsulates these three answers. It is the verse which describes humanity's need for companionship: "And God the Lord said, 'It is not good for Adam to be alone. I will make for him an *ezer kenegdo*'" (Gen. 2:18).

The idea brought to the forefront in our mishna, that we can't do things alone, is highlighted in the first part of the verse. In the second half of the verse, we learn the reason why: because we require an *ezer kenegdo*. What does this mean? *Ezer* means "an assistant" or "helper" and *kenegdo* means "opposite" or "against" him. We shouldn't judge alone but instead go to all lengths to create space for other voices. Our own voice needs "assistance" (the first answer above) because we can't see all sides of the story. And at times an "opposite" view (*kenegdo*) aids in strengthening or sharpening our own opinions (the second and third answers above).

Fun Judaism Is Not Enough

רַבִּי יוֹנָתָן אוֹמֵר: כָּל הַמְקַיֵּם אֶת הַתּוֹרָה מֵעֹנִי, סוֹפוֹ לְקַיְּמָהּ מֵעֹשֶׁר.
וְכָל הַמְבַטֵּל אֶת הַתּוֹרָה מֵעֹשֶׁר, סוֹפוֹ לְבַטְּלָהּ מֵעֹנִי.

Rabbi Yonatan said: Whoever fulfills the Torah out of a state of poverty, their end will be to fulfill it out of a state of wealth. And whoever discards The Torah out of a state of wealth, their end will be to discard it out of a state of poverty.

Empirical data shows that there are many people who discard the Torah out of a state of wealth and nevertheless remain wealthy upon doing so. Similarly, there are many who fulfill the Torah amid poverty and remain poor afterward. Rabbi Berel Wein therefore offers that the mishna is describing two orientations to Torah observance: one based on true Torah values and another based on societal concerns.

When one is committed to true Torah values and performs the commandments from a genuine and educated mindset, any shifts in financial status will not greatly impact one's observance. Conversely, one who performs commandments for less idealistic reasons is more at risk for abandoning the Torah when their financial status changes.

In this latter category, Rabbi Wein lists people who perform commandments due to their "environment and current financial situation." I would include those who follow the Torah because they learned to do so at home but never really cultivated a genuine connection of their own; those who enjoy the social aspect of Judaism but do not internally connect to Torah and mitzvot; and those who stay connected for some other external cause—because it's fun or some other reward or benefit.

This is the lesson of the mishna. One who genuinely observes the Torah while poor will be less enticed to abandon the Torah when they come upon great wealth: "Their end will be to fulfill it out of a state of wealth." And one who doesn't fully live Torah while rich will most likely not have the spiritual stamina and values to help them maintain that same level of observance should their financial luck change for the worse: "Their end will be to discard it out of a state of poverty."

This mishna is a wake-up call for Jewish educators. We surely must provide all the fun we can while teaching. I remember getting "bribed" by my rabbis to come and learn Torah with all kinds of good food and fun games. But if we do not provide content that is inspiring, if we do not firmly ground our students and children in Jewish texts and empower them to forge a real and lasting connection to Yiddishkeit, we have not fulfilled our task. It's not enough to provide "fun Judaism." We must prepare the next generation so that when they are faced with temptations as they grow older, their "end will be to fulfill" the Torah and not abandon our cherished tradition. May Hashem assist us in this holy work!

4:12

Spiritual Growth—A Step at a Time

רַבִּי מֵאִיר אוֹמֵר: הֱוֵי מְמַעֵט בְּעֵסֶק, וַעֲסֹק בַּתּוֹרָה. וֶהֱוֵי שְׁפַל רוּחַ בִּפְנֵי כָל אָדָם. וְאִם בָּטַלְתָּ
מִן הַתּוֹרָה, יֶשׁ לְךָ בְּטֵלִים הַרְבֵּה כְנֶגְדָּךְ. וְאִם עָמַלְתָּ בַתּוֹרָה, יֶשׁ לוֹ שָׂכָר הַרְבֵּה לִתֶּן לָךְ.

Rabbi Meir said: Engage but little in business, and busy yourself with the Torah. Be of humble spirit before all people. If you have neglected the Torah, you will have many who bring you to neglect it, but if you have labored at the study of Torah, there is much reward to give to you.

The *Ruach Chaim* commentary on *Ethics of the Fathers* brings attention to Rabbi Meir's second word: ממעט. Above, this was translated to "engage but little," but it can also mean "gradually reduce" as in "gradually reduce your business affairs and busy yourself with Torah." One who is overly engaged in matters of this world is instructed to gradually reduce their engagement to make space for loftier spiritual pursuits.

This instruction to take things slowly is crucial in one's spiritual work. Rabbi Kook highlights two forms of repentance: sudden and gradual.

> Sudden repentance comes about as a result of a certain spiritual flash that enters the soul. At once the person senses all the evil and the ugliness of sin, and they are converted into a new being; already they experience inside themselves a complete transformation for the better.

157

There is also a gradual form of repentance. No sudden flash of illumination dawns upon the person to make them change from the depth of evil to the good, but they feel that they must mend their way of life, their will, their pattern of thought. By heeding this impulse, they gradually acquire the ways of equity, they correct their morals, they improve their actions, and they condition themselves increasingly to becoming a good person, until they reach a high level of purity and perfection. (*Orot HaTeshuva*, ch. 2)

Sometimes we are blessed with a "spiritual flash" that enables us, in a moment's notice, to "sense all the evil and ugliness of sin." This flash transforms us instantly "into a new being." However, most of the time we are involved in a gradual process, a step at a time, until we reach our goal. This is the correct path because if we push too fast when we are supposed to go slow, it can prove disastrous.

In Judaism we surely welcome miracles such as these "spiritual flashes," but we do not depend upon them (see *Talmud Bavli*, Kiddushin 39b). If you find yourself overworked or overextended to the point that you are not growing spiritually, it's worth gradually shifting out of this life pattern. This goes for many areas—even our own worries and thoughts, which can withhold us from flourishing in Torah and mitzvah performance.

Many think that to improve, one must cut off from one's vice "cold turkey." Sometimes this works, but many times, what is more effective is weaning oneself a step at time. The difficulty with this path is that as one grows gradually, one is keenly aware of the fact that one is still "sinning," or not living up to their ideal, each step of the way (albeit a bit less each time). This can be frustrating and deflating, but the alternative can prove even more devastating: going too fast and spiraling downward.

I'll give you an example. I had a year during which I didn't work out at all. I had been exercising with a trainer for around a year, and then, for different reasons, my workouts just tailed off. My personal exercise regimen then tailed off as a result. I am pretty good when it comes to spiritual work, but when it comes to physical exercise, I sometimes (okay, most of the time!) require others to get me going. Without a trainer, my favorite carbs welcomed me back with open arms, and I slowly grew out of shape once more. Getting back into shape afterward was a grueling and slow process. I made sure I took the process a step at a time. I offered a safe example here, but this applies to all forms of negative behavior.

The continuation of the mishna adds an important element. As one slowly reduces the frequency of sin, one must toil in Torah. It is hard to stay away from sin if one does not fill in the void with something positive. The combination of separating slowly from negative behavior alongside constant spiritual growth and progress will ensure that there will be "much reward to give unto you."

Transforming Accusers into Advocates

רַבִּי אֱלִיעֶזֶר בֶּן יַעֲקֹב אוֹמֵר: הָעוֹשֶׂה מִצְוָה אַחַת, קוֹנֶה לוֹ פְּרַקְלִיט אֶחָד. וְהָעוֹבֵר עֲבֵרָה אַחַת, קוֹנֶה לוֹ קַטֵּגוֹר אֶחָד. תְּשׁוּבָה וּמַעֲשִׂים טוֹבִים, כִּתְרִיס בִּפְנֵי הַפֻּרְעָנוּת.

Rabbi Eliezer ben Yakov said: One who performs one commandment acquires for themselves one advocate, and one who commits one transgression acquires for themselves one accuser. Repentance and good deeds are a shield against punishment.

Rabbi Eliezer reminds us that it's important to think about the amazing gift of teshuva (repentance) all year round. Around Rosh Hashanah and Yom Kippur, rabbis speak a lot about teshuva, but in truth, teshuva is needed all the time because each of our actions creates either positive or negative energy, advocates or accusers. Repentance and good deeds protect us from the negative effects of these behaviors.

Rabbi Eliezer is highlighting one positive effect of teshuva: protection from punishment. Reish Lakish, a later authority, goes a step further and adds that teshuva has the power to transform sins into merits: "Repentance is so great that sins are accounted as though they were merits" (*Talmud Bavli*, Yoma 86b). Teshuva does not only protect from the "accuser"; it transforms it into an advocate. That is amazing!

How does this work? How can sins be transformed into good deeds by means of teshuva? Rabbi Kook explains that in every sin there is a mixture of good and bad, both an accuser and an advocate (*Shemonah Kevatzim* 1:240). We may have had good intentions as we transgressed, or we may have been doing a kind act but just at the wrong time and place. There are many examples of these "hybrid" sins.

For instance, Rabbi Kook was critical of the young "settlers" of his days, the residents in the "new settlement," due to their abandonment of the Torah. He nevertheless depicted them in a positive light, stressing that they only left religion because they were looking for higher and greater ideals, believing Judaism didn't have much to offer them on this front. He made it one of his life goals to develop and teach a lofty and idealistic Torah to help bring these individuals closer to Judaism.

Rabbi Kook encourages us to "lift" the good intention or aspect from within the overall sin and strengthen it. By doing so, we will "in actuality" transform our previous sin into merit. In Rabbi Kook's words:

> And even more so does one need to define the good which is present in the depths of the bad and to strengthen it, with the same amount of strength one used to escape from the evil. [By means of strengthening the good in the bad] the teshuva process leads to a positive outcome; it, in actuality, transforms the sins into merits.

One final example: assume you get in many fights with your sibling. You end up going to therapy to speak about it and find out that what you are really looking for in the relationship is to be heard and recognized. Nothing is wrong with that! You stop fighting and surround yourself with people who *do* hear and appreciate you. In time you come to hear and appreciate yourself as well.

By doing all of this, you transformed your sin into a merit because you now are even stronger than you were beforehand. This is the power of teshuva—to not only protect us from the accuser but to turn the accuser into an advocate and elevate us to higher plateaus in our service of Hashem.

Speaking from Your Core

רַבִּי יוֹחָנָן הַסַּנְדְּלָר אוֹמֵר: כָּל כְּנֵסִיָּה שֶׁהִיא לְשֵׁם שָׁמַיִם, סוֹפָהּ
לְהִתְקַיֵּם. וְשֶׁאֵינָהּ לְשֵׁם שָׁמַיִם, אֵין סוֹפָהּ לְהִתְקַיֵּם.

Rabbi Yochanan Hasandlar said: Every assembly which is for the sake of heaven, will in the end endure. And every assembly which is not for the sake of heaven, will in the end not endure.

In an earlier commentary (to *Ethics of the Fathers* 3:11–12), we discussed two meanings of the word להתקיים that appears in our mishna. It can mean both "to endure" and "to apply." I'd like to understand our mishna based on this first interpretation.

When we are passionately fighting for a cause, it is imperative to assess the source of our passion. Are we fighting for something that is true, or are ulterior motives masking themselves behind righteous rationalizations? Sometimes you can tell just by assessing whether your inner core is speaking or whether some other, external side of your ego is at play. The former feels more alive and *enduring* than the latter.

This is what our mishna is alluding to. One can sense when one is in an assembly for the sake of heaven, when one's arguments are coming from a true place. When the arguments emerge from superficial and false motives, the words come from a less "enduring" part of one's being.

Heavenly Relationships

רַבִּי אֶלְעָזָר בֶּן שַׁמּוּעַ אוֹמֵר: יְהִי כְבוֹד תַּלְמִידְךָ חָבִיב עָלֶיךָ כְּשֶׁלָּךְ,
וּכְבוֹד חֲבֵרְךָ כְּמוֹרָא רַבְּךָ, וּמוֹרָא רַבְּךָ כְּמוֹרָא שָׁמָיִם.

Rabbi Elazar ben Shammua said: Let the honor of your student be as dear to you as your own, and the honor of your friend as the reverence for your teacher, and the reverence for your teacher as the reverence of heaven.

The Maharal and others offer an alternative version to the first part of the text. Instead of the text reading "as dear to you as your own," it reads: "as dear to you as your friend's." Based on this, the Maharal points out, one statement naturally leads into the other: the honor for your student should be like the honor for your friend, the honor for your friend should be like the reverence for your teacher, and the reverence for your teacher should be like your reverence of heaven. Based on this reading, all of our relationships are related to our reverence for heaven because in the end they, one after another, lead to this final form of reverence.

Based on this version, it is possible that Rabbi Elazar ben Shammua is urging us to "upgrade" our relationships in terms of our respect and reverence for the other. One way to achieve this level of reverence is to see these connections as relationships placed in our lives by Hashem. When we view connections as divinely ordained, our appreciation for them grows stronger. This may be the connection to reverence for heaven: we must respect our friends, students, and teachers because they were placed in our lives by Hashem.

Looking back, I know I have had teachers and guides who were sent to me at different intervals by Hashem. I have also taught classes to others who were meant, in some respects, to teach me divine lessons. When we view things this way, we engender more reverence for our relationships because we understand Hashem wants them to be this way. This also pushes us to be better people in the relationship because we view our behavior in the relationship as a means of serving Hashem.

The same goes for one's spousal relationship. If this is the match Hashem planned for us, we should act accordingly and have reverence for our loved one. When seen this way, relationships become "heavenly" encounters, unique opportunities to serve Hashem.

4:16–17

Striving for Excellence

רַבִּי יְהוּדָה אוֹמֵר: הֱוֵי זָהִיר בַּתַּלְמוּד, שֶׁשִּׁגְגַת תַּלְמוּד עוֹלָה זָדוֹן. רַבִּי שִׁמְעוֹן אוֹמֵר: שְׁלֹשָׁה כְתָרִים הֵם: כֶּתֶר תּוֹרָה, וְכֶתֶר כְּהֻנָּה, וְכֶתֶר מַלְכוּת, וְכֶתֶר שֵׁם טוֹב עוֹלֶה עַל גַּבֵּיהֶן.

Rabbi Yehuda said: Be careful in study, for a (nondeliberate) error in study counts as a deliberate sin. Rabbi Shimon said: There are three crowns: the crown of Torah, the crown of priesthood, and the crown of royalty, but the crown of a good name supersedes them all.

Many editions of *Ethics of the Fathers* combine the statements of Rabbi Yehuda and Rabbi Shimon into one mishna. This juxtaposition teaches us a lot about the nature of "the crown of a good name" to which we all should aspire.

Rabbi Shimon lists three crowns: Torah, priesthood, and royalty. He then states that the crown of a good name supersedes them all. What makes this crown stand out in relation to the others? This is where Rabbi Yehuda's words come in. One achieves a good name by worrying about even a nondeliberate error while learning and teaching others. This personality trait of being thorough and dependable cultivates a good name for oneself among one's peers. The individual depicted in the beginning of the mishna is so precise with themselves that they view their nondeliberate errors as deliberate ones.

This is something I tried to implement as I worked on my dissertation at Bar-Ilan University. A large portion of the time was devoted to editing. I wanted my paper to be accepted and valued by my peers, so I took all the precautions. I didn't want there to be blatant errors. Even nondeliberate errors were of concern, and due to this, I didn't take shortcuts, reviewing each paragraph and sentence with a fine comb to ensure I didn't miss anything. I pray this will earn me a good name with those who read it.

This attitude should be a way of life: working hard in all we do and not cutting corners—striving for excellence. The first three crowns can be inherited. However, earning a good name through hard work, worrying that one's initiatives will be as error free as possible, is something that supersedes the others.

Exiling Ourselves to Torah

רַבִּי נְהוֹרַאי אוֹמֵר: הֱוֵי גוֹלֶה לְמָקוֹם תּוֹרָה, וְאַל תֹּאמַר שֶׁהִיא תָבֹא אַחֲרֶיךָ, שֶׁחֲבֵרֶיךָ יְקַיְּמוּהָ בְיָדֶךָ. וְאֶל בִּינָתְךָ אַל תִּשָּׁעֵן (משלי ג).

Rabbi Nehorai said: Go as a [voluntary] exile to a place of Torah and say not that it will come after you, for [it is] your fellow [students] who will make it permanent in your hand. "And do not lean upon your own understanding" (Prov. 3:5).

Our mishna opens urging us to exile ourselves to "a place of Torah." The simple reading of the mishna teaches us to leave our physical locale, if need be, in order to surround ourselves with Torah. It won't come after us, our chevrutas (Torah study partners) won't make it happen for us, and we shouldn't depend on our own intellect. Instead, we should uproot and surround ourselves with a Torah community.

The Maharal's reading sees the exile in more of an internal manner, as an attitude. We must understand that the Torah is beyond us. It is something holy, separate. We must exile ourselves to *this* place of Torah. This can be applied to our approach to innovation in Torah. While it's fine and often praiseworthy to extrapolate new teachings and apply modern principles to ancient texts, we must also remember that the Torah is beyond all of this. We must fit ourselves to the Torah, exiling ourselves from our modern outlook to the mandates and teachings of our sacred, age-old tradition.

The mishna tells us to not think the Torah will come after us. One can possibly read this as "do not think the Torah should follow you"

("שתבא אחריך"), hinting that we should follow the Torah's lead and not the opposite. It then goes on to list two areas which prove obstacles to this approach. The first is societal influences. The thoughts, movements, and pressures of the times can strongly influence us. This is what the mishna refers to with the words "שחבריך יקימוה בידך." This can be read as "your friends, societal influences, establish the Torah for you." We must beware of being swayed too much by this.

Another area from which we must exile ourselves is our own intellect. This sounds harsh, and it surely does not mean we should suspend our own personal analysis. It's warning us to not rely *solely* on our understanding ("ואל בינתך אל תשען") but instead to tap into the rich reservoir of wisdom and guidance from previous generations.

The language of "exile" used by the mishna is strong. Sometimes the only way to be sure we are following the Torah is to divest ourselves of or temporarily suspend our modern sensibilities. Upon emerging from this internal exile, we can then better engage the text in a way that is balanced and fitting to the holy and sacred Torah.

4:19

It's Not Your Fault

רַבִּי יַנַּאי אוֹמֵר: אֵין בְּיָדֵינוּ לֹא מִשַּׁלְוַת הָרְשָׁעִים וְאַף לֹא מִיִּסּוּרֵי הַצַּדִּיקִים.

Rabbi Yannai said: It is not in our hands either the security of the wicked, or even the afflictions of the righteous.

Rabbi Yannai talks about something being or not being "in our hands." This is often understood as referring to our comprehension. It is not in our hands to understand these tragedies!

Another possible reading views the mishna's "hands" as representative of one's responsibility for given tragedies. There is a tendency when one sees bad things to blame oneself for these occurrences, to see one's own "hands" as playing a part. This is not wrong in and of itself, as our texts do ask us to assess our actions (*Talmud Bavli*, Berachot 5a) and to believe our actions have a wider spiritual reach than our own private lives (*Mishneh Torah*, Teshuva 3:4; *Nefesh HaChaim* 1:3).

However, this personal accountability is only a partial truth. There are many reasons why tragedies happen that are not connected to us. Or in the language of our mishna: these causes are beyond the scope of "our hands." It may simply be because Hashem granted humans free will, which can be used to society's detriment. And there are many other factors. Even if we do see where our actions have had an impact, we must be careful to not go overboard with self-blame. This blame can be destructive to our inner peace and detrimental to our spiritual growth.

The mishna may be hinting at a remedy to this form of self-defeating blame. Focus on what *is* in your hands. Don't over dwell on what was. Focus on the present, making the world a better place and improving the lives of others. Through being proactive, our hands can actively tilt the scale toward bringing justice to the wicked and fitting reward to the righteous.

Building Healthy, Balanced Relationships

רַבִּי מַתְיָא בֶן חָרָשׁ אוֹמֵר: הֱוֵי מַקְדִּים בִּשְׁלוֹם כָּל אָדָם,
וֶהֱוֵי זָנָב לָאֲרָיוֹת, וְאַל תְּהִי רֹאשׁ לַשּׁוּעָלִים.

Rabbi Mattia ben Charash said: Upon meeting people, be the first to extend greetings, and be a tail unto lions, and not a head unto foxes.

Being in service of others is a very Jewish thing. Avraham's tent was famously open on all four sides, symbolizing his welcoming in of all kinds of people from the four corners of the Earth.

Our mishna opens directing us to be in service of others. The first directive is often read as guidance to be the first to extend greetings to others, with *bishlom* (בשלום) signifying the inquiring of others' well-being (seeking their peace, *shalom*). However, one could also read this more generally, prodding us to be in service of others, making sure they are *bishlom*, at peace. And the language of *makdim* (מקדים) is a hint for us to be the first to extend ourselves to others—the essence of good service.

This first directive is true for all individuals, as the mishna says: "כל אדם" (lit., all people). Indeed, this was Avraham's modus operandi with his guests. The second part of the mishna, however, transitions to people we surround ourselves with on a consistent basis. This is noted by the switch to two social groups in the mishna: "foxes" and "lions."

When it comes to these groups, one should be more selective. If we find ourselves "serving" foxes, sly and opportunistic individuals, our generous service will quickly devolve into exploitation, and we will end up depleted and being taken advantage of. This is hinted at through the description of one being at the head of this group of foxes. In this position, one is not receiving but rather leading them constantly by servicing all their needs. These relationships are liable to be toxic and should be avoided.

Instead, we should pursue relationships with individuals who are similar to "lions." Lions are the "head" of the jungle. They are independent and are well able to take care of themselves. We should find individuals who will value our service and will allow us at times to be at the "tail," the recipients of their service and care. This is a more balanced relationship, where our service of others will not deplete us but rather strengthen and deepen our relationship with those whom we are serving.

4:21

Living in the World to Come—In This World

רַבִּי יַעֲקֹב אוֹמֵר: הָעוֹלָם הַזֶּה דּוֹמֶה לִפְרוֹזְדוֹר בִּפְנֵי הָעוֹלָם הַבָּא. הַתְקֵן עַצְמְךָ בַּפְּרוֹזְדוֹר, כְּדֵי שֶׁתִּכָּנֵס לַטְּרַקְלִין.

Rabbi Yakov said: This world is like a vestibule before the world to come. Prepare yourself in the vestibule, so that you may enter the banquet hall.

The simple reading of this mishna instructs us to view this world as a means to an end: the next world, the afterlife. There are many versions of this theme in Jewish tradition. For example, a parallel source teaches: "Whoever toils on Sabbath eve will have what to eat on the Sabbath" (*Talmud Bavli*, Avodah Zarah 3a). They all point to the same message: our world is not the final destination.

Many people put all their efforts into improving their status in this world. Our mishna reminds us that this is a mistake. Imagine someone putting all their renovation budget into the vestibule, the lobby, while completely ignoring the final destination: the banquet hall. When seen from the perspective of what is beyond the vestibule, this is a gross misappropriation of funds.

As mentioned, this mishna highlights a central theme in Jewish thought in relation to this world. However, there is another strand of thought that views this world and its elevation as an ideal within itself.

In more modern terms this is called *tikkun olam* (repair of the world). In chassidic texts this is portrayed as God's desire to inhabit the lower worlds (*dira batachtonim*). Based on this, we were placed here to elevate and repair this world. Even Adam and Eve, who inhabited a very refined world, were requested to "till and guard" the Garden of Eden, which can be understood as a reparation of this world. This was even before they sinned—an ideal in and of itself.

In his explanation to our mishna, the *Sfat Emet* (Vayikra, Emor, s.v. olam hazeh) offers a synthesis of the two views. He creatively reads the whole mishna as guidance for us in this world. Our world is full of illusions and temptations. Our goal should be to look beyond these "veils" and see the inner truth behind things. This is how he explains the "world to come" in our mishna. As he explains, we are able to live in a "world to come" consciousness while living in this world (compare *Nefesh HaChaim* 1:11 and related sources in ibid., ch. 1, footnote 57). How is this done? By passing through the vestibule to enter the banquet hall—the deeper approach, beyond the veils and veneers of this world.

This view focuses on this world and the next one at one and the same time, urging us to live in the "world to come" while at the same time remaining engaged in this world. The more good we see and the more we view our current reality through a positive prism, the more we can taste from the world to come. Working hard to see the next world in this world will benefit us all, lifting us to higher "banquet-like" worlds, along with all of those around us.

The Freedom of the Present Moment

הוּא הָיָה אוֹמֵר: יָפָה שָׁעָה אַחַת בִּתְשׁוּבָה וּמַעֲשִׂים טוֹבִים בָּעוֹלָם הַזֶּה מִכָּל חַיֵּי הָעוֹלָם הַבָּא. וְיָפָה שָׁעָה אַחַת שֶׁל קוֹרַת רוּחַ בָּעוֹלָם הַבָּא מִכָּל חַיֵּי הָעוֹלָם הַזֶּה.

He used to say: More precious is one hour in repentance and good deeds in this world than all the life of the world to come. And more precious is one hour of the tranquility of the world to come than all the life of this world.

One of the greatest and least appreciated blessings we all enjoy is the present moment. Life in this world is made up of one present moment after another. We often overlook this by remaining stuck in the past or in the future. The beginning of our mishna highlights this unique gift by comparing it to life in the world to come. The world to come is a place in which we will enjoy immense reward; however, it will be a static state of bliss. In that reality, we will not be able to grow or advance in spirituality. In contrast, our mishna discusses one "שעה" in this world. The word "שעה" can translate to a single moment. Even one moment in this world is greater than all the world to come. Why so? Because the present moment contains within it potential for change and growth.

I remember many years ago while working on my graduate degree reading (what I understood!) of Jean Paul Sartre's works on existentialism. Throughout his writings, he makes an argument for the immense freedom that is packed into every new moment. Here is an example:

For if indeed existence precedes essence, one will never be able to explain one's action by reference to a given and specific human nature; in other words, there is no determinism—man is free, man is freedom. (*Existentialism and Human Emotions*)

I believe this is what our mishna is impressing upon us. As long as we are in this world, we are not locked into any set "essence." What we were yesterday or will be tomorrow does not and should not dictate who we are in the present. In the present, we can be anything: we can do teshuva! And we can choose to be the best version of ourselves by engaging in good deeds. When seen this way, every moment is packed with immense potential. This is a very uplifting and liberating thought. "More precious is one hour in repentance and good deeds in this world than all the life of the world to come!"

Respecting Others in their Time of Distress

רַבִּי שִׁמְעוֹן בֶּן אֶלְעָזָר אוֹמֵר: אַל תְּרַצֶּה אֶת חֲבֵרְךָ בִּשְׁעַת כַּעֲסוֹ, וְאַל תְּנַחֲמֶנּוּ
בְּשָׁעָה שֶׁמֵּתוֹ מֻטָּל לְפָנָיו, וְאַל תִּשְׁאַל לוֹ בִּשְׁעַת נִדְרוֹ, וְאַל תִּשְׁתַּדֵּל לִרְאוֹתוֹ
בִּשְׁעַת קַלְקָלָתוֹ. שְׁמוּאֵל הַקָּטָן אוֹמֵר (משלי כד): בִּנְפֹל אוֹיִבְךָ אַל תִּשְׂמָח
וּבִכָּשְׁלוֹ אַל יָגֵל לִבֶּךָ, פֶּן יִרְאֶה ה' וְרַע בְּעֵינָיו וְהֵשִׁיב מֵעָלָיו אַפּוֹ.

Rabbi Shimon ben Elazar said: Do not try to appease your friend during their hour of anger, nor comfort them at the hour while their dead still lies before them, nor question them at the hour of their vow, nor strive to see them in the hour of their disgrace. Shmuel Hakatan said: "If your enemy falls, do not exult. If they trip let your heart not rejoice, lest the Lord see it and be displeased and avert His wrath from them" (Prov. 24:17-18).

One can read these two mishnas as one unit. Together, the mishnas list five directives, five improper ways to react to another in their moment of struggle. These five directives can be further organized into three groups.

The first group, composed of the first three directives mentioned by Rabbi Shimon, discusses coming to the aid of the other with a sincere desire to help them in their time of need. Many of us possess a similar inclination to "fix" things and make them better. This is a praiseworthy trait. However, when acted upon at the wrong time, it can prove counterproductive.

Our mishna opens with three failed attempts to "fix" others' situations. One who is in a fit of rage may only have their rage exacerbated upon our engagement with them in the heat of the moment. One who is processing a loved one's loss may not be able to welcome conversation; they may just need to be left alone as they overcome their initial shock. And one who is making a vow, if approached and offered ways out of their vow at that very moment, may do the opposite and double down on their vow, deeming it unconditional (see Rashi, ad loc.). As a result, they may close off the option for annulment at a later period. All of these cases deal with good intentions, a desire to fix and help the other, accompanied by a faulty, wrongly timed application.

Rabbi Shimon's fourth statement represents the second group. It deals with a certain voyeuristic tendency, prevalent in our culture, that needs correction: the desire to see others in their time of disgrace. Our mishna reminds us to resist this tendency and allow others to retain their pride and composure as they endure personal travails.

The first group intends to help the other. The second group's intentions are not good, but they aren't overly malicious. Shmuel's directive presents a more malevolent version, a third group, who intentionally take joy in others' downfall. This may not only be referring to an objective enemy, such as the slanderers discussed in a prayer composed for our daily amidah prayer by none other than Shmuel himself; it may be referring to those whom we subjectively view as enemies due to resentment, jealousy, bias, or hatred.

The main theme as it relates to all three groups is to respect the space and dignity of others in their times of need and distress. Nobody is perfect. When we find others at their lowest, it is up to us to rise higher, working to keep their best aspirations in mind and thinking creatively about how to assist them when they need it.

4:25

Learning Like a Child

אֱלִישָׁע בֶּן אֲבוּיָה אוֹמֵר: הַלּוֹמֵד יֶלֶד לְמַה הוּא דוֹמֶה? לִדְיוֹ כְתוּבָה עַל נְיָר חָדָשׁ. וְהַלּוֹמֵד זָקֵן לְמַה הוּא דוֹמֶה? לִדְיוֹ כְתוּבָה עַל נְיָר מָחוּק.

Elisha ben Avuyah said: One who learns when a child, to what are they compared? To ink written upon a new writing sheet. And one who learns when an old person, to what are they compared? To ink written on a rubbed writing sheet.

What makes a young student so impressionable? Aside from the fact that there is not as much competing information in their head at this early developmental stage, another factor at play is their open and innocent attitude when it comes to receiving Torah knowledge. As we grow older, we become, rightfully so, more critical and selective. However, it's still important to maintain, even at this later stage, a simplicity and innocence when it comes to learning Torah.

Our mishna reminds us to remain innocent and open to "learn like a child" ("לומד ילד")—even as an adult—so that the teachings of the Torah will be "written upon a new writing sheet." Being overly critical when processing information can, at times, hinder the Torah's ability to directly impact us and speak to our hearts.

On Passover, we address four children: the wise, the wicked, the simple, and the child who doesn't know how to ask. Many think that the first two (wise and wicked) and last two (simple and doesn't know how to ask) are pairs, with the first of each pair being the remedy to the other.

However, the Abarbanel (on the Haggadah) teaches that the true anti-dote to the wicked child is not the wise child. The wise child pairs well with the child who does not know how to ask by helping them learn how to ask the right questions. The simple child is the wicked child's match.

Wisdom can lead us to become overly sophisticated and, as a result, disconnected from our simple, inner faith. The simple child, just by being who they are, bypasses these complications. The simple child's strong faith protects them from the wicked child's heresy. At times the consistency of the simple child's faith and purity can be a stronger influence on the wicked child than any of the wise child's sophisticated answers.

The Wonderful Fruits of the Younger Generation

רַבִּי יוֹסֵי בַר יְהוּדָה אִישׁ כְּפַר הַבַּבְלִי אוֹמֵר: הַלּוֹמֵד מִן הַקְּטַנִּים לְמַה
הוּא דוֹמֶה? לְאֹכֵל עֲנָבִים קֵהוֹת וְשׁוֹתֶה יַיִן מִגִּתּוֹ. וְהַלּוֹמֵד מִן הַזְּקֵנִים
לְמַה הוּא דוֹמֶה? לְאֹכֵל עֲנָבִים בְּשֵׁלוֹת וְשׁוֹתֶה יַיִן יָשָׁן.

Rabbi Yosi ben Yehuda a man of Kfar ha-Bavli said: One who learns from the young, to what are they compared? To one who eats unripe grapes, and drinks wine from their vat. And one who learns from the old, to what are they compared? To one who eats ripe grapes, and drinks old wine.

Rabbi Yosi ben Yehuda continues the discussion of the previous mishna on Torah learning among youths and adults. The Maharal distinguishes between the young and the elderly in terms of potential versus actualization. The vat with the unripe grapes and the wine from one's vat hold immense potential but are difficult to consume. The Maharal attributes this to the fact that in one's youth, one's intellect is "embedded" in one's body. As one ages, the body and its needs become less dominant, and one's intellect, a spiritual force in itself, is unleashed and able to actualize its potential (for more on this, see our commentary to *Ethics of the Fathers* 5:25).

I'd like to focus on this potential versus actuality dynamic. The Maharal does not say this, but one could argue, based on this model, for

RABBI DR. ELI YOGGEV

the validity of statements and teachings of the youth. The unripe grape and the wine in the vat contain everything that will emerge later on when developed and cultivated under the right conditions. I do not believe our mishna is guiding us to ignore the words of the youth. It may be hinting at the opposite: to probe the depths of what they are saying, thinking, and feeling and then find ways, based on the elderly's life experience and perspective, to help actualize this potential.

The new generation is often looked at as suspect by their elders. Because the youth have been reared in completely different conditions and social structures, they think and react differently to life. In contemporary times, Gen Zers don't "get" millennials, and millennials don't always understand the baby boomer generation. This is just the way it is and the way it will be between different generations for years to come. This experience disparity doesn't objectively mean that the younger generation is wrong. They may at times even have greater perspective because their idealistic views have yet to be affected by life's ups and downs.

The youth often don't have the right words to express what they are feeling or thinking. When the youth do share their revealed (grapes) and hidden (wine) understandings, they don't always articulate them in a moderate fashion. And sometimes, due to lack of experience, their approaches are not fully grounded in reality. However, this does not by any means translate into a lack of potential and deep truth among the youth! The opposite is true: the finest, most expensive wines were once unripe grapes and wine in a vat. The older generation must be cognizant of this and remain on the lookout for these wonderful grapes.

4:27

Looking Beyond External Characteristics

רַבִּי אוֹמֵר: אַל תִּסְתַּכֵּל בַּקַּנְקַן, אֶלָּא בְּמַה שֶּׁיֵּשׁ בּוֹ. יֵשׁ קַנְקַן
חָדָשׁ מָלֵא יָשָׁן, וְיָשָׁן שֶׁאֲפִלּוּ חָדָשׁ אֵין בּוֹ.

Rabbi said: Don't look at the container but at that which is in it. There is a new container full of old wine, and an old [container] in which there is not even new [wine].

It is not clear who the author of this mishna is. Some say it is Rabbi Yehuda HaNasi; others say it is Rabbi Meir. If it is the latter, it is befitting that Rabbi Meir would offer this guidance. Rabbi Meir is well known for having chased down Elisha Ben Avuyah, a rabbi-turned-heretic, to learn Torah. His reasoning for doing so was that he "found a pomegranate and ate its contents while throwing away its peel" (*Talmud Bavli*, Chagigah 15b). Rabbi Meir was focused on the inner content and did not get distracted by externalities. On the outside, Elisha was sinning and causing others to sin. Rabbi Meir was able to see beyond this and extract the good while disposing of the unwanted waste. Not an easy feat!

As a society we are often quick to judge based on outward characteristics. We all do this. Sadly, we are still plagued by many -isms: ageism, ableism, sexism, racism, and much more. Rabbi Meir reminds us to shift focus to what's on the inside.

Our mishna teaches that at times, the external reality may mask a completely different internal reality. The conclusion of our mishna drives this point home. You may find an old container and expect it to hold old wine. However, there are times when it doesn't even hold new wine: it is just completely empty! There is so much more in this world than what meets the eye. We must always stay open and push through the external reality—to connect with what is truly "inside the container!"

4:28

Staying Grounded in Your Own World

רַבִּי אֶלְעָזָר הַקַּפָּר אוֹמֵר: הַקִּנְאָה, וְהַתַּאֲוָה, וְהַכָּבוֹד מוֹצִיאִין אֶת הָאָדָם מִן הָעוֹלָם.

Rabbi Elazar Hakappar said: Envy, lust, and honor put a person out of the world.

We are already familiar from previous mishnas with the danger of a trait or behavior "putting a person out of this world." From these repeated warnings, it appears this greatly worried the Sages. They wanted to ensure we remain with our feet grounded "in the world."

One way that these three traits—envy, lust, and honor—remove us from the world is through engaging our imagination. They thrust us into an imaginary and illusionary world. One of my rabbis urged my peers and me to divorce ourselves from all illusions. He used to say that living in illusions is not living a real life. He asked us to go through events from our past and see how we still view them today from an illusionary perspective, perhaps based on incorrect, childish reactions. He then guided us to correct our thinking and see things for what they really were. I found this exercise extremely helpful. It is effective for illusional thinking in the present as well.

This is one way to understand our mishna. We may be living in a studio apartment and lusting after a large house. Sometimes this can take up more real estate in our minds than we'd like! We may be excelling at work but, nevertheless, experiencing jealousy throughout the day toward a coworker. We may be worrying about our honor and imagining how episodes in our life *should* have played out: "I should have received that honor"; "I should be positioned in front of that group." Many times, we envision how things *should have* looked, and this mental picture, this illusion, sticks with us and haunts us.

Imagination is a wonderful thing. We must dream of big things in life. However, when we allow it to cloud our connection to and grasp of reality, it is dangerous. It does not allow one to truly deal with what one needs to focus on in life because one is always "in another world"—an imaginary one.

Another way to understand the "world" imagery adopted by our mishna is to see each one of us as having our own world. The Sages taught that each one of us is "A world unto themselves" (*Avot de Rebbe Natan* 31). When we focus on our world, we grow and progress from a safe and calm place. However, when these three traits draw us away from our world, we spend unnecessary time in others' worldscapes and lose our ability to improve and properly progress in our own lives.

Let me share a personal anecdote. With great fondness, I recall first joining my graduate program at Bar-Ilan University. I felt so proud of my accomplishments. I had just finished at Herzog College in Alon Shvut, Israel, and felt like I really had moved up in life. I looked forward with anticipation to my new academic life and stature. I joined the yeshiva on the Bar-Ilan Campus and started to learn Torah as I pursued my degree. I felt on top of the world. At that point, I started to look around and paid attention to the many doctoral students who filled our beit midrash (study center) on the campus. Instead of being happy with my lot and open to learning from these advanced scholars, these three traits kicked in and got the best of me. I was envious of their accomplishments and at times "lusted" after their honorable position. How quickly I had forgotten how happy I was when I first joined the university! A good friend of mine woke me up to this and lifted me out of this negative place. He reminded me to stay focused on my world instead of others, and that's what I did.

Granted, the highest level is not to struggle at all inside with these three obstacles, but not all of us are at this level. I forced myself to shift focus to my own world, which greatly helped. When we spend all our time in someone else's world, we end up neglecting our own. We are all worlds unto ourselves. Let's do all we can to make our own world a better place!

4:29

Knowledge of God
versus Fear of Punishment

הוּא הָיָה אוֹמֵר: הַיִּלּוֹדִים לָמוּת, וְהַמֵּתִים לְהַחֲיוֹת, וְהַחַיִּים לִדּוֹן, לֵידַע לְהוֹדִיעַ וּלְהִוָּדַע
שֶׁהוּא אֵל, הוּא הַיּוֹצֵר, הוּא הַבּוֹרֵא, הוּא הַמֵּבִין, הוּא הַדַּיָּן, הוּא עֵד, הוּא בַּעַל דִּין, וְהוּא
עָתִיד לָדוּן. בָּרוּךְ הוּא, שֶׁאֵין לְפָנָיו לֹא עַוְלָה, וְלֹא שִׁכְחָה, וְלֹא מַשּׂוֹא פָנִים, וְלֹא מִקַּח
שֹׁחַד, שֶׁהַכֹּל שֶׁלּוֹ. וְדַע שֶׁהַכֹּל לְפִי הַחֶשְׁבּוֹן. וְאַל יַבְטִיחֲךָ יִצְרְךָ שֶׁהַשְּׁאוֹל בֵּית מָנוֹס לָךְ.
שֶׁעַל כָּרְחֲךָ אַתָּה נוֹצָר, וְעַל כָּרְחֲךָ אַתָּה נוֹלָד, וְעַל כָּרְחֲךָ אַתָּה חַי, וְעַל כָּרְחֲךָ אַתָּה מֵת,
וְעַל כָּרְחֲךָ אַתָּה עָתִיד לִתֵּן דִּין וְחֶשְׁבּוֹן לִפְנֵי מֶלֶךְ מַלְכֵי הַמְּלָכִים הַקָּדוֹשׁ בָּרוּךְ הוּא.

He used to say: The ones who were born are to die, and the ones who have died are to be brought to life, and the ones brought to life are to be judged. So that one may know, make known and have the knowledge that He is God. He is the designer, He is the creator, He is the discerner, He is the judge, He is the witness, He is the complainant, and that He will summon to judgment. Blessed be He, before Whom there is no iniquity, nor forgetting, nor respect of persons, nor taking of bribes, for all is His. And know that all is according to the reckoning.

And let not your impulse assure you that the grave is a place of refuge for you. For against your will were you formed, against your will were you born, against your will you live, against your will you will die, and against your will you will give an account and reckoning before the King of the kings of kings, the Holy One, blessed be He.

Our mishna can be separated into two parts. The first part deals with knowledge: "One may know, make known and have the knowledge that He is God"; "And know that all is according to reckoning." The second deals with our impulses: "And let not your impulse assure you."

The first section is urging us to intellectually probe the depths of Hashem's judgment: Hashem's multiple roles and attributes and Hashem's honest and unbiased judgment. This should bring us closer to Hashem and generate within us awe and respect for the true Judge. To this end, the mishna offers aspects upon which we can reflect and strengthen this reverence. Hashem is the designer, creator, discerner, etc. Each one of these descriptions is packed with rich meaning when it comes to Hashem's guidance and providence.

This level isn't always easy to attain. That is why Rabbi Elazar introduces another directive to help us overcome our impulses, our *yetzer harah*, in a more direct and expedited manner. In the second half of the mishna, we are reminded to focus on the ramifications of this judgment for our lives: that we will all be brought to judgment. This will happen whether we like it or not: "against our will."

There is definitely a place for fear of punishment in our divine service. This oftentimes appeals to our emotions and impulses and helps us remain in line with our purpose in this world. However, the more we can cultivate reverence from a place of knowledge, the more we can follow the first direction in our mishna, and the more elevated our service will be.

5:1

Our World Is a Beautiful Place—
Let's Keep it That Way

בַּעֲשָׂרָה מַאֲמָרוֹת נִבְרָא הָעוֹלָם. וּמַה תַּלְמוּד לוֹמַר, וַהֲלֹא בְמַאֲמָר אֶחָד יָכוֹל לְהִבָּרְאוֹת? אֶלָּא לְהִפָּרַע מִן הָרְשָׁעִים שֶׁמְּאַבְּדִין אֶת הָעוֹלָם שֶׁנִּבְרָא בַּעֲשָׂרָה מַאֲמָרוֹת, וְלִתֵּן שָׂכָר טוֹב לַצַּדִּיקִים שֶׁמְּקַיְּמִין אֶת הָעוֹלָם שֶׁנִּבְרָא בַּעֲשָׂרָה מַאֲמָרוֹת.

With ten utterances the world was created. And what does this teach, for surely it could have been created with one utterance? But this was so in order to punish the wicked who destroy the world that was created with ten utterances, and to give a good reward to the righteous who maintain the world that was created with ten utterances.

Our world is a beautiful place. We have a responsibility to upkeep and maintain it. This is hinted at in the dual role prescribed to Adam and Eve in the Garden of Eden: "To tend it and to guard it" (Gen. 2:15). This is a twofold mission: we must both develop the world, tending to it, and also protect and guard it. This means improving life here on Earth through using its natural resources to our advantage (see Ramban on Gen. 1:28). It also means keeping our Earth clean, trying to minimize our carbon footprint, and treating the Earth not only as a treading ground to help us achieve our personal goals but also as a living creation of God, into which God put much thought and attention in the process of its creation.

Our mishna alludes to this by depicting Hashem undergoing much "effort" to create the world. Hashem can do anything. Hashem nevertheless chose to model for us a slow and detailed creation of our world—with ten utterances. The number ten connotes a complete act, as is often pointed out by the Maharal.

This ought to bring to our attention that it is not enough to focus on our own lives or even our own four cubits of Jewish law. We have a responsibility to our world and to the environment. We are the caretakers of this beautiful planet! If Hashem was willing to go through all this effort to create the world and then command Adam and Eve to protect and develop it, we ourselves must follow suit.

The mishna relays this by stating that the wicked are punished for not upkeeping the world that was created with ten utterances. The opposite is true for the righteous. If the world had been created solely with one utterance, there might have been an argument for more modest reactionary measures when it comes to our behavior. Now that Hashem has shown us how important the world is, if we take care of it, we are performing a good deed, and in turn, "a good reward" awaits us. The opposite is the case when one who denies this and proceeds to profane and destroy Hashem's beautiful creation.

All of Humanity Is Precious to Hashem

עֲשָׂרָה דוֹרוֹת מֵאָדָם וְעַד נֹחַ, לְהוֹדִיעַ כַּמָּה אֶרֶךְ אַפַּיִם לְפָנָיו. שֶׁכָּל הַדּוֹרוֹת הָיוּ מַכְעִיסִין
וּבָאִין, עַד שֶׁהֵבִיא עֲלֵיהֶם אֶת מֵי הַמַּבּוּל. עֲשָׂרָה דוֹרוֹת מִנֹּחַ וְעַד אַבְרָהָם, לְהוֹדִיעַ כַּמָּה אֶרֶךְ
אַפַּיִם לְפָנָיו. שֶׁכָּל הַדּוֹרוֹת הָיוּ מַכְעִיסִין וּבָאִין, עַד שֶׁבָּא אַבְרָהָם וְקִבֵּל עָלָיו שְׂכַר כֻּלָּם.

There were ten generations from Adam to Noah, to make known what long-suffering is His; for all those generations kept on provoking Him, until He brought upon them the waters of the flood. [There were] ten generations from Noah to Avraham, to make known what long-suffering is His; for all those generations kept on provoking Him, until Avraham, came and received the reward of all of them.

Our two mishnas point to the universalistic mission of Am Yisrael in the world. Hashem's original plan was for all of humanity to be rewarded and blessed. In fact, this desire was so strong that when Hashem witnessed humanity's steep decline ("provoking") generation after generation, Hashem did not punish them collectively but rather patiently waited ("long-suffering") until they mended their ways. At a certain point, the situation was helpless, and Hashem hit restart with the deluge.

After the flood, Hashem waited once more for humanity to live up to its potential and be rewarded—"making it known that long-suffering is His"—but again this did not come to pass. After ten more generations followed this path, finally, one person, Avraham, emerged, and Hashem chose to bestow the blessing on his progeny. Avraham's offspring would now receive the original blessing Hashem had planned to offer all of humanity. This is what is meant by Avraham "receiving the reward of all of them."

Our two mishnas highlight how long Hashem waited for humanity to "get it together." Twenty or so generations! We can learn from Hashem's "long-suffering" in both mishnas. It reveals Hashem's true desire: that all humanity be elevated and close to Hashem. Our mishnas remind us to not fall into seclusionist thinking. Am Yisrael was bestowed the reward of all the generations so that they would share it with everyone and help push forward Hashem's original goal. There is so much that needs fixing in the world! Hashem waited and waited because all of humanity is so precious to Hashem. We must cultivate this same love for all of humanity and spread Hashem's blessing to all who are open to receive it.

Choosing Hashem as Our Candidate

עֲשָׂרָה נִסְיוֹנוֹת נִתְנַסָּה אַבְרָהָם אָבִינוּ עָלָיו הַשָּׁלוֹם וְעָמַד בְּכֻלָּם,
לְהוֹדִיעַ כַּמָּה חִבָּתוֹ שֶׁל אַבְרָהָם אָבִינוּ עָלָיו הַשָּׁלוֹם.

With ten trials was Avraham, our father (may he rest in peace), tried, and he withstood them all; to make known how great was the love of Avraham, our father (peace be upon him).

Rabbi Berel Wein brings attention to the unique language used in our mishna to describe Avraham's trials: "ועמד בכלם." This literally means: "and he stood for all of them." The simple explanation is that Avraham passed all his trials. Rabbi Wein, however, shifts the focus to the conclusion of the trial; upon passing each trial, Avraham stood up and went even higher. Each successive trial built his character.

It is possible to highlight another aspect of "ועמד בכלם." It may signify the importance of Avraham showing up in the first place or each of the trials. It's not so much the passing of the trial nor the growth that emerged as a result that is being stressed but Avraham's eagerness to go through the trials in the first place—to *stand up*, ready for the ensuing trial and challenge.

Passionate love can bring one to put themselves on the line for the object of their love. You see this in strong marriages and family connections. You also see this, for example, when candidates are seeking to be elected to governmental positions. People are often willing to do all that is in their power to ensure their nominee gets the vote. No one is forcing them to do so. Knocking on doors, being involved in media campaigns, cold calling—all of these actions and more are undertaken out of love and admiration for their choice candidate.

Avraham was lovesick for his choice candidate: Hashem. This is alluded to in the concluding words of our mishna: "להודיע כמה חיבתו של אברהם." This can be read as "how much was the love for Avraham (from Hashem)"; however, it can also mean: "how much love from Avraham (for Hashem)." This is what pushed him to keep standing up, ready for each new challenge (see Rashi on Gen. 22:3, s.v. vayashkem).

Avraham demonstrated a high level of love and devotion; therefore, our mishna provides an important tip for helping us get there: take it a step at a time! This is the secret behind the ten trials mentioned in our mishna. Ten is a complete number. It teaches that Avraham endured a long process until he was able to fully exhibit his love for Hashem. One trial after another built up Avraham's love until he finally arrived, poised and ready, to pass the most difficult test of them all: the binding of his beloved son, Yitzchak.

The "Thank You, Hashem" Game

עֲשָׂרָה נִסִּים נַעֲשׂוּ לַאֲבוֹתֵינוּ בְמִצְרַיִם, וַעֲשָׂרָה עַל הַיָּם. עֶשֶׂר מַכּוֹת
הֵבִיא הַקָּדוֹשׁ בָּרוּךְ הוּא עַל הַמִּצְרִיִּים בְּמִצְרַיִם, וְעֶשֶׂר עַל הַיָּם.

Ten miracles were wrought for our ancestors in Egypt, and ten at the sea. Ten plagues did the Holy one, blessed be He, bring upon the Egyptians in Egypt and ten at the sea.

Our mishna discusses Hashem's providence during the two stages of redemption from Egypt: the plagues in Egypt and the splitting of the sea. Many of us are familiar with the miracles wrought in Egypt, the ten plagues, from the reading of the Haggadah each year at the Passover Seder. These ten miracles get the most "airtime" in sermons and in the Torah, with the splitting of the sea and its miracles often going under the radar.

We tend to think of the splitting of the sea as one single miracle. The commentators on our mishna (see Rambam and Rabbeinu Yonah based on *Avot DeRebbe Natan* 33), however, paint a more intricate picture. As the Jews moved through the sea, they enjoyed ten miracles within the overall miracle of the splitting sea. Miracles within a miracle! Some of the miracles included: tunnels that were formed in the sea, transparent walls that allowed each tribe to see the other, and sweet drinking water for the Jews to enjoy. There were also ten full plagues on the Egyptians at the sea, just like in Egypt. Some of these included: loud noises, arrows, swords, and stones. These, too, are lesser-known miracles within a miracle.

What does all of this have to teach us today? We do not only experience miracles on a day-to-day basis but also miracles within miracles. Some are there to enhance our lives, like the ten miracles at the sea. Others are there to protect us from calamities that might befall us, like the ten plagues at the sea. Our mishna is bringing to the fore the concept of recognizing miracles within the miracles we experience in our lives.

I have a game I sometimes play with a friend of mine—now a rabbi—from my rabbinical school days. Yes, it's a rabbi game! But in truth, if done correctly, it can help everyone experience their own personal splitting of the sea. No less! We call it "Thank You, Hashem." We basically go back and forth, each one of us sharing one thing we are grateful for, each time starting with the words "Thank you, Hashem." It gets harder after a while as you try to think of more and more things for which to thank Hashem. But truthfully, there really are so many things for which we can offer thanks! As you move along, the energy keeps getting stronger, and the gratitude swells up. It's fun playing with someone else, but you can also play by yourself. We usually play this while walking or driving somewhere together. For some reason this makes it easier to keep it going.

This game drives home the idea of miracles within miracles. These submiracles are often as little recognized by us as the submiracles at the sea relayed to us by our tradition! No matter what is happening in our lives, we all experience an abundance of kindnesses within kindnesses. This is what is alluded to in our mishna with the number ten, which is, as we mentioned, a whole and complete number in our tradition.

5:6

It's Okay to Question and Doubt

עֲשָׂרָה נִסְיוֹנוֹת נִסּוּ אֲבוֹתֵינוּ אֶת הַמָּקוֹם בָּרוּךְ הוּא בַּמִּדְבָּר, שֶׁנֶּאֱמַר
(במדבר יד): וַיְנַסּוּ אֹתִי זֶה עֶשֶׂר פְּעָמִים וְלֹא שָׁמְעוּ בְּקוֹלִי.

With ten trials did our ancestors try God, blessed be He, as it is said, "And they have tried Me these ten times and they have not listened to my voice" (Num. 14:22).

The Talmud (*Talmud Bavli*, Arachin 15a) lists the different trials mentioned in our mishna: "Two at the sea, and two with water, two with the manna, two with the quail, one with the golden calf, and one in the wilderness of Paran." Hashem's forgiveness and patience are themes that are often stressed by commentators upon explicating our mishna. In all these instances, Am Yisrael wavered in their trust in Hashem; Hashem nevertheless forgave them and did not forsake them.

Our mishna may also be alluding to an additional theme: the positive role of doubt and "trials" in our spiritual growth. In all these cases, Hashem allowed the nation to "try" Hashem. Hashem could have terminated the connection after each trial, but this was not the case. This was to provide space for Am Yisrael to develop deep and authentic faith in Hashem.

Rabbi Kook teaches that it is through trials and questioning that we arrive at true faith: "True faith is attained through the possibility of heresy" (*Midot HaReayah*, Emunah 15). The relevant kernel here is that we must allow ourselves freedom to ask questions, and in this sense "try Hashem," in order to arrive at even higher levels of connection and faith.

I once watched a religious movie about a woman who was banished from her church due to her questioning of the fundamentals of her faith. They demanded a level of blind faith from her that she was unable to uphold. Our mishna reminds us that faith is less about perfect obedience and more about being *in a relationship* with Hashem. We aren't going to be perfect. We are going to waver at times in our faith, especially when times are tough, as in Am Yisrael's experience in the desert.

Additionally, some of us (but not all of us: ibid., 18) will only be able to develop our faith through exploring, asking questions, doubting, and revisiting key principles and ideas of Jewish faith. Our mishna assures us that this is okay. This is all part of being in a relationship with Hashem, which, like most relationships, endures ups and downs and requires much work and even "trials" from time to time in order to flourish.

Not at All Times Should
One "Bow" to Others

עֲשָׂרָה נִסִּים נַעֲשׂוּ לַאֲבוֹתֵינוּ בְּבֵית הַמִּקְדָּשׁ. לֹא הִפִּילָה אִשָּׁה מֵרֵיחַ בְּשַׂר הַקֹּדֶשׁ, וְלֹא הִסְרִיחַ בְּשַׂר הַקֹּדֶשׁ מֵעוֹלָם, וְלֹא נִרְאָה זְבוּב בְּבֵית הַמִּטְבָּחַיִם, וְלֹא אֵרַע קֶרִי לְכֹהֵן גָּדוֹל בְּיוֹם הַכִּפּוּרִים, וְלֹא כִּבּוּ גְּשָׁמִים אֵשׁ שֶׁל עֲצֵי הַמַּעֲרָכָה, וְלֹא נָצְחָה הָרוּחַ אֶת עַמּוּד הֶעָשָׁן, וְלֹא נִמְצָא פְסוּל בָּעֹמֶר וּבִשְׁתֵּי הַלֶּחֶם וּבְלֶחֶם הַפָּנִים, עוֹמְדִים צְפוּפִים וּמִשְׁתַּחֲוִים רְוָחִים, וְלֹא הִזִּיק נָחָשׁ וְעַקְרָב בִּירוּשָׁלַיִם מֵעוֹלָם, וְלֹא אָמַר אָדָם לַחֲבֵרוֹ: צַר לִי הַמָּקוֹם שֶׁאָלִין בִּירוּשָׁלַיִם.

Ten wonders were wrought for our ancestors in the Temple. No woman miscarried from the odor of the sacred flesh; the sacred flesh never became putrid; no fly was ever seen in the slaughterhouse; no emission occurred to the high priest on the Day of Atonement; the rains did not extinguish the fire of the woodpile; the wind did not prevail against the column of smoke; no defect was found in the omer, or in the two loaves, or in the showbread; the people stood pressed together, yet bowed down and had enough room; never did a serpent or a scorpion harm anyone in Jerusalem; and no person said to another, "The place is too congested for me to lodge overnight in Jerusalem."

Several commentators explain the eighth miracle, "עומדים צפופים ומשתחוים רוחים—the people stood pressed together, yet bowed down and had enough room," in a creative manner. They point out that when one stands up straight, not humbling themselves in front of others or working with them as a team, then everything feels stuffed and "pressed together." However, when one works selflessly with others, then there is room for everyone: people feel comfortable, and everyone gets along and works well with each other.

Similarly, reading this line out of its original context, I'd like to offer a different interpretation. There are times when standing straight actually leads to positive results. Not at all times should one "bow" to others. There are times when people will surround us (צפופים) and apply pressure to have us fulfill their wishes. However, attending to their requests at these moments is not always in their best interest.

Anyone with children knows this to be true. If we were to comply with all their requests, we would not be doing them a favor. It can be hazardous to their development if they believe the world will always "bow" to their needs. Sometimes standing up straight is just the remedy for such behavior, and it can lead to great results in the end. When we do give, after appropriately standing our ground, we do so from a place of strength and intention. This can be the greatest kindness to those around us.

This lesson is relayed through this line of our mishna when its two components are read in succession. When we stand straight (עומדים) amid pressure (צפופים), then our giving and acceding to others (משתחוים) will breed positive results (רווחים—which can also mean "earnings").

Why the Ba'al Teshuva Is More Elevated Than the Wholly Righteous

עֲשָׂרָה דְבָרִים נִבְרְאוּ בְּעֶרֶב שַׁבָּת בֵּין הַשְּׁמָשׁוֹת, וְאֵלוּ הֵן: פִּי הָאָרֶץ, וּפִי הַבְּאֵר, וּפִי הָאָתוֹן, וְהַקֶּשֶׁת, וְהַמָּן, וְהַמַּטֶּה, וְהַשָּׁמִיר, וְהַכְּתָב, וְהַמִּכְתָּב, וְהַלּוּחוֹת. וְיֵשׁ אוֹמְרִים: אַף הַמַּזִּיקִין, וּקְבוּרָתוֹ שֶׁל מֹשֶׁה, וְאֵילוֹ שֶׁל אַבְרָהָם אָבִינוּ. וְיֵשׁ אוֹמְרִים: אַף צְבָת בִּצְבָת עֲשׂוּיָה.

Ten things were created on the eve of the Sabbath at twilight, and they are: The mouth of the earth, the mouth of the well, the mouth of the donkey, the rainbow, the manna, the staff [of Moses], the shamir, the letters, the writing, and the tablets. And some say: Also the demons, the grave of Moses, and the ram of Avraham, our father. And some say: And also tongs, made with tongs.

The *Sfat Emet* explains why all these miraculous creations transpired specifically at twilight of creation's Sabbath Eve. Adam had just repented from his sin, and Hashem wanted to reward him. All active creation from Hashem's side was to cease on Shabbat; therefore, Hashem "snuck in" these ten creations during twilight, immediately prior to the commencement of Shabbat.

Based on this explanation, we can offer another possible reason why Hashem chose this twilight period to bestow the miracles: this liminal time hints, symbolically, at the turbulent life of the ba'al teshuva (lit., "the one who returns" to Judaism, the penitent). The ba'al teshuva is in a constant tug-of-war between "night" and "day." They are all too familiar with the attraction of sin (night), and due to their past enmeshment in sin, they are naturally drawn toward it. This attraction accompanies them as they grow spiritually and can become a menace to them, especially in dark times. The greatness of the ba'al teshuva is that they nevertheless choose the correct path (day).

This is why, according to our rabbis, the ba'al teshuva is on a higher level than a completely righteous individual (*tzaddik gamur*). The righteous never tasted sin in the first place; they, therefore, don't experience the same continuous push and pull with these dark forces.

Hashem blessed Adam with the potential for these miracles during twilight in praise of his choice of the side of life and light despite the draw to sin. Our mishna reminds us that, like Adam, miracles and blessings await us when we liberate ourselves from the clutches of sin and choose the path of light over darkness.

The Truth is Between
the Alefs and Tavs

שִׁבְעָה דְבָרִים בַּגֹּלֶם וְשִׁבְעָה בֶחָכָם. חָכָם אֵינוֹ מְדַבֵּר בִּפְנֵי מִי שֶׁהוּא גָדוֹל
מִמֶּנּוּ בְּחָכְמָה וּבְמִנְיָן, וְאֵינוֹ נִכְנָס לְתוֹךְ דִּבְרֵי חֲבֵרוֹ, וְאֵינוֹ נִבְהָל לְהָשִׁיב, שׁוֹאֵל
כָּעִנְיָן וּמֵשִׁיב כַּהֲלָכָה, וְאוֹמֵר עַל רִאשׁוֹן רִאשׁוֹן וְעַל אַחֲרוֹן אַחֲרוֹן, וְעַל מַה
שֶׁלֹּא שָׁמַע, אוֹמֵר לֹא שָׁמַעְתִּי, וּמוֹדֶה עַל הָאֱמֶת. וְחִלּוּפֵיהֶן בַּגֹּלֶם.

There are seven things [characteristic] in a clod, and seven in a wise
person. A wise person does not speak before one who is greater than
them in wisdom; and does not break into their fellow's speech; and is not
hasty to answer. They ask what is relevant, and answer to the point; and
they speak of the first [point] first, and of the last [point] last; and con-
cerning that which they have not heard, they say: I have not heard; and
they acknowledge the truth. And the reverse of these [are characteristic]
in a clod.

The Maharal, in discussing the final trait that deems one wise,
"acknowledgement of the truth," compares the word אמת ("truth") to
שקר ("falsehood"). Some think that seeing the truth entails being closed
to other views and being one-sided, but this is not the case.

In contrast, the Maharal demonstrates how the word אמת connotes
balanced thinking. The alef (א) is on one side of the aleph-bet, and the
letter tav (ת) is on the other. The letter mem (מ) falls in between and
balances between them. The word שקר, in contrast, is lopsided and

imbalanced, comprised of three of the final letters of the aleph-bet. Acknowledging truth is far from one-sidedness. It requires humility and patience to hear different views. This balance is hinted at in the letters אמת. Those who are connected to שקר, on the other hand, many times see only one side of things and surround themselves with those who voice the same opinion.

Many have drawn attention to the special friendship between the late Justice Ruth Bader Ginsburg and her also-deceased colleague Justice Antonin Scalia. They were on polar opposites of the political spectrum, one on the א side and the other on the ת side, but they managed to coexist and still be friends. We need this so much in these polarized days! Sadly, today, the alefs can't speak with the tavs and vice versa.

Being wise is not being the only one who is right. It is understanding that the truth is oftentimes found in between the alefs and tavs or at least through taking the different letters into consideration!

The Satisfaction of Giving

שִׁבְעָה מִינֵי פֻּרְעָנִיּוֹת בָּאִין לָעוֹלָם עַל שִׁבְעָה גוּפֵי עֲבֵרָה. מִקְצָתָן מְעַשְׂרִין וּמִקְצָתָן אֵינָן מְעַשְׂרִין: רָעָב שֶׁל בַּצֹרֶת בָּאָה, מִקְצָתָן רְעֵבִים וּמִקְצָתָן שְׂבֵעִים. גָּמְרוּ שֶׁלֹּא לְעַשֵּׂר: רָעָב שֶׁל מְהוּמָה וְשֶׁל בַּצֹרֶת בָּאָה. וְשֶׁלֹּא לִטֹּל אֶת הַחַלָּה: רָעָב שֶׁל כְּלָיָה בָּאָה.

Seven kinds of punishment come to the world for seven categories of transgression. When some of them give tithes, and others do not give tithes, a famine from drought comes, some go hungry and others are satisfied. When they have all decided not to give tithes, a famine from tumult and drought comes. [When they have, in addition, decided] not to set apart the dough-offering, an all-consuming famine comes.

Our mishna continues with the lists of number sevens as it delineates three successive levels of neglect of contributions. For each level, a different calamity is administered: a famine from drought in which some go hungry, a famine from tumult and drought, and an all-consuming famine.

Rashi presents the second form of punishment, tumult (מהומה), as the retribution in the following verse: "ואכלתם ולא תשבעו—And you will eat, yet not be satisfied" (Lev. 26:26). I believe Rashi is hinting that when there is no place in our life for giving to others, we will not properly enjoy all the good with which we are blessed. You will eat but not feel satisfied!

There is a certain joy and exuberance that comes from giving to others. It's hard to describe it in words, but the more one embraces this way of life, the more happiness and satisfaction one experiences. Our mishna is teaching that one can have all the riches—in produce and grain—but if these are not channeled outward (through tithes, challah, and other forms of charity), one will still feel a certain void, an inner "drought" or "famine" which will not be satiated until one includes others in their blessing.

5:11

We Are Guests in Hashem's Home— Let's Behave Accordingly!

דֶּבֶר בָּא לָעוֹלָם עַל מִיתוֹת הָאֲמוּרוֹת בַּתּוֹרָה שֶׁלֹּא נִמְסְרוּ לְבֵית דִּין וְעַל פֵּרוֹת שְׁבִיעִית. חֶרֶב בָּאָה לָעוֹלָם עַל עִנּוּי הַדִּין, וְעַל עִוּוּת הַדִּין, וְעַל הַמּוֹרִים בַּתּוֹרָה שֶׁלֹּא כַהֲלָכָה.

Pestilence comes to the world for sins punishable by death according to the Torah, but which have not been referred to the court, and for neglect of the law regarding the fruits of the Shemita (Sabbatical) year. The sword comes to the world for the delay of judgment, and for the perversion of judgment, and because of those who teach the Torah not in accordance with the accepted law.

דבר often translates to pestilence. However, it is also used in our texts as a general reference to plagues or pandemics. Our mishna offers two reasons why plagues strike humanity. For our purposes, I'd like to focus on the second reason: plagues befall Am Yisrael due to "neglect of the law regarding the fruits of the Shemitah year."

The Shemitah laws teach us that the land is Hashem's. We attest to this fact through refraining from tilling the land and benefiting from its produce during the Shemitah year. It can therefore be deduced that one reason plagues transpire is due to our forgetting that the land is Hashem's. I like to see this as less of a punishment and more as a reminder of our lack of control over reality. This is what plagues bring to the fore through the instability and trepidation they inject into our lives.

But why is this so important to remember? As I am writing this commentary to our mishna, I am being hosted at someone's home. There is a lot of Torah to be learned from the difference between how we behave in our own homes versus our behavior as a guest in another's dwelling. When we are being hosted, we are (hopefully!) on our best behavior. We act civilly toward those around us, clean up after ourselves, and refrain from certain behavior that might embarrass us while in mixed company.

This is how we should feel as we are "hosted" all of our days here on Earth, in Hashem's home. As guests, we should behave kindly to each other, clean up after ourselves (take care of the environment), and just be on our best behavior as we are hosted here for the duration of our stay. It's really as simple as that!

The Shemitah year comes every seven years to shift us from an owner mentality to a guest mentality. The hope is that this understanding will continue with us for the next six years as we till the land and tend to our fields and produce. When the Shemitah year no longer serves this purpose, due to our "neglect" of its laws, Hashem ensures this attitude is cultivated through other means—to remind us to Whom the land belongs and that we must behave accordingly.

5:12

Holiness, Life-Giving, and Service of Hashem

חַיָּה רָעָה בָּאָה לָעוֹלָם עַל שְׁבוּעַת שָׁוְא וְעַל חִלּוּל הַשֵּׁם. גָּלוּת בָּאָה לָעוֹלָם עַל
עוֹבְדֵי עֲבוֹדָה זָרָה, וְעַל גִּלּוּי עֲרָיוֹת, וְעַל שְׁפִיכוּת דָּמִים, וְעַל הַשְׁמָטַת הָאָרֶץ.

Wild beasts come to the world for swearing in vain, and for the profanation of the Name. Exile comes to the world for idolatry, for sexual sins and for bloodshed, and for [transgressing the commandment of] Shemitah.

Our mishna lists the sixth and seventh punishments that appear in our series of mishnas: wild animals and exile. The exile that is mentioned is our current exile from the land of Israel and the Temple worship. Out of the seven punishments, exile must be the gravest of them all as it occurs because of the three cardinal sins (*Talmud Bavli*, Sanhedrin 74a): idol worship, illicit sexual acts, and murder.

When it comes to the destruction of the Second Temple, we are taught that the source of the calamity was baseless, or unconditional, hatred (ibid., Yoma 9b). Regarding this, Rabbi Kook famously taught that what would lead to its rebuilding is just the opposite: unconditional love (*Shemonah Kevatzim* 8:47). With Rabbi Kook's approach in mind, it is worth thinking about what will end our current exile by considering the opposite of each one of the cardinal sins. If we were exiled due to these sins, we must be redeemed, based on Rabbi Kook, through strengthening the opposite.

The first is foreign worship. The opposite of this is service of Hashem. The second is illicit sexual acts. According to the Maharal's commentary on our mishna, the opposite of this is holiness. And the final sin is murder. The opposite of this is life-giving. Interestingly, these three align well with the first three blessings of the amidah. The first blessing discusses each of our forefathers' unique service of Hashem, the second blessing is about giving life, and the third blessing is about holiness.

There is a tendency in religious circles to go to extremes. In more progressive segments of Judaism, life-giving is heavily focused upon, in a broad sense, through social action, or *tikkun olam*. On the more traditional side, there is constant progress and growth in terms of holiness; however, engagement in the world outside of one's immediate circles is often viewed as less central.

The purpose of Am Yisrael is to be both a ממלכת כהנים, a kingdom of priests, who give life to others, and a גוי קדוש, a holy nation. In this sense, we all have much to learn from each other. However, these engagements are not sufficient if they are not expressed and manifested within the framework of our tradition. Both must be expressed in the service of Hashem, the opposite of the third sin, foreign worship.

When we find ourselves strong and committed to all three ideals, we will be worthy of being redeemed, equipped with what we will need to fulfill our national and global mission.

Extras for Some Are Bare
Essentials for Others

בְּאַרְבָּעָה פְרָקִים הַדֶּבֶר מִתְרַבֶּה: בָּרְבִיעִית, וּבַשְּׁבִיעִית, וּבְמוֹצָאֵי שְׁבִיעִית,
וּבְמוֹצָאֵי הֶחָג שֶׁבְּכָל שָׁנָה וְשָׁנָה. בָּרְבִיעִית, מִפְּנֵי מַעְשַׂר עָנִי שֶׁבַּשְּׁלִישִׁית.
בַּשְּׁבִיעִית, מִפְּנֵי מַעְשַׂר עָנִי שֶׁבַּשִּׁשִּׁית. וּבְמוֹצָאֵי שְׁבִיעִית, מִפְּנֵי פֵרוֹת
שְׁבִיעִית. וּבְמוֹצָאֵי הֶחָג שֶׁבְּכָל שָׁנָה וְשָׁנָה, מִפְּנֵי גֶזֶל מַתְּנוֹת עֲנִיִּים.

At four times pestilence increases: in the fourth year, and in the seventh year, and at the conclusion of the seventh year, and at the conclusion of Sukkot in every year. In the fourth year, on account of the tithe of the poor which is due in the third year. In the seventh year, on account of the tithe of the poor which is due in the sixth year. At the conclusion of the seventh year, on account of the produce of the seventh year. And at the conclusion of Sukkot in every year, for robbing the gifts to the poor.

Our mishna begins a series of mishnas with counts of four. All four periods that are mentioned are connected to withholding gifts from the poor: the tithe of the poor in the third and sixth years; the produce meant to be left aside for the poor throughout the Shemitah year; and the produce we should have left for those in need during our harvest around Sukkot time, such as leket, peiah, and shichika. What stands out in the final statement is the language "גזל מתנות עניים." This literally means: "the stealing of the poor person's gifts."

If it's a gift, how is it stealing? One way to reconcile this is to say that indeed it is a gift, but it is a gift from Hashem. We have been assigned as Hashem's emissaries to dispense these gifts. However, this extra produce was never really ours in the first place. When we withhold it, it is akin to stealing. The following words of the Chafetz Chaim help clarify the message, reminding us that what is "extra" for some are bare essentials for others.

> Indeed, the amount of money owned by a person in excess of his needs is a trust fund deposited by the Master of the Universe, Who appointed him to administer it, to take pity on the unfortunate, and to extend favors to the needy. (*Ahavat Chesed*, pp. 133–34)

> Whatever the poor really needs belongs to him. It is deposited with you on his behalf; therefore, you must not withhold it from him. (Ibid., p. 134)

The Maharal explains why pestilence is a fitting punishment for withholding these gifts. Other punishments, such as the sword (חרב), affect the body, while the soul remains intact. Pestilence, on the other hand, runs deep. One may look intact on the outside while being completely plagued with pestilence on the inside. Perhaps pestilence is a reminder to those who withhold their "extras" from those who so desperately need them. What is *external* for you, extra cash or produce, is for them the most basic of needs, *internal* matters of necessity.

The mishna goes on to teach that one cannot sit still and claim they did not actively do anything wrong by not segregating these amounts for those in need. This is hinted at in the language "pestilence increases." These needs keep growing, and the internal struggles demand attention. Inaction only foments this. Increased pestilence is meant as a hint to those with means to change their ways and recognize the increasing daily struggles of the less fortunate.

5:14

Self-Care as a Prerequisite to Selflessness

אַרְבַּע מִדּוֹת בָּאָדָם. הָאוֹמֵר שֶׁלִּי שֶׁלִּי וְשֶׁלְּךָ שֶׁלָּךְ, זוֹ מִדָּה בֵּינוֹנִית. וְיֵשׁ אוֹמְרִים: זוֹ מִדַּת סְדוֹם. שֶׁלִּי שֶׁלְּךָ וְשֶׁלְּךָ שֶׁלִּי, עַם הָאָרֶץ. שֶׁלִּי שֶׁלְּךָ וְשֶׁלְּךָ שֶׁלָּךְ, חָסִיד. שֶׁלִּי שֶׁלִּי וְשֶׁלְּךָ שֶׁלִּי, רָשָׁע.

There are four types of character in human beings. One that says, "Mine is mine, and yours is yours," is a commonplace type, and some say this is a Sodom-type of character. One that says, "Mine is yours and yours is mine," is an unlearned person (am ha'aretz). One that says, "Mine is yours and yours is yours," is a pious person. One that says, "Mine is mine, and yours is mine," is a wicked person.

Our mishna runs through four traits. For me, only one of its conclusions is clear-cut. The one who says "What's mine is mine, and what's yours is mine" is clearly a wicked person or at least thinking in a "wicked" manner if this is their modus operandi.

The other extreme, "What's mine is yours, and what's yours is yours," is less clear-cut. Some might even call this person a pushover! However, our mishna goes in the exact opposite direction, deeming this individual a חסיד, a pious individual. I will share a bit more on this below.

The mishna defines someone who says "What's mine is yours, and what's yours is mine" as an ignoramus or an unlearned person. When I taught this mishna to my congregants, this was met with pushback. One of them said, "Isn't this basically learning how to share with each other?"

One way to answer is that when taken to an extreme, this total divestment of personal property can be hazardous. Although my friends who lived in a kibbutz several years ago in Israel would argue just the opposite!

What I'd like to focus on, however, is the one who says, "What's mine is mine, and what's yours is yours." On this perspective, our mishna offers two reflections. It defines this person as a בינוני, which is translated above as a "commonplace type" and states that this person could also be defined as a Sodom-type of character.

I'd like to explain the difference as follows. Our tradition teaches us that the people of Sodom were out for themselves. They passed laws forbidding people from the outside to enter their plush real estate for fear that they would taint it. They were selfish and greedy, and this is why Hashem chose to destroy the area in the time of Avraham.

Notwithstanding, there are times when it is fitting to apply this attitude of "I do my thing, and you do yours." This can be seen as an approach of self-care and noninterference with the property of the others—when applied in moderation. Self-care is extremely vital in one's life and divine service. When taken to the extreme, this can turn into the way of Sodom, but when practiced in a measured way and as a springboard to arrive at a higher level of selflessness toward others, this trait is commendable.

I believe this is what the mishna is referring to when it uses the word בינוני. This word contains within it the word בין which means "in-between." This trait should not be our final destination. Otherwise, we will end up in Sodom territory. Instead, it should be an intermediate state, a trait of בין, "in between." When we take good care of ourselves, we can offer more to others. This allows us to recognize everyone's right to their own property and self-definition—"What's mine is mine, and what's yours is yours"—and extend from this place of strength to a position of selfless giving to others.

Interestingly, this also answers our question when it comes to the one who says, "What's mine is yours, and what's yours is yours." This individual is only a "pushover" when they forget about themselves completely. However, when there is a healthy sense of self to start with, the intermediate stage of "what's mine is mine, and what's yours," one can then safely embody the highest level mentioned in our mishna: "What's mine is yours, and what's yours is yours."

Hard Work Will Get You Far

אַרְבַּע מִדּוֹת בַּדֵּעוֹת. נוֹחַ לִכְעֹס וְנוֹחַ לִרְצוֹת, יָצָא שְׂכָרוֹ בְהֶפְסֵדוֹ. קָשֶׁה לִכְעֹס וְקָשֶׁה לִרְצוֹת,
יָצָא הֶפְסֵדוֹ בִשְׂכָרוֹ. קָשֶׁה לִכְעֹס וְנוֹחַ לִרְצוֹת, חָסִיד. נוֹחַ לִכְעֹס וְקָשֶׁה לִרְצוֹת, רָשָׁע.

There are four kinds of temperaments. Easy to become angry, and easy to be appeased: their gain disappears in their loss. Hard to become angry, and hard to be appeased: their loss disappears in their gain. Hard to become angry and easy to be appeased: a pious person. Easy to become angry and hard to be appeased: a wicked person.

Our mishna presents four temperaments—all dealing with anger. Let's begin with the two extremes. Someone who is quick to become angry and slow to be appeased is clearly the worst on this list. This is equivalent to someone getting angry very easily and then never letting go of their grudge. On the other side of the spectrum is someone who is difficult to make angry, and when they do get angry, they quickly forgive and let go of their grudge. This person is called a חסיד, a pious individual.

The question that remains is which of the middle traits is worse: someone who gets angry easily but is easy to appease or someone who is slow to anger, but when they get angry, they are tough to appease? The first of these middle temperaments has an advantage in that they are easily appeased. Even though they are quick to get angry, they mend this by easily becoming appeased. The latter has an advantage in that they don't easily get angry in the first place. However, when they do, it's difficult for them to forgive.

According to the Meiri and others, the first of the two temperaments is preferable. This is based on a different version of the mishna that says that one who easily becomes angry and is easily appeased finds their loss disappear in their gain, while one who is slow to anger but also slow to be appeased finds their gain disappear in their loss, which is clearly worse. According to my understanding, although the first person gets angry more often, there is hope for them to improve if they continuously self-correct. The other individual may get angry less often, but they hold onto a grudge. When one does this, there is less hope for growth.

Based on this version of the mishna, the message is clear. You may start out with disadvantages in life—like this individual who gets angry more often; however, with work and constant self-correction, you can rise above your current reality, and in time, perhaps, even surpass the one who is more successful at the onset. It's all about work and investment. When one puts in the work, in a consistent and diligent manner, the sky's the limit (see *Ohr LeTzion: Zichron Hadassah: Chochmah U'mussar*, p. 23 s.v. ume'idach).

5:16

Quit Swiping and Start Living

אַרְבַּע מִדּוֹת בַּתַּלְמִידִים. מַהֵר לִשְׁמֹעַ וּמַהֵר לְאַבֵּד, יָצָא שְׂכָרוֹ בְהֶפְסֵדוֹ. קָשֶׁה לִשְׁמֹעַ וְקָשֶׁה לְאַבֵּד, יָצָא הֶפְסֵדוֹ בִשְׂכָרוֹ. מַהֵר לִשְׁמֹעַ וְקָשֶׁה לְאַבֵּד, חָכָם. קָשֶׁה לִשְׁמֹעַ וּמַהֵר לְאַבֵּד, זֶה חֵלֶק רָע.

There are four types of disciples. Quick to comprehend, and quick to forget: their gain disappears in their loss. Slow to comprehend, and slow to forget: their loss disappears in their gain. Quick to comprehend, and slow to forget: a wise person. Slow to comprehend, and quick to forget: this is an evil portion.

In the first case, the mishna discusses one who is "quick to comprehend and quick to forget." The Maharal describes the two parts of this statement in a causal manner. Someone who only listens in a superficial manner will quickly forget what they learned. In our generation, social media and constant "swiping" on our smartphones and tablets for newer and more exciting content have changed the way we think and absorb information.

There are positive sides to this, of course. I remember in the not-so-distant past having to physically drive to the library (during open hours, of course) and "swipe" through a card catalog to find information I needed. Now, I literally have it all at my fingertips. The flip side of this, however, is that in many ways we have become more superficial. We are quick to absorb and swipe through information but less connected to what we are doing.

This may be what the mishna is referring to when it says "מהר לאבד."
This is often translated to "quick to forget," but the literal translation is
"quick to lose," and it could be referring to the quickness with which one
loses an internal connection to the content being absorbed.

It's not only about being present in the moment. It's about allowing
ideas to "cook" and "brew" in our heads for an extended period of time,
taking time to thoroughly analyze a prayer, or spending hours reading a
good book. There is so much good that can come from zoning in on one
topic and uncovering all the good that is lying beneath its surface. This
is something that we miss out on with the constant swipes.

Secrets to Success in a Group Setting

אַרְבַּע מִדּוֹת בְּנוֹתְנֵי צְדָקָה. הָרוֹצֶה שֶׁיִּתֵּן וְלֹא יִתְּנוּ אֲחֵרִים: עֵינוֹ רָעָה בְּשֶׁל אֲחֵרִים. יִתְּנוּ אֲחֵרִים וְהוּא לֹא יִתֵּן: עֵינוֹ רָעָה בְּשֶׁלּוֹ. יִתֵּן וְיִתְּנוּ אֲחֵרִים: חָסִיד. לֹא יִתֵּן וְלֹא יִתְּנוּ אֲחֵרִים: רָשָׁע.

There are four types of charity givers. One who wishes to give, but that others should not give: their eye is evil to that which belongs to others. One who wishes that others should give, but that they should not give: their eye is evil toward that which is their own. One who desires that they should give, and that others should give: this is a pious person. One who desires that they should not give and that others too should not give: this is a wicked person.

Our mishna refers to four ways of giving charity. I'd like to expand this to all just causes based on a looser understanding of the of the term *tzedakah* in our mishna, whose root is צ-ד-ק, which means "just." Our mishna offers the proper attitude for working toward these lofty goals in a group setting.

On a personal level, everyone wants to excel—at work, in sports, and in life overall. However, one must always keep in mind the greater good of the group in which one is functioning. On the one hand, one must not leave one's work for others to do ("one who wishes that others should give, but that they should not give"). That's not only inconsiderate, but it displays a lack of ambition and personal accountability ("their eye is evil toward that which is their own"). Consideration and accountability are required traits for one to excel and maximize their potential. On the

RABBI DR. ELI YOGGEV

other hand, one must not be overly ambitious to the point that one seeks to overshadow others ("one who wishes to give, but that others should not give: their eye is evil to that which belongs to others"). If one's underlying goal is the success of the group and the just cause, one will be happy when others succeed because it makes the group even better.

This balancing act is very tough because overly focusing on one can lead to forgetting the other. This is a litmus test for those who strive to excel in a group setting. While you are, thank God, excelling and doing well, are you still able to be happy for others in your group when they succeed? Will you make space for them to grow as they even surpass your performance if that's in the group's best interest? If so, then you have struck the right balance mentioned in our mishna: "one who desires that they should give, and that others should give." This is what our mishna calls a pious person. We can call it being a real team player!

Don't Discount the JFKers!

אַרְבַּע מִדּוֹת בְּהוֹלְכֵי לְבֵית הַמִּדְרָשׁ. הוֹלֵךְ וְאֵינוֹ עוֹשֶׂה: שָׂכָר הֲלִיכָה בְּיָדוֹ. עוֹשֶׂה וְאֵינוֹ הוֹלֵךְ: שָׂכָר מַעֲשֶׂה בְּיָדוֹ. הוֹלֵךְ וְעוֹשֶׂה: חָסִיד. לֹא הוֹלֵךְ וְלֹא עוֹשֶׂה: רָשָׁע.

There are four types among those who frequent the beit hamidrash (study hall). One who attends but does not practice: they receive a reward for attendance. One who practices but does not attend: they receive a reward for practice. One who attends and practices: a pious person. One who neither attends nor practices: a wicked person.

Many in shul bemoan the reality of "JFK" shul goers. No, this has nothing to do with a former US president; the initials stand for people who come Just For Kiddush. The main discomfort with this is obvious: we want people to come to shul not just for the hot cholent and l'chaims but for the spiritual nourishment as well! Is there value nevertheless in visits to the shul even when one doesn't enter the sanctuary itself? In short: when it comes to one who comes to shul ("frequents the beit hamidrash") but doesn't actually daven with the shul ("practices"), can we find some good in this endeavor as well?

Let me say up front that I wholeheartedly suggest coming to daven in person and attending services and classes. In the following, I am searching for good in the act of attending despite not "practicing." Our mishna seems to find some good by indicating that one receives reward for just showing up: "one who attends but does not practice: they receive a reward for attendance." What is the nature of that reward?

Our senior rabbi at Beth Tfiloh Congregation, Rabbi Mitchell Wohlberg, says that whatever brings people into the building (of course, as long as it's halachic) is worth it because it's better they are here than doing something else on Shabbos. He also adds that what is sometimes called the "the hallway minyan" at our shul can at times (we hope more times than not!) spill over from the hallway into the sanctuary. If they were not in the building at all, there would be no chance of this happening.

This may be the understanding of the reward listed, "שכר הליכה," for one who simply attends the beit hamidrash. The literal meaning of this is "the reward for walking," but it can also be read as the "reward of walking." The reward for showing up and walking in the door is actually more walking: from kiddush into the shul to hear a sermon from time to time or to daven and develop a deeper connection to the community.

Another positive result is laid forth by the *Netivot Shalom* (Breishit, p. 61). The *Netivot Shalom* brings the verse from Psalms 133:1: "הנה מה טוב ומה נעים שבת אחים גם יחד—How good and pleasant it is for people to dwell together," to explain that when Jews come together, even if not for the sake of holy endeavors, a certain aspect of divinity is revealed. I will admit that when I first came across this source, I had to read it again to make sure this is the correct reading. However, this is what is written: "And even for a superficial gathering [בציבור חיצוני], when ten (or more) Jews come together, it is the reality that whenever there are ten together the divine presence resides, and as we said, this is even when they do not speak on the topic fear of God...[T]he gathering itself of people with positive intrinsic traits draws in the divine presence."

Based on this, there is spiritual value to the gathering even if "JFK goers" do not make their way into the main sanctuary. Jews coming together and being together has value in itself! The relationship and connection draw in the divine. This may be another understanding of the "reward of walking." Walking connotes movement. The movement of one Jew toward another is valuable in and of itself. And this is its intrinsic reward—two Jews moving toward each other and connecting is "good and pleasant."

5:19

Jewish Values Begin at Home

אַרְבַּע מִדּוֹת בְּיוֹשְׁבִים לִפְנֵי חֲכָמִים. סְפוֹג, וּמַשְׁפֵּךְ, מְשַׁמֶּרֶת, וְנָפָה. סְפוֹג, שֶׁהוּא סוֹפֵג אֶת הַכֹּל. מַשְׁפֵּךְ, שֶׁמַּכְנִיס בְּזוֹ וּמוֹצִיא בְזוֹ. מְשַׁמֶּרֶת, שֶׁמּוֹצִיאָה אֶת הַיַּיִן וְקוֹלֶטֶת אֶת הַשְּׁמָרִים. וְנָפָה, שֶׁמּוֹצִיאָה אֶת הַקֶּמַח וְקוֹלֶטֶת אֶת הַסֹּלֶת.

There are four types among those who sit before the sages: a sponge, a funnel, a strainer, and a sieve. A sponge soaks up everything. A funnel takes in at one end and lets out at the other. A strainer lets out the wine and retains the sediment. A sieve lets out the coarse meal and retains the choice flour.

For the Rambam, our mishna deals with true and false claims and which vessel best arrives at these intellectual truths. Rashi takes things in a whole different direction. Our mishna does not deal with true versus false but rather essential (עיקר) versus peripheral (טפל) information.

On this understanding, Rashi ranks the four vessels. The funnel is the worst. It allows for the essential to be lost along with the nonessential. Then comes the strainer, which holds on to the unimportant aspects while disposing of the essential. For Rashi, it is preferable to have peripheral information than none at all! Next in line is the sponge, which absorbs the essential but lacks the ability to neutralize the peripheral. And lastly is the sieve, which holds on to what is important and lets go of the rest.

Rashi's explanation better reflects our everyday experiences and life decisions than the Rambam's. Many times, it is not a choice between true and false that stands before us (Rambam) but a choice between a positive and a less positive option—between what is essential versus what is nonessential. One could say that for Rashi the emphasis is less on an intellectual decision (Rambam) and more on embracing *the right set of values.* The more one knows what is of value, the easier it will be to prefer one good option over the other.

I find it interesting that the Sages are not seen in our mishna as the ones effecting this value preference. Pay attention, the students are seated in front of the Sages, but they, nevertheless, in three out of the four cases, are not influenced by the rabbis to prefer the essential over the nonessential. Perhaps this hints at our roles as parents in this process. It's important to enroll our children in Jewish schools and to "seat them" in front of wise sages and educators, but if we don't model for them at home what is important and valuable in life, they will not know how to see the forest for the trees. We must help them know what to take and what to discard so that later on, as they are no longer seated but rather moving about in life, they will have the knowledge along with the moral compass to make the correct decisions.

5:20

Just Showing Up Makes
All the Difference

כָּל אַהֲבָה שֶׁהִיא תְּלוּיָה בְדָבָר, בָּטֵל דָּבָר, בָּטְלָה אַהֲבָה. וְשֶׁאֵינָהּ תְּלוּיָה
בְדָבָר, אֵינָהּ בְּטֵלָה לְעוֹלָם. אֵיזוֹ הִיא אַהֲבָה הַתְּלוּיָה בְדָבָר? זוֹ אַהֲבַת
אַמְנוֹן וְתָמָר. וְשֶׁאֵינָהּ תְּלוּיָה בְדָבָר? זוֹ אַהֲבַת דָּוִד וִיהוֹנָתָן.

All love that depends on something, when the thing ceases, the love ceases; and all love that does not depend on anything, will never cease. What is an example of love that depended on something? Such was the love of Amnon for Tamar. And what is an example of love that did not depend on anything? Such was the love of David and Yonatan.

This is a wonderful mishna whose simple reading offers a powerfully true message: love others for the right reasons. When our love is contingent on "a something," an ulterior motive, when this "something" no longer exists, the love fades along with it. David and Yonatan are exemplars of this true love that never ceased, despite all the obstacles (such as Yonatan's father!) that could have kept them apart.

An interesting explanation to the mishna focuses on the word דבר, translated above as "a something." The word דבר also means "word." A possible reading, based on this understanding, teaches that our love can and should be expressed in avenues that stretch far beyond words. I experienced this firsthand while working as a chaplain one summer. My adviser taught me not to worry too much about what to say and to shift to an orientation of being present for the other. This was sage advice. In fact, most of the love and care I offered my patients came through nonverbal communication.

One of my rabbis once said that the most effective way to show care for another in their time of need is to just "show up." Having one's expressions of love be contingent upon verbal communication limits the ways we can be there for others: "When the דבר (word) ceases, the love ceases." Sometimes a hug is all someone needs. Sometimes just sitting in silence for as long as is required is the most helpful way to show that someone cares. It's oftentimes not about the words but about being there. There are times when listening intently can be cathartic.

Many times we get caught up in "What is the right thing to say?" or "How can I most eloquently express what needs to be heard?" This is a mistake. Of course, it's important to offer words that are helpful and come from a place of love, but in the end, love truly knows no bounds. For love to "not cease," we need to be open to expressing that love through many mediums—many of which are "not dependent on a דבר (word)."

The Limits of Jewish Pluralism

כָּל מַחֲלֹקֶת שֶׁהִיא לְשֵׁם שָׁמַיִם, סוֹפָהּ לְהִתְקַיֵּם. וְשֶׁאֵינָהּ לְשֵׁם שָׁמַיִם,
אֵין סוֹפָהּ לְהִתְקַיֵּם. אֵיזוֹ הִיא מַחֲלֹקֶת שֶׁהִיא לְשֵׁם שָׁמַיִם? זוֹ מַחֲלֹקֶת
הִלֵּל וְשַׁמַּאי. וְשֶׁאֵינָהּ לְשֵׁם שָׁמַיִם? זוֹ מַחֲלֹקֶת קֹרַח וְכָל עֲדָתוֹ.

Every dispute that is for the sake of heaven, will in the end endure. And one that is not for the sake of heaven, will not endure. Which is the controversy that is for the sake of heaven? Such was the controversy of Hillel and Shammai. And which is the controversy that is not for the sake of heaven? Such was the controversy of Korach and all his congregation.

When I was in rabbinical school, I attended a Shabbaton for rabbis-in-training. Over the weekend, a rabbinical student shared about how the Talmud already spoke in pluralistic terms much before our modern, pluralistic culture stepped onto the scene. In support of this argument, a well-known Talmudic adage was put forward: "These and those are the words of the living God" (*Talmud Bavli*, Eruvin 13b). This text highlights how both Hillel and Shammai's views are correct and valid, even though they almost always stand in stark contradiction to one another.

I remember at the time chatting about this with a colleague and arguing that this Talmudic "pluralism" has its limits. I shared how this is hinted at in the final words of the aforementioned adage, "words of the living God." The views must be part of God's living word. This excludes views, unlike those of Hillel and Shammai, that are antithetical to God's word. Another way to explain this is to say there is a playing field which has space for many views. All views which align with the words of the living God are on the field. Others which do not fit these criteria are left off. This is not true pluralism because the latter is much less selective.

Another famous adage quantifies how many "players" are allowed to play. It's admittedly a high number, but it isn't pluralism in its purest sense. The midrash speaks of "seventy faces of the Torah" (*Bamidbar Rabbah* 13:16): seventy acceptable approaches to varied topics. Another text speaks about forty-eight valid ways to purify an object (*Talmud Bavli*, Eruvin 13b).

Our mishna continues this theme by speaking of what made Hillel and Shammai's debate one that lasted until our day (סופה להתקיים). Their debate was for the sake of heaven, *shamayim* (לשם שמיים). This may be understood as a debate which expands upon the Torah, given from *shamayim*, heaven.

Our mishna brings an example of an approach cast to the sidelines: that of Korach and his congregation. They openly contradicted tenets of Jewish faith by denying God's appointed leaders. And their ideas did not make it into the corpus of accepted opinions (אין סופה להתקיים). There is a limit to the Talmud's "pluralism." We must therefore be selective and careful to ensure we are always playing on the right field.

5:22

Elevate Others and You Will Be Elevated

כָּל הַמְזַכֶּה אֶת הָרַבִּים, אֵין חֵטְא בָּא עַל יָדוֹ. וְכָל הַמַּחֲטִיא אֶת הָרַבִּים, אֵין מַסְפִּיקִין בְּיָדוֹ
לַעֲשׂוֹת תְּשׁוּבָה. מֹשֶׁה זָכָה וְזִכָּה אֶת הָרַבִּים, זְכוּת הָרַבִּים תָּלוּי בּוֹ, שֶׁנֶּאֱמַר (דברים לג)
צִדְקַת ה' עָשָׂה וּמִשְׁפָּטָיו עִם יִשְׂרָאֵל. יָרָבְעָם חָטָא וְהֶחֱטִיא אֶת הָרַבִּים, חֵטְא הָרַבִּים תָּלוּי בּוֹ,
שֶׁנֶּאֱמַר (מלכים א טו): עַל חַטֹּאות יָרָבְעָם (בֶּן נְבָט) אֲשֶׁר חָטָא וַאֲשֶׁר הֶחֱטִיא אֶת יִשְׂרָאֵל.

Whoever causes the multitudes to be righteous, sin will not occur on their account. And whoever causes the multitudes to sin, they are not given the ability to repent. Moshe was righteous and caused the multitudes to be righteous, therefore the righteousness of the multitudes is hung on him, as it is said, "He executed the Lord's righteousness and His decisions with Israel" (Deut. 33:21). Yerovam sinned and caused the multitudes to sin, therefore the sin of the multitudes is hung on him, as it is said, "For the sins of Yerovam which he sinned, and which he caused Israel to sin thereby" (I Kings 15:30).

Living one's life in service of others brings with it many blessings— first and foremost for the community but also for oneself. One such benefit is that it protects one from sin: "Sin will not occur on his account."

What is the mechanism behind this? Teaching and instructing others in a manner that "causes them to be righteous" involves an immense amount of work, preparation, and involvement. For this purpose, one's Torah must be on a high level so that it will be able to affect many people

231

("multitudes"), and it will transform them into "righteous" individuals. In other words, for one to be on one's A-game, one needs to be on a high level oneself. This in turn protects one from sin.

This message of the mishna is hinted at in the fact that at the beginning, the text speaks solely about one's effect on others: "causing others to be righteous." Then, when it brings a real-life example, it says of Moshe that he was foremost "זכה," righteous, and then "וזכה את הרבים," he was able to cause the multitude to be righteous. This involvement of Moshe's with the community elevated him as well!

I see this all the time in my own modest, rabbinic position. Preparing classes and being involved in *chesed* (lovingkindness) opportunities throughout the day not only keeps me busy and positive; it also locks me in on doing the right thing in my own life. When I teach others what to stay away from, I, myself, baruch Hashem, find it harder for "sin to occur on my account." Want to be protected from sin? Be involved in protecting others from sin!

5:23

Properly Channeling Our Unique Gifts

כָּל מִי שֶׁיֵּשׁ בְּיָדוֹ שְׁלֹשָׁה דְבָרִים הַלָּלוּ, מִתַּלְמִידָיו שֶׁל אַבְרָהָם אָבִינוּ. וּשְׁלֹשָׁה דְבָרִים אֲחֵרִים, מִתַּלְמִידָיו שֶׁל בִּלְעָם הָרָשָׁע. עַיִן טוֹבָה, וְרוּחַ נְמוּכָה, וְנֶפֶשׁ שְׁפָלָה, מִתַּלְמִידָיו שֶׁל אַבְרָהָם אָבִינוּ. עַיִן רָעָה, וְרוּחַ גְּבוֹהָה, וְנֶפֶשׁ רְחָבָה, מִתַּלְמִידָיו שֶׁל בִּלְעָם הָרָשָׁע. מַה בֵּין תַּלְמִידָיו שֶׁל אַבְרָהָם אָבִינוּ לְתַלְמִידָיו שֶׁל בִּלְעָם הָרָשָׁע? תַּלְמִידָיו שֶׁל אַבְרָהָם אָבִינוּ, אוֹכְלִין בָּעוֹלָם הַזֶּה וְנוֹחֲלִין בָּעוֹלָם הַבָּא, שֶׁנֶּאֱמַר (משלי ח): לְהַנְחִיל אֹהֲבַי יֵשׁ, וְאֹצְרֹתֵיהֶם אֲמַלֵּא. אֲבָל תַּלְמִידָיו שֶׁל בִּלְעָם הָרָשָׁע יוֹרְשִׁין גֵּיהִנֹּם וְיוֹרְדִין לִבְאֵר שַׁחַת, שֶׁנֶּאֱמַר (תהלים נה): וְאַתָּה אֱלֹהִים תּוֹרִידֵם לִבְאֵר שַׁחַת, אַנְשֵׁי דָמִים וּמִרְמָה לֹא יֶחֱצוּ יְמֵיהֶם, וַאֲנִי אֶבְטַח בָּךְ.

Whoever possesses these three things is of the disciples of Avraham, our father; and [whoever possesses] three other things is of the disciples of Bilaam, the wicked. A good eye, a humble spirit, and a moderate appetite is of the disciples of Avraham, our father. An evil eye, a haughty spirit, and a limitless appetite is of the disciples of Bilaam, the wicked.

What is the difference between the disciples of Avraham, our father, and the disciples of Bilaam, the wicked? The disciples of Avraham, our father, enjoy this world, and inherit the world to come, as it is said: "I will endow those who love me with substance, I will fill their treasuries" (Prov. 8:21). But the disciples of Bilaam, the wicked, inherit Gehinnom, and descend into the nethermost pit, as it is said: "For you, O God, will bring them down to the nethermost pit those murderous and treacherous men; they shall not live out half their days; but I trust in You" (Ps. 55:24).

One of my rabbis, Rabbi Uri Sherki, shared an interesting observation on the following well-known Talmudic statement: "There are three distinguishing marks of the Jewish nation: they are merciful, they are shamefaced, and they perform acts of kindness" (*Talmud Bavli*, Yevamot 79a). The Talmud explains that this was a litmus test the Gibeonite nation did not pass, leading King David to decree that they should not be allowed into the nation of Israel. Rabbi Sherki shared that these wonderful and defining traits are the same ones that at times have gotten us in trouble over the years. There were times that Jews adopted an overly passive, humble, and kindhearted orientation—to the point that we were taken advantage of and abused to no end. He shared that our defining traits need to be tempered by their counterparts.

In a similar fashion, our mishna teaches that the students of Avraham are demarcated by three traits: "A good eye, a humble spirit, and a moderate appetite." These praiseworthy characteristics can pose a similar danger. If one is overly optimistic, overly humble, and overly moderate in their appetite, they may lose their footing in this world and be taken advantage of.

Our mishna may be hinting at the proper usage of these traits by means of the positive reward enjoyed by Avraham's students in this world. When we compare the fate of Avraham's students to that of Bilaam's, we find an incongruency. Bilaam's students suffer two levels of punishment, both in the next world: they "inherit Gehinnom and descend into the nethermost pit." The students of Avraham, on the other hand, "enjoy this world and inherit the world to come." They benefit from this world as well. They literally eat, אוכלין, in this world.

This may be hinting at Avraham's students' healthy application of the three traits mentioned in the mishna. They embody these three important traits yet remain grounded in this world throughout. This protects them from any negative misapplications of these lofty traits. We as a nation are blessed with incredible gifts. When we utilize them the right way, we can attain the highest of spiritual levels: "I will endow those who love me with substance, I will fill their treasuries."

Serving Hashem through Intuition and Common Sense

יְהוּדָה בֶן תֵּימָא אוֹמֵר: הֱוֵי עַז כַּנָּמֵר, וְקַל כַּנֶּשֶׁר, וְרָץ כַּצְּבִי, וְגִבּוֹר כָּאֲרִי, לַעֲשׂוֹת רְצוֹן אָבִיךָ שֶׁבַּשָּׁמָיִם. הוּא הָיָה אוֹמֵר: עַז פָּנִים לְגֵיהִנֹּם וּבֹשֶׁת פָּנִים לְגַן עֵדֶן. יְהִי רָצוֹן מִלְּפָנֶיךָ ה' אֱלֹהֵינוּ שֶׁתִּבָּנֶה עִירְךָ בִּמְהֵרָה בְיָמֵינוּ וְתֵן חֶלְקֵנוּ בְּתוֹרָתֶךָ.

Yehuda ben Tema said: Be strong as a leopard, light as an eagle, swift as a gazelle, and brave as a lion, to do the will of your Father in heaven. He used to say: The shameless go to Gehinnom and those with a sense of shame go to the Garden of Eden. May it be the will, Hashem our God, that your city be rebuilt speedily in our days and set our portion in the studying of your Torah.

A rabbi of mine encouraged us to use common sense when it comes to the application of Jewish law. In this respect, he spoke of a "fifth section" of the Shulchan Aruch. We spoke about this above (see commentary to *Ethics of the Fathers* 1:16). Technically, the code of Jewish law, the Shulchan Aruch, consists of four sections. The "fifth section" is the place we must make for common sense, something that can't be put down in words.

The *Mei Hashiloach* takes this to the next level by discussing serving Hashem based on intuition. He calls this *binat halev*, "wisdom of the heart." According to the *Mei Hashiloach*, the more we are connected to Hashem, the better we are able to ascertain what Hashem wants from us in any given situation. This is needed because not every life situation is addressed in the four volumes of the Shulchan Aruch: "Even if one is careful to perform all of the Shulchan Aruch it is still doubtful whether one will be in congruence with the deeper will of God, because God's will is very deep, who can find it?" (*Mei Hashiloach*, 2, pp. 87–88, s.v. im). Sometimes the strict law cannot dictate precisely how to act. Hashem's will is "very deep" and can't be assessed strictly on the basis of the set law. In these moments, one must use intuition to decipher the proper mode of action.

This idea is at the heart of our mishna. Hashem's will for us is always changing—based on ever-changing realities. Sometimes Hashem's will mandates being light; at others, strong. At other moments, we must be brave, and other times Hashem's will mandates running away swiftly, like a gazelle, from a perceived threat. As the *Mei Hashiloach* puts it: the will of Hashem is very deep! We must be flexible and adapt—using common sense and, at times, intuition—in order to fulfill "the will of our Father in heaven."

5:25

The Wonderful Gifts of Old Age

הוּא הָיָה אוֹמֵר: בֶּן חָמֵשׁ שָׁנִים לַמִּקְרָא, בֶּן עֶשֶׂר לַמִּשְׁנָה, בֶּן שְׁלֹשׁ עֶשְׂרֵה לַמִּצְוֹת,
בֶּן חֲמֵשׁ עֶשְׂרֵה לַתַּלְמוּד, בֶּן שְׁמֹנֶה עֶשְׂרֵה לַחֻפָּה, בֶּן עֶשְׂרִים לִרְדּוֹף, בֶּן שְׁלֹשִׁים
לַכֹּחַ, בֶּן אַרְבָּעִים לַבִּינָה, בֶּן חֲמִשִּׁים לָעֵצָה, בֶּן שִׁשִּׁים לַזִּקְנָה, בֶּן שִׁבְעִים לַשֵּׂיבָה, בֶּן
שְׁמֹנִים לַגְּבוּרָה, בֶּן תִּשְׁעִים לָשׁוּחַ, בֶּן מֵאָה כְּאִלּוּ מֵת וְעָבַר וּבָטֵל מִן הָעוֹלָם.

He used to say: At five years of age, the study of scripture; at ten, the study of mishna; at thirteen, the commandments; at fifteen, the study of Talmud; at eighteen, the bridal canopy; at twenty, for pursuit; at thirty, the peak of strength; at forty, wisdom; at fifty, able to give counsel; at sixty, old age; at seventy, ripe old age; at eighty, the age of strength; at ninety, a bent body; at one hundred, as good as dead and gone completely out of the world.

Whenever I teach this mishna to my congregants, the elder members chuckle without fail. At face value, the descriptions of the latter epochs are far from flattering: "old age," "ripe old age," "bent body," and "completely out of the world." Notwithstanding, I view this mishna as incredibly empowering for those in their "later years." This is based on an alternative, spiritualized explanation for each of these latter stages (based on Artscroll's *The Pirkei Avos Treasury: Ethics of the Fathers*).

Granted, old age often brings with it a diminution of physical capabilities. However, this also can result in enhanced spiritual awareness and opportunity for spiritual growth. The neutralization of the body and its machinations in old age can make space for a true blossoming of the soul. This is what our mishna is relaying at each stage.

Sixty—old age, זקנה. This Hebrew word is also an acronym for זה (חכמה) קנה, meaning: "This one acquired (knowledge)" (see *Talmud Bavli*, Kiddushin 32b). At sixty, one is wiser due to life experience. One can amass knowledge and actively arrive at new comprehensions based on this acquired knowledge.

Seventy—ripe old age, שֵׂיבָה. The Hebrew word שֵׂיבָה hints at the ability to do teshuva (תשובה), repentance (from the root ש-ו-ב which means "return"). When the body is less of an obstacle, one's soul can be more easily summoned to improve one's character and religious life.

Eighty—strength, גבורה. As the body becomes weaker, the soul becomes stronger.

Ninety—a bent body, לשוח. This word not only means "bent" but also "to pray" or "discuss." One's body may be weak, but the power of prayer is always available. In fact, prayers of an elder can be on a higher level than those who are younger as they are one step (or maybe many steps) closer to the "next world."

One hundred—as good as dead and gone completely out of this world, כאילו מת ועבר ובטל מן העולם. No, this isn't another way of saying "incredible" as in "you are out of this world!" However, this does hint at the elevated spiritual state of those who have achieved old age. Their souls are ever so close to the next world, "as good as dead," and bound up tightly with the divine, "out of this world." When my Sabba (grandfather), of blessed memory, was in his final days—he passed at age ninety-five—I felt so much divinity in that hospital room. This final statement reminds me of this elevated spiritual state.

Our mishna, when read this way, encourages those at a later stage in life to invest in their spirituality. It's not only because "it's never too late" to grow. Old age offers unique opportunities that are not always available at an earlier stage in life. In short, whether we are young or old, there is always hope, promise, and an upward path for self-actualization waiting for us if we choose to follow it.

If You Look Hard, You Can Find It in Judaism

בֶּן בַּג בַּג אוֹמֵר: הֲפֹךְ בָּהּ וַהֲפֹךְ בָּהּ, דְּכֹלָּא בָהּ. וּבָהּ תֶּחֱזֵי, וְסִיב וּבְלֵה בָּהּ, וּמִנַּהּ
לֹא תָזוּעַ, שֶׁאֵין לְךָ מִדָּה טוֹבָה הֵימֶנָּה. בֶּן הֵא הֵא אוֹמֵר: לְפוּם צַעֲרָא אַגְרָא.

Ben Bag Bag said: Turn it over, and again turn it over, for all is therein. And look into it and become gray and old therein. And do not move away from it, for you have no better portion than it. Ben Hei Hei said: According to the labor is the reward.

I like to share in my Jewish philosophy classes that one can look to the Jewish realm to find what one is interested in. Are you spiritual? We have Kabbalah. Into psychology? There is a wealth of texts, including chassidic works, that deal with psychological themes. A rationalist? Try the medieval thinkers, especially Rambam. Looking for a personal connection to Hashem? Try Rebbe Nachman of Breslov. Meditation? We have that too! And the list of options goes on.

In my classes I share that if one idea or philosophy doesn't resonate, be patient. Listen to other approaches, and there is a good chance one will end up clicking—and sometimes it will take a conglomerate of texts or modes of thinking to finally click. And when it does, it will enable you to connect more deeply to Torah. For me, this happened with Rabbi Avraham Yitzchak HaKohen Kook and Rabbi Mordechai Yosef Leiner, best known for his work *Mei Hashiloach*. When I found their Torah, it opened worlds for me and greatly enhanced my connection to Yiddishkeit.

This is all put forth in our mishna.

"Turn it over, and again turn it over, for all is therein." This may be teaching that one can find many directions and approaches in the Torah. It can also mean that "all" you are looking for can be found in Torah—that your deepest passions and inclinations can find expression through the holy Torah.

"And look into it and become gray and old therein. And do not move away from it, for you have no better portion than it." The more you "look into it," the more you will be drawn in because you will find it gives expression to your inner voice. When that happens, you will learn Torah more consistently ("become gray and old") and will unite with the Torah on a deeper level ("do not move away from it"). I still remember the time I "discovered" Rabbi Kook's writings. It felt like I was being restored. He was sharing so much of what I was feeling. When you find what fits, there is "no better portion."

Ben Hei Hei then reminds us that when it comes to this, "according to the labor is the reward." Once you find what you connect to, you must put in the work to grow and progress. The more effort you put in, the greater will be your fulfillment. Hashem has blessed us with so many Torah approaches so that we will turn them over until we find those that were made for us. When we do so, "there is no better portion!"

Projecting Torah onto all Areas of Life

שָׁנוּ חֲכָמִים בִּלְשׁוֹן הַמִּשְׁנָה. בָּרוּךְ שֶׁבָּחַר בָּהֶם וּבְמִשְׁנָתָם. רַבִּי מֵאִיר אוֹמֵר: כָּל הָעוֹסֵק בַּתּוֹרָה לִשְׁמָהּ, זוֹכֶה לִדְבָרִים הַרְבֵּה. וְלֹא עוֹד אֶלָּא שֶׁכָּל הָעוֹלָם כֻּלּוֹ כְּדַי הוּא לוֹ. נִקְרָא רֵעַ, אָהוּב, אוֹהֵב אֶת הַמָּקוֹם, אוֹהֵב אֶת הַבְּרִיּוֹת, מְשַׂמֵּחַ אֶת הַמָּקוֹם, מְשַׂמֵּחַ אֶת הַבְּרִיּוֹת. וּמַלְבַּשְׁתּוֹ עֲנָוָה וְיִרְאָה, וּמַכְשַׁרְתּוֹ לִהְיוֹת צַדִּיק וְחָסִיד וְיָשָׁר וְנֶאֱמָן, וּמְרַחַקְתּוֹ מִן הַחֵטְא, וּמְקָרַבְתּוֹ לִידֵי זְכוּת, וְנֶהֱנִין מִמֶּנּוּ עֵצָה וְתוּשִׁיָּה בִּינָה וּגְבוּרָה, שֶׁנֶּאֱמַר (משלי ח): לִי עֵצָה וְתוּשִׁיָּה אֲנִי בִינָה לִי גְבוּרָה. וְנוֹתֶנֶת לוֹ מַלְכוּת וּמֶמְשָׁלָה וְחִקּוּר דִּין, וּמְגַלִּין לוֹ רָזֵי תוֹרָה, וְנַעֲשֶׂה כְּמַעְיָן הַמִּתְגַּבֵּר וּכְנָהָר שֶׁאֵינוֹ פוֹסֵק, וֶהֱוֵי צָנוּעַ וְאֶרֶךְ רוּחַ, וּמוֹחֵל עַל עֶלְבּוֹנוֹ, וּמְגַדַּלְתּוֹ וּמְרוֹמַמְתּוֹ עַל כָּל הַמַּעֲשִׂים.

The Sages taught in the language of the mishna. Blessed be He who chose them and their teaching. Rabbi Meir said: Whoever occupies themselves with the Torah for its own sake, merits many things; not only that but they are worth the whole world. They are called beloved friend, one that loves God, one that loves humankind, one that gladdens God, one that gladdens humankind. And the Torah clothes them in humility and reverence, and equips them to be righteous, pious, upright and trustworthy. It keeps them far from sin and brings them near to merit. And people benefit from their counsel, sound knowledge, understanding and strength, as it is said, "Counsel is mine and sound wisdom; I am understanding, strength is mine" (Prov. 8:14). And it bestows upon them royalty, dominion, and acuteness in judgment. To them are revealed the secrets of the Torah, and they are made as an ever-flowing spring, and like a stream that never ceases. And they become modest, long-suffering, and forgiving of insult. And it magnifies them and exalts them over everything.

The whole upcoming chapter, chapter six, is dedicated to Torah learning and its positive effects on the individual. Its teachings are no longer called mishnas. They are *beraitas*, which means "on the outside," because they are Tannaitic teachings that were not included by Rebbe in the official mishna. Nevertheless, our beraita tells us the Sages taught these teachings "in the language of the mishna."

Our chapter opens by listing the benefits of learning Torah for the sake of heaven. One of the accolades is that "to them are revealed the secrets of the Torah, and they are made as an ever-flowing spring, and like a stream that never ceases." There is a Talmudic saying that was often quoted in my yeshiva: "How foolish are the rest of the people who stand before a Torah scroll that passes before them, and yet they do not stand before a great Torah scholar" (*Talmud Bavli*, Makkot 22b). This was meant to impress on us to not only stand in reverence when the Torah is removed from the Ark but also when a *talmid chacham* (Torah scholar) enters the room or even walks by. It's a mistake to think there is more holiness in the Torah scroll than in a Torah scholar! Our beraita reminds us of this when it teaches how *talmidei chachamim* can become walking Torahs themselves from which new and exciting divrei Torah flow—like "springs" and "streams."

When I was in yeshiva, I took this teaching very seriously. I followed my rabbis around because I wanted to see and learn firsthand how to live life from "living Torahs." I recall one time being in the back of a car on the way to a wedding with two of my rebbes. I had hopes of gleaning important lessons during that ride, so you can imagine how let down I was when they began speaking about Israeli politics. But soon enough, I realized the conversation was about something much deeper.

At the time, a rabbi from an affiliated yeshiva had just become a member of the Israeli parliament, and my rabbis were debating whether it was a smart move for an esteemed rabbi to be involved in politics in the first place. One argued that this wasn't a good use of his time. It was a shame that now he wouldn't be able to learn and teach like he used to. The other shared that this was the ideal way to elevate the political sphere and that through serving in the parliament, he was fulfilling our purpose as a "holy nation" (גוי קדוש) in the world (a nation with an army, political presence, etc., that is also holy).

My initial discomfort quickly abated as I realized I was in the middle of a debate on lofty topics we talk about in the beit midrash: the role of the material and political in the life of a developing Jewish nation in the land of Israel. What stood out for me was that the rabbis took their Torah with them outside of the yeshiva, into the car. They were applying it to current events as well. I loved this. Something mundane was transformed into a deep Torah debate!

The idea of Torah being compared to water is not new in our tradition. We are taught: "There is no water aside from Torah" (ibid., Bava Kamma 82a). I think our beraita may hint at an aspect of this connection by comparing it to streams and springs. These sources project water outward, spreading it over other areas. This is the beauty of one who learns Torah for the sake of heaven. When there is a real connection to Torah, one not only learns Torah, one also projects it onto all areas of one's life—proving that "whoever occupies himself with the Torah for its own sake, merits many things."

6:2

Making Torah Relevant
for Our Generation

אָמַר רַבִּי יְהוֹשֻׁעַ בֶּן לֵוִי: בְּכָל יוֹם וָיוֹם בַּת קוֹל יוֹצֵאת מֵהַר חוֹרֵב וּמַכְרֶזֶת וְאוֹמֶרֶת, אוֹי
לָהֶם לַבְּרִיּוֹת מֵעֶלְבּוֹנָהּ שֶׁל תּוֹרָה. שֶׁכָּל מִי שֶׁאֵינוֹ עוֹסֵק בַּתּוֹרָה נִקְרָא נָזוּף, שֶׁנֶּאֱמַר
(משלי יא): נֶזֶם זָהָב בְּאַף חֲזִיר אִשָּׁה יָפָה וְסָרַת טָעַם. וְאוֹמֵר (שמות לב): וְהַלֻּחֹת
מַעֲשֵׂה אֱלֹהִים הֵמָּה וְהַמִּכְתָּב מִכְתַּב אֱלֹהִים הוּא חָרוּת עַל הַלֻּחֹת. אַל תִּקְרָא חָרוּת אֶלָּא
חֵרוּת, שֶׁאֵין לְךָ בֶּן חוֹרִין אֶלָּא מִי שֶׁעוֹסֵק בְּתַלְמוּד תּוֹרָה. וְכָל מִי שֶׁעוֹסֵק בְּתַלְמוּד
תּוֹרָה הֲרֵי זֶה מִתְעַלֶּה, שֶׁנֶּאֱמַר (במדבר כא): וּמִמַּתָּנָה נַחֲלִיאֵל וּמִנַּחֲלִיאֵל בָּמוֹת.

Rabbi Yehoshua ben Levi said: Every day a *bat kol* (a heavenly voice) goes forth from Mount Horeb and makes proclamation and says: "Woe unto humankind for their contempt toward the Torah," for whoever does not occupy themselves with the study of Torah is called *nazuf* (the rebuked). As it is said, "Like a gold ring in the snout of a pig is a beautiful woman bereft of sense" (Prov. 11:22). And it says, "And the tablets were the work of God, and the writing was the writing of God, graven upon the tablets" (Exod. 32:16). Read not *harut* ['graven'] but *herut* ['freedom']. For there is no free person but one who occupies themselves with the study of the Torah. And whoever regularly occupies themselves with the study of the Torah is surely exalted, as it is said, "And from Mattanah to Nachaliel; and Nachaliel to Bamot" (Num. 21:19).

I once heard a rabbi share a funny story that went something like this:

The other day, I shared with my students the Talmudic teaching that in the future, in the world to come, our main preoccupation will be learning Talmud all day long. They didn't seem nearly as excited as I was about this prospect. When I asked them why they seemed so indifferent to the idea, they responded: "Rebbe, we enjoyed the story, but please tell us one thing: are you describing heaven or hell?"

Unfortunately, this is how many young women and men experience Torah learning—with a certain disconnect or even as a heavy burden. Our beraita teaches us the opposite! Great freedom and joy can be attained through Torah learning: "For there is no free person but one that occupies themselves with the study of the Torah." Our beraita derives this from a wordplay. חרות means "engraved." We read it instead as "חירות," which means "freedom."

However, there may be another layer here: that the actual engraving itself leads to freedom! What do we know about how the words were engraved on the tablets? The Torah says, "They were inscribed on the one side and on the other" (Exod. 32:15). This means that the engraving began on one side and pierced through to the other.

There are some deep lessons when it comes to this. One is that our Torah should be one that makes space for seeing things from multiple perspectives, allowing both sides to be voiced and understood "on one side and on the other." Our teaching should make space for dialogue and sharing of multiple views. Another is that the engraving reached the other side of the tablets. This shows that the Torah we teach should be deep, not surface layer. Lastly, the other side, when read as is, comes out to read something else entirely. For instance, the words "שמור" would read "רומש". And apparently, it still was understood! Or perhaps it was intended to mean something completely different. This is the art of Jewish hermeneutics—being open to reinterpretation and rereading of texts.

When we offer our students Torah that encourages dialogue, when we present deeper understandings which extend far beyond the simple reading of the text, and when we make space for them to interpret the Torah (of course, within the confines of the tradition—they must be a part of the tablets!)—all of this brings the Torah to life. This is the secret to turning Talmud learning and other Torah study into a "heavenly" pursuit!

Recognizing Good Within the Good

הַלּוֹמֵד מֵחֲבֵרוֹ פֶּרֶק אֶחָד אוֹ הֲלָכָה אַחַת אוֹ פָסוּק אֶחָד אוֹ דִּבּוּר אֶחָד אוֹ אֲפִלּוּ אוֹת אַחַת,
צָרִיךְ לִנְהוֹג בּוֹ כָּבוֹד, שֶׁכֵּן מָצִינוּ בְּדָוִד מֶלֶךְ יִשְׂרָאֵל, שֶׁלֹּא לָמַד מֵאֲחִיתֹפֶל אֶלָּא שְׁנֵי דְבָרִים
בִּלְבָד, קְרָאוֹ רַבּוֹ אַלּוּפוֹ וּמְיֻדָּעוֹ, שֶׁנֶּאֱמַר (תהלים נה): וְאַתָּה אֱנוֹשׁ כְּעֶרְכִּי אַלּוּפִי וּמְיֻדָּעִי.
וַהֲלֹא דְבָרִים קַל וָחֹמֶר. וּמַה דָּוִד מֶלֶךְ יִשְׂרָאֵל, שֶׁלֹּא לָמַד מֵאֲחִיתֹפֶל אֶלָּא שְׁנֵי דְבָרִים
בִּלְבָד קְרָאוֹ רַבּוֹ, אַלּוּפוֹ, וּמְיֻדָּעוֹ, הַלּוֹמֵד מֵחֲבֵרוֹ פֶּרֶק אֶחָד אוֹ הֲלָכָה אַחַת אוֹ פָסוּק אֶחָד
אוֹ דִּבּוּר אֶחָד אוֹ אֲפִלּוּ אוֹת אַחַת, עַל אַחַת כַּמָּה וְכַמָּה שֶׁצָּרִיךְ לִנְהוֹג בּוֹ כָּבוֹד. וְאֵין כָּבוֹד
אֶלָּא תוֹרָה, שֶׁנֶּאֱמַר (משלי ג): כָּבוֹד חֲכָמִים יִנְחָלוּ, (משלי כח) וּתְמִימִים יִנְחֲלוּ טוֹב,
וְאֵין טוֹב אֶלָּא תוֹרָה, שֶׁנֶּאֱמַר (משלי ד): כִּי לֶקַח טוֹב נָתַתִּי לָכֶם תּוֹרָתִי אַל תַּעֲזֹבוּ.

One who learns from their friend one chapter, or one halacha, or one verse, or one word, or even one letter, is obligated to treat them with honor; for so we find with David, King of Israel, who learned from Achitophel no more than two things, yet called him his master, his guide, and his beloved friend, as it is said, "But it was you, a man mine equal, my guide and my beloved friend" (Ps. 55:14). Is this not [an instance of the argument] "from the less to the greater" (*kal vachomer*)? If David, King of Israel, who learned from Achitophel no more than two things, nevertheless called him his master, his guide, and his beloved friend; then in the case of one who learns from their fellow one chapter, or one halacha, or one verse, or one word, or even one letter, all the more so are they under obligation to treat them with honor. And "honor'" means nothing but Torah, as it is said, "It is honor that sages inherit" (Prov. 3:35). "And the perfect shall inherit good" (Prov. 28:10). And "good" means nothing but Torah, as it is said, "For I give you good instruction; do not forsake my Torah" (Prov. 4:2).

Hakarat hatov, gratitude (lit., recognition of the good), is the foundation of all Yiddishkeit, and it's the foundation of our beraita as well. I love how our teaching drives home this message by slowly zoning in on each good, from the general to the specific: from one chapter, to one halacha, to one verse, to one word, and then "even one letter." This reminds us of a message mentioned earlier in our commentary: that within each good there is another concealed good. One chapter encompasses one halacha, that has one verse, and so on. This is true in all areas of life. One good from which we benefit really contains other blessings as well.

There is a midrash that picks up on this theme by asking why Moshe did not strike the Nile as he brought the plague of blood and frogs onto Egypt (*Shemot Rabbah* 9:10, 10:7). It answers that the Nile was involved in saving Moshe's life when he was a baby: he was placed in a basket in the Nile and later saved. Therefore, as an act of gratitude, he did not want to bring the plagues onto the water. Pay attention to the sensitivity: water is an inanimate object!

There were many other factors involved as well: his mother had the instinct to hide him, his sister protected him, Pharaoh's daughter brought him in, others were involved in raising him, and Hashem, of course, was there the whole time to ensure the survival of our cherished leader. But Moshe did not forget the water! He acknowledged all factors that contributed to his preservation and survival. Let's follow King David and Moshe's lead and not forget to recognize good things that happen within other good experiences in our lives!

6:4

Finding Spirituality in the Modern World

כַּךְ הִיא דַּרְכָּהּ שֶׁל תּוֹרָה: פַּת בְּמֶלַח תֹּאכַל, וּמַיִם בִּמְשׂוּרָה תִשְׁתֶּה, וְעַל
הָאָרֶץ תִּישַׁן, וְחַיֵּי צַעַר תִּחְיֶה, וּבַתּוֹרָה אַתָּה עָמֵל. אִם אַתָּה עֹשֶׂה כֵן, (תהלים
קכח) אַשְׁרֶיךָ וְטוֹב לָךְ. אַשְׁרֶיךָ בָּעוֹלָם הַזֶּה וְטוֹב לָךְ לְעוֹלָם הַבָּא.

Such is the way [of a life] of Torah: You shall eat bread with salt, drink rationed water, sleep on the ground, live a life of privation, and labor in Torah. If you do this, "Happy shall you be, and it shall be good for you" (Ps. 128:2). "Happy shall you be" in this world, "and it shall be good for you" in the world to come.

Every religious denomination has its go-to sources and "mantras." For instance, when I was in Israel attending National Religious seminaries, our rabbis relayed their deep belief that we were in the midst of the Redemption after a long exile through key sayings from the Talmud. One such source highlighted all the signs listed in the Talmud that point to our "flowering of redemption" (*Talmud Bavli*, Sanhedrin 98a). They argued that these signs were indeed coming true in our days, and I remember how these teachings injected excitement into the students.

In this respect, the Modern Orthodox community is no different. Shmuel's reason for the nazarite's obligatory sacrifice upon terminating his abstention from wine (ibid., Ta'anit 11a–11b) is often quoted in support of enjoying life and the pleasures it provides us. Shmuel states that despite the holy intentions accompanying the abstention from physical pleasures, the nazarite is still considered a sinner precisely *because* he

249

denied himself these very pleasures! From here it is deduced that someone who fasts is considered a "sinner" as well. This pleasure-positive
text is often coupled with another similar source text from the Jerusalem
Talmud (*Talmud Yerushalmi*, Kiddushin 4:12) which proclaims: "In the
future people will be judged on everything they saw and were allowed to
benefit from but abstained, nevertheless, from doing so."

With these teachings in mind, it may be a bit shocking to come across
a beraita like ours, which seems to relay the opposite message. Our beraita
talks about eating bread and salt, rationed water, sleeping on the ground,
and just overall privation. Many explain that our teaching is not a directive
to be embraced *ab initio*, in the first place. Instead, if one is faced with
such dire circumstances, one should learn Torah, nevertheless. This, of
course, is true and sadly has been the experience of many pious Jews over
the course of Jewish history. Notwithstanding, one can derive a lot from
this beraita when read as "unfiltered" as well. We are being reminded that
the world of the spirit is very rich and vast. We mustn't forget that our
happiness isn't limited to the pleasures of this world. When we tap into the
divine, "happy we will be"—also in this world!

Indeed, some of my most defining moments, and the most enjoyable ones that I have experienced in my life, involved temporarily sus-
pending my physical pleasures to make space for the spiritual. One such
memory stands out. It was late in the afternoon on Shabbat. At the time,
I was attending yeshiva in Jerusalem, and I was walking from one side of
town to the other. I hadn't eaten for hours and was physically worn from
the trek. I arrived at a serene tree-laden area on my way from Rechavia
to Bayit Vegan when suddenly I felt this deep spirituality bubble up from
inside me. I can't really explain it in words and have been seeking to
restore it for years. I can only describe it as a mystical experience. It was
filled with such beauty. It was heaven. I never wanted it to end! Many
conditions contributed to this moment but perhaps most predominantly
was the physical displacement, fatigue, and general deprivation I was
experiencing at that moment. Granted, these agendas, the material and
spiritual, do not have to conflict, and many times they work in unison;
however, the physical body and its drives can also weigh us down and
withhold us from soaring spiritually.

Our beraita when read this way is a tempering text, serving as an
important reminder for the modern Jew. Shmuel's view on fasting is
often highlighted in modern circles, but there is another view on fasting

in that very same source that goes overlooked! Rabbi Elazar teaches, based on the nazarite (!), that one who fasts is not only not considered a sinner but is deemed holy! In other words: we must always beware that our "modern" pursuits do not stand in the way or withhold us from all of the beauty and happiness that a spiritual life has to offer!

6:5

Making Peace with Our Current Lot

אַל תְּבַקֵּשׁ גְּדֻלָּה לְעַצְמְךָ, וְאַל תַּחְמֹד כָּבוֹד. יוֹתֵר מִלִּמּוּדְךָ עֲשֵׂה. וְאַל תִּתְאַוֶּה לְשֻׁלְחָנָם שֶׁל מְלָכִים, שֶׁשֻּׁלְחָנְךָ גָּדוֹל מִשֻּׁלְחָנָם, וְכִתְרְךָ גָּדוֹל מִכִּתְרָם. וְנֶאֱמָן הוּא בַּעַל מְלַאכְתְּךָ שֶׁיְּשַׁלֶּם לְךָ שְׂכַר פְּעֻלָּתֶךָ.

Do not seek greatness for yourself, and do not covet honor. Practice more than you learn. Do not yearn for the table of kings, for your table is greater than their table, and your crown is greater than their crown, and faithful is your employer to pay you the reward of your labor.

Our beraita lists three directives to aid us in our spiritual growth. It then brings three comments relating to each of these directives.

It opens saying we should not seek greatness. In relation to this, it later teaches that we shouldn't yearn for the table of kings, for "our table is greater than their table." It then commands us not to covet honor, afterward reminding us that our crown is greater than that of kings. It also teaches to "practice more than our learning." In relation to this, it reminds us that "our employer" is faithful to pay us the reward of our labor.

Our beraita reminds us to be content with our current place in life. Instead of looking around us at what kings—celebrities, friends, neighbors—have and enjoy, know that each one of us has exactly what we need right now from Hashem. At times this is hard to accept, but a person of faith should strive to see things this way. Thus, the emphasis on *"your* table" and *"your* crown." Our table may not be as glamorous as others', and our crown may not be that of kings and queens, but *for us,* this is what Hashem wants for us right now. If this is the case, this is greater because this is exactly what we need.

Nevertheless, this shouldn't lead to complacency. This is the third directive. Keep doing more than your current status requires of you—in order that you advance and progress. Instead of competition or comparison to others being the impetus to growth, let your intentions be for Hashem, for your "employer." Through this, you will faithfully be rewarded for all of your actions and advance to higher levels.

Our beraita provides a path toward both internal and external happiness. We must find contentment with our current lot but always strive to improve and grow—for the right reasons. When we live this way, we release ourselves from much worry, stress, and sadness and in the end enjoy "the reward of our labor."

6:6

The Truth Will Set You Free

גְּדוֹלָה תוֹרָה יוֹתֵר מִן הַכְּהֻנָּה וּמִן הַמַּלְכוּת. שֶׁהַמַּלְכוּת נִקְנֵית בִּשְׁלֹשִׁים מַעֲלוֹת, וְהַכְּהֻנָּה בְּעֶשְׂרִים וְאַרְבַּע, וְהַתּוֹרָה נִקְנֵית בְּאַרְבָּעִים וּשְׁמֹנָה דְבָרִים. וְאֵלּוּ הֵן: בְּתַלְמוּד, בִּשְׁמִיעַת הָאֹזֶן, בַּעֲרִיכַת שְׂפָתַיִם, בְּבִינַת הַלֵּב, בְּשִׂכְלוּת הַלֵּב, בְּאֵימָה, בְּיִרְאָה, בַּעֲנָוָה, בְּשִׂמְחָה, בְּטָהֳרָה, בְּשִׁמּוּשׁ חֲכָמִים, בְּדִקְדּוּק חֲבֵרִים, וּבְפִלְפּוּל הַתַּלְמִידִים, בְּיִשּׁוּב, בַּמִּקְרָא, בַּמִּשְׁנָה, בְּמִעוּט סְחוֹרָה, בְּמִעוּט דֶּרֶךְ אֶרֶץ, בְּמִעוּט תַּעֲנוּג, בְּמִעוּט שֵׁינָה, בְּמִעוּט שִׂיחָה, בְּמִעוּט שְׂחוֹק, בְּאֶרֶךְ אַפַּיִם, בְּלֵב טוֹב, בֶּאֱמוּנַת חֲכָמִים, וּבְקַבָּלַת הַיִּסּוּרִין, הַמַּכִּיר אֶת מְקוֹמוֹ, וְהַשָּׂמֵחַ בְּחֶלְקוֹ, וְהָעוֹשֶׂה סְיָג לִדְבָרָיו, וְאֵינוֹ מַחֲזִיק טוֹבָה לְעַצְמוֹ, אָהוּב, אוֹהֵב אֶת הַמָּקוֹם, אוֹהֵב אֶת הַבְּרִיּוֹת, אוֹהֵב אֶת הַצְּדָקוֹת, אוֹהֵב אֶת הַמֵּישָׁרִים, אוֹהֵב אֶת הַתּוֹכָחוֹת, מִתְרַחֵק מִן הַכָּבוֹד, וְלֹא מֵגִיס לִבּוֹ בְּתַלְמוּדוֹ, וְאֵינוֹ שָׂמֵחַ בְּהוֹרָאָה, נוֹשֵׂא בְעֹל עִם חֲבֵרוֹ, מַכְרִיעוֹ לְכַף זְכוּת, מַעֲמִידוֹ עַל הָאֱמֶת, וּמַעֲמִידוֹ עַל הַשָּׁלוֹם, מִתְיַשֵּׁב לִבּוֹ בְּתַלְמוּדוֹ, שׁוֹאֵל וּמֵשִׁיב, שׁוֹמֵעַ וּמוֹסִיף, הַלוֹמֵד עַל מְנָת לְלַמֵּד וְהַלוֹמֵד עַל מְנָת לַעֲשׂוֹת, הַמַּחְכִּים אֶת רַבּוֹ, וְהַמְכַוֵּן אֶת שְׁמוּעָתוֹ, וְהָאוֹמֵר דָּבָר בְּשֵׁם אוֹמְרוֹ. הָא לָמַדְתָּ, שֶׁכָּל הָאוֹמֵר דָּבָר בְּשֵׁם אוֹמְרוֹ מֵבִיא גְאֻלָּה לָעוֹלָם, שֶׁנֶּאֱמַר (אסתר ב): וַתֹּאמֶר אֶסְתֵּר לַמֶּלֶךְ בְּשֵׁם מָרְדֳּכָי.

Greater is learning Torah than the priesthood and greater than royalty, for royalty is acquired by thirty stages, and the priesthood by twenty-four, but the Torah by forty-eight things. By study, attentive listening, proper speech, by an understanding heart, by an intelligent heart, by awe, by fear, by humility, by joy, by attending to the Sages, by critical give and take with friends, by fine argumentation with disciples, by clear thinking, by study of scripture, by study of mishna, by a minimum of sleep, by a minimum of chatter, by a minimum of pleasure, by a minimum of frivolity, by a minimum of preoccupation with worldly matters, by long-suffering, by generosity, by faith in the Sages, by acceptance of suffering. Learning of Torah is also acquired by one who recognizes their place, who rejoices in their portion, who makes a fence about their words, who takes no credit for themself, who is loved, who loves God, who loves their fellow creatures, who loves righteous ways, who loves reproof, who loves uprightness, who keeps themselves far from honors, who does not let their heart become swelled on account of their learning, who does not delight in giving legal decisions, who shares in the bearing of a burden with their colleague, who judges with the scales weighted in their favor, who leads them on to truth, who leads them on to peace, who composes themselves at their study, who asks and answers, who listens [to others], and adds [to their knowledge], who learns in order to teach, who learns in order to practice, who makes their teacher wiser, who is exact in what they have learned, and who says a thing in the name of one who said it. Thus, you have learned that all those who say a thing in the name of one who said it, bring redemption into the world, as it is said: "And Esther told the king in Mordechai's name" (Esther 2:22).

Each one of these forty-eight traits are worthy of their own commentary. Nevertheless, I'd like to focus on the final trait: "Saying a thing in the name of one who said it." In relation to this we are taught: "All those who say a thing in the name of one who said it, bring redemption into the world." How does this bring redemption to the world, and how does this contribute to one's acquisition of the Torah?

Omitting the sources of one's Torah ideas has a negative impact on one's soul. "Passing off" others' ideas as one's own is deceitful; it is plagiarism. The path to freeing, "redeeming," oneself from this, is to be honest and name the source when one is borrowing from another.

The Sages teach us that "ניכרין דברי אמת—words of truth can be recognized" (Talmud Bavli, Sotah 9b). It's hard to put one's finger on it, but there are times when one is around another and one can just discern, from their energy, that they are being dishonest. It's a certain stuck, nervous energy, almost like they are tightly holding on to a falsehood, working extra hard to conceal the truth. Letting go of these behaviors can be extremely liberating.

This is the idea that being true and transparent when it comes to our sourcing brings redemption to the world. This free-flowing energy makes our inner world more relaxed and fuller of life and allows those around us to be more comfortable as well. To be sure, this holds true for all forms of covering up and deception. It is from this honest place that Torah can be acquired. When one's energy is open and not "stuck" due to lies and deceit, it opens channels for real reception of Torah into one's life.

6:7

Creating Connection through Jewish Education

גְּדוֹלָה תוֹרָה שֶׁהִיא נוֹתֶנֶת חַיִּים לְעֹשֶׂיהָ בָּעוֹלָם הַזֶּה וּבָעוֹלָם הַבָּא, שֶׁנֶּאֱמַר (משלי ד): כִּי חַיִּים הֵם לְמֹצְאֵיהֶם וּלְכָל בְּשָׂרוֹ מַרְפֵּא. וְאוֹמֵר (שם ג): רִפְאוּת תְּהִי לְשָׁרֶךָ וְשִׁקּוּי לְעַצְמוֹתֶיךָ. וְאוֹמֵר (שם ג): עֵץ חַיִּים הִיא לַמַּחֲזִיקִים בָּהּ וְתֹמְכֶיהָ מְאֻשָּׁר. וְאוֹמֵר (שם א): כִּי לְוְיַת חֵן הֵם לְרֹאשֶׁךָ וַעֲנָקִים לְגַרְגְּרֹתֶיךָ. וְאוֹמֵר (שם ד): תִּתֵּן לְרֹאשְׁךָ לְוְיַת חֵן עֲטֶרֶת תִּפְאֶרֶת תְּמַגְּנֶךָּ. וְאוֹמֵר (שם ט): כִּי בִי יִרְבּוּ יָמֶיךָ וְיוֹסִיפוּ לְךָ שְׁנוֹת חַיִּים. וְאוֹמֵר (שם ג): אֹרֶךְ יָמִים בִּימִינָהּ בִּשְׂמֹאולָהּ עֹשֶׁר וְכָבוֹד. וְאוֹמֵר (שם): כִּי אֹרֶךְ יָמִים וּשְׁנוֹת חַיִּים וְשָׁלוֹם יוֹסִיפוּ לָךְ. וְאוֹמֵר (שם): דְּרָכֶיהָ דַרְכֵי נֹעַם וְכָל נְתִיבוֹתֶיהָ שָׁלוֹם.

Great is Torah for it gives life to those that practice it, in this world, and in the world to come, as it is said: "For they are life unto those that find them, and health to all their flesh" (Prov. 4:22). And it says: "It will be a cure for your navel and marrow for your bones" (ibid., 3:8). And it says: "She is a tree of life to those that grasp her, and whoever upholds her is happy" (ibid., 3:18). And it says: "For they are a graceful wreath upon your head, a necklace about your throat" (ibid., 1:9). And it says: "She will adorn your head with a graceful wreath; crown you with a glorious diadem" (ibid., 4:9). And it says: "Indeed, through me your days shall be increased, and years of life shall be added to you" (ibid., 9:11). And it says: "In her right hand is length of days, in her left riches and honor" (ibid., 3:9). And it says: "For lengthy days and years of life, and peace shall they add to you" (ibid., 3:2). And it says: "For they will bestow on you length of days, years of life and peace" (ibid., 3:17).

Several years ago, I taught at a Hebrew school affiliated with the Reform movement. When I interviewed for the position, I was asked to share my educational philosophy. I reassured them that while I was a strictly Orthodox Jew, I was open to all levels of observance and to making space for others to connect to Yiddishkeit at their own level. They appreciated my direction and, thankfully, I got the job.

In the interview, I explained my outlook on the backdrop of one of the aforementioned verses: "She is a tree of life to those that grasp her, and whoever upholds her is happy." Indeed, most of my outreach as an Orthodox rabbi has revolved around this verse and, more specifically, around its first part: "She is a tree of life to those that grasp her."

Over my years in education, I have found my role to be less centered on "converting" others to my line of thinking and level of observance and more on presenting the full beauty of Torah to students in the hopes that they "grasp" onto the "tree of life." Of course, my hopes are that, due to my teachings, they would be drawn to uphold the Torah and all its laws and, as a result, find happiness in their lives, "ותומכיה מאושר" (the second part of the verse: "Whoever upholds her is happy"). And whenever my students express interest, I guide them on how best to perform the details of Jewish law and live an observant life. Notwithstanding, on the ground, most of my experiences, including as a Hebrew school teacher, have been geared toward creating avenues for others to grasp onto the Torah—each at their own level.

The Torah is a tree of life, and it is our obligation to assist others in grasping onto it. Some will grasp onto a leaf and others a branch while others may latch onto its trunk or even its roots. The tree imagery is powerful in that it reminds us how education can also be about connection, "life," even if it doesn't always lead to full observance. It's not all-or-nothing, and every bit of life is precious in itself. The spatial element of the tree imagery allows for these varied levels of connection.

With all of its verses on the life-giving Torah, our beraita teaches us that there is a lot of room for growth and development in the gap between nonobservance and full Torah observance. The order of the statements in the aforementioned verse reminds us that the more we connect those around us to this source of life, the more we help bridge this gap and bring about happy, fulfilled lives: "She is a tree of life to those that grasp her—and whoever upholds her is happy."

6:8

Physicality and Aesthetics as Adornments to the Torah

רַבִּי שִׁמְעוֹן בֶּן יְהוּדָה מִשּׁוּם רַבִּי שִׁמְעוֹן בֶּן יוֹחַאי אוֹמֵר: הַנּוֹי, וְהַכֹּחַ, וְהָעֹשֶׁר, וְהַכָּבוֹד,
וְהַחָכְמָה, וְהַזִּקְנָה, וְהַשֵּׂיבָה, וְהַבָּנִים נָאֶה לַצַּדִּיקִים וְנָאֶה לָעוֹלָם, שֶׁנֶּאֱמַר (שם טז):
עֲטֶרֶת תִּפְאֶרֶת שֵׂיבָה בְּדֶרֶךְ צְדָקָה תִּמָּצֵא. וְאוֹמֵר (שם כ): תִּפְאֶרֶת בַּחוּרִים כֹּחָם
וַהֲדַר זְקֵנִים שֵׂיבָה. וְאוֹמֵר (שם יד): עֲטֶרֶת חֲכָמִים עָשְׁרָם. וְאוֹמֵר (שם יז): עֲטֶרֶת
זְקֵנִים בְּנֵי בָנִים וְתִפְאֶרֶת בָּנִים אֲבוֹתָם. וְאוֹמֵר (ישעיה כד): וְחָפְרָה הַלְּבָנָה וּבוֹשָׁה
הַחַמָּה, כִּי מָלַךְ ה' צְבָאוֹת בְּהַר צִיּוֹן וּבִירוּשָׁלַיִם וְנֶגֶד זְקֵנָיו כָּבוֹד. רַבִּי שִׁמְעוֹן בֶּן
מְנַסְיָא אוֹמֵר: אֵלּוּ שֶׁבַע מִדּוֹת שֶׁמָּנוּ חֲכָמִים לַצַּדִּיקִים, כֻּלָּם נִתְקַיְּמוּ בְרַבִּי וּבְבָנָיו.

Rabbi Shimon ben Yehuda said in the name of Rabbi Shimon ben Yochai: Beauty, strength, riches, honor, wisdom, old age, gray hair, and children are becoming to the righteous, and becoming to the world. As it is said: "Gray hair is a crown of glory (beauty); it is attained by way of righteousness" (Prov. 16:31). And it says: "The ornament of the wise is their wealth" (ibid., 14:24). And it says: "The glory of youths is their strength; and the beauty of old men is their gray hair" (ibid., 20:29). And it says: "Grandchildren are the glory of their elders, and the glory of children is their parents" (ibid., 17:6). And it says: "Then the moon shall be ashamed, and the sun shall be abashed. For the Lord of Hosts will reign on Mount Zion and in Jerusalem, and God's Honor will be revealed to His elders" (Isa. 24:23). Rabbi Shimon ben Menasya said: These seven qualities, which the Sages have listed as becoming to the righteous, were all fulfilled in Rebbe and his sons.

In an earlier mishna (*Ethics of the Fathers* 4:1), four of the seven traits which appear in our mishna were cast in a "spiritualized" light. They were not seen as valuable within themselves but instead reinterpreted and only then promoted. "Wealthy" meant someone who is happy with their lot; "honorable," one who honors others; "wise," one who learns from others; and "strong," one who overcomes their evil inclination.

Our beraita, in contrast, finds value in each of these traits within themselves and adds on other descriptions as well. A similar teaching appears in *Talmud Bavli*, Shabbat 92a: "The Divine Presence only rests upon a person who is wise, mighty, wealthy, etc." Nowhere in this text are these traits qualified or explained in a spiritualized manner. They are understood as valuable within themselves and even imperative to achieving the Divine Presence. How does our beraita square away with the mishna in 4:1?

The verses brought in our beraita point to the correct answer. Most reference a crown, עטרה (*atarah*). A crown comes to mark one's current status, to reinforce or strengthen a reality that is already active and in place. Royalty is royalty with or without a crown or head covering. The latter comes to enforce this position and mark for all that this is the case.

Beauty, strength, riches, honor, and wisdom find importance when they come to embolden and beautify an already present status of holiness. Being physically fit helps one grow in Torah. Seeing beautiful sites and people can enhance one's spirituality, or as the Sages say, "A beautiful home, a beautiful spouse (lit., wife), and beautiful home decor expand one's consciousness" (*Talmud Bavli*, Berachot 57b). General knowledge can add to one's Torah. The teachings of Rabbi Lord Jonathan Sacks on the Torah portion highlight this. He interweaves secular knowledge throughout, and, at least in my opinion, it enhances his Torah lessons.

So it is for the other traits. For instance, our synagogue, Beth Tfiloh Congregation, houses one of the more beautiful sanctuaries I have seen. If we focus solely on its beauty, then we have missed the mark. The beauty and grandeur are "befitting" our holy congregation when they expand our consciousness and uplift our spirits—propelling us even higher in spirituality.

This is how we can reconcile the two teachings. To arrive at a spiritual state, one must apply the directives from the earlier mishna: respecting and learning from others, overcoming one's desires, and being happy with one's lot. Once this is in place, one can revisit and embrace these traits for what they are and use them to crown and adorn one's spirituality.

Is the Chabad Outreach
Model for Everyone?

אָמַר רַבִּי יוֹסֵי בֶּן קִסְמָא: פַּעַם אַחַת הָיִיתִי מְהַלֵּךְ בַּדֶּרֶךְ וּפָגַע בִּי אָדָם אֶחָד, וְנָתַן לִי שָׁלוֹם,
וְהֶחֱזַרְתִּי לוֹ שָׁלוֹם. אָמַר לִי: רַבִּי, מֵאֵיזֶה מָקוֹם אַתָּה? אָמַרְתִּי לוֹ: מֵעִיר גְּדוֹלָה שֶׁל חֲכָמִים
וְשֶׁל סוֹפְרִים אָנִי. אָמַר לִי: רַבִּי, רְצוֹנְךָ שֶׁתָּדוּר עִמָּנוּ בִמְקוֹמֵנוּ, וַאֲנִי אֶתֵּן לְךָ אֶלֶף אֲלָפִים
דִּינְרֵי זָהָב וַאֲבָנִים טוֹבוֹת וּמַרְגָּלִיּוֹת? אָמַרְתִּי לוֹ: בְּנִי, אִם אַתָּה נוֹתֵן לִי כָּל כֶּסֶף וְזָהָב וַאֲבָנִים
טוֹבוֹת וּמַרְגָּלִיּוֹת שֶׁבָּעוֹלָם, אֵינִי דָר אֶלָּא בִמְקוֹם תּוֹרָה. וְלֹא עוֹד, אֶלָּא שֶׁבִּשְׁעַת פְּטִירָתוֹ שֶׁל
אָדָם אֵין מְלַוִּין לוֹ לָאָדָם לֹא כֶסֶף וְלֹא זָהָב וְלֹא אֲבָנִים טוֹבוֹת וּמַרְגָּלִיּוֹת, אֶלָּא תוֹרָה וּמַעֲשִׂים
טוֹבִים בִּלְבַד, שֶׁנֶּאֱמַר (משלי ו): בְּהִתְהַלֶּכְךָ תַּנְחֶה אֹתָךְ, בְּשָׁכְבְּךָ תִּשְׁמֹר עָלֶיךָ, וַהֲקִיצוֹתָ
הִיא תְשִׂיחֶךָ. בְּהִתְהַלֶּכְךָ תַּנְחֶה אֹתָךְ, בָּעוֹלָם הַזֶּה. בְּשָׁכְבְּךָ תִּשְׁמֹר עָלֶיךָ, בַּקֶּבֶר. וַהֲקִיצוֹתָ
הִיא תְשִׂיחֶךָ, לָעוֹלָם הַבָּא. וְכֵן כָּתוּב בְּסֵפֶר תְּהִלִּים עַל יְדֵי דָוִד מֶלֶךְ יִשְׂרָאֵל (תהלים קיט):
טוֹב לִי תוֹרַת פִּיךָ מֵאַלְפֵי זָהָב וָכָסֶף. וְאוֹמֵר (חגי ב): לִי הַכֶּסֶף וְלִי הַזָּהָב אָמַר ה' צְבָאוֹת.

Rabbi Yosi ben Kisma said: Once I was walking along the way when a man met me and greeted me, and I greeted him. He said to me, "Rabbi, where are you from?" I said to him, "I am from a great city of Sages and scribes." He said to me, "Rabbi, would you consider living with us in our place? I would give you a thousand thousand denarii of gold, and precious stones and pearls." I said to him: "My son, even if you were to give me all the silver and gold, precious stones and pearls that are in the world, I would not dwell anywhere except in a place of Torah. For when a person passes away they are accompanied by neither gold nor silver, nor precious stones nor pearls, but Torah and good deeds alone, as it is said, 'When you walk it will lead you. When you lie down it will watch

over you; and when you are awake it will talk with you' (Prov. 6:22).
'When you walk it will lead you' in this world. 'When you lie down it
will watch over you' in the grave. 'And when you are awake it will talk
with you' in the world to come. And thus it is written in the book of
Psalms by David, King of Israel, 'I prefer the teaching You proclaimed
to thousands of pieces of gold and silver' (Ps. 119:72). And it says: 'Mine
is the silver, and mine the gold, says the Lord of Hosts' (Chaggai 2:8)."

Rabbi Ben Tzion Abba Shaul offers an interesting observation on
our beraita (*Ohr LeTzion, Zichron Hadassah: Chochmah U'mussar*, pp.
33–34). He tracks the sequence of events and asks: "How did Rabbi Yosi
ben Kisma end up in this predicament—being enticed to leave a center of Torah—in the first place?" He answers that it all began from his
casual stroll: "Once I was walking along the way." He explains that a
yeshiva student should focus solely on their studies. "Strolling" outside
of the yeshiva when one should really be learning exposes one to the
lures of the "outside world" that distance one from Torah. Yosi ben
Kisma was approached to leave Torah because he himself abandoned it
by going out on a stroll! These are all the insidious machinations of the
yetzer harah, the evil inclination.

I recall once listening to a class in which Rabbi Ovadia Yosef asked a
question on this beraita that seemed to contradict Rabbi Ben Tzion's (his
study partner of many years) direction. He asked, "Why not just move
to that area and make it a place of Torah yourself?!" This is more of a
Chabad model, where a Chabad family moves to a location and slowly
transforms it into a Jewish center. The views of these two towering Torah
leaders appear to contradict one another. However, they can also work in
tandem, and our beraita may be hinting at this path of reconciliation.

There is a time to distance oneself from spaces devoid of Torah
and a time for integration. When I first became more observant, I went
through a phase where I didn't leave the yeshiva's four walls (aside from
a few exercise runs around the neighborhood) for several months. At the
time, I was learning at Yeshivat Mercaz Harav and wanted to soak in
all the holiness without being distracted by the outside world. I experienced and categorized all external stimuli as unwanted diversions from
this mission. Eventually, I emerged from this introverted stage, but to be
sure, this was a formative time for me. I thank Hashem for the opportunity to currently be able to influence others and help make my congre-

gation a place of Torah; however, if it wasn't for me staying focused, not "strolling around," during my impressionable yeshiva years, there is no way I would have the strong foundations today for the communal work in which I am involved.

Our beraita offers direction specifically for this first, centripetal stage of one's development. This is hinted at in the opening language: "Once I was walking along the way." The dangers of the outside world are linked in particular to a reality of leaving a place of Torah in order to "walk along the way." This departure is not for the sake of elevating others and transforming a location to a place of Torah. When it comes to the latter agenda, our beraita may agree that one should go out and effect change. One with strong foundations will be shielded from the negative influences encountered during this form of outreach. However, for the one who is not spiritually ready, whose departures from the Torah centers are simply "to walk along the way," it is by far preferable for them to continue learning. This will equip them later, if needed, to follow Rabbi Ovadia Yosef's direction and transform communities into places of Torah.

Was Everything Created
for the Sake of Israel?

חֲמִשָּׁה קִנְיָנִים קָנָה לוֹ הַקָּדוֹשׁ בָּרוּךְ הוּא בְּעוֹלָמוֹ, וְאֵלּוּ הֵן: תּוֹרָה קִנְיָן אֶחָד, שָׁמַיִם וָאָרֶץ
קִנְיָן אֶחָד, אַבְרָהָם קִנְיָן אֶחָד, יִשְׂרָאֵל קִנְיָן אֶחָד, בֵּית הַמִּקְדָּשׁ קִנְיָן אֶחָד. תּוֹרָה מִנַּיִן?
דִּכְתִיב (משלי ח): ה' קָנָנִי רֵאשִׁית דַּרְכּוֹ קֶדֶם מִפְעָלָיו מֵאָז. שָׁמַיִם וָאָרֶץ קִנְיָן אֶחָד מִנַּיִן?
דִּכְתִיב (ישעיה סו): כֹּה אָמַר ה' הַשָּׁמַיִם כִּסְאִי וְהָאָרֶץ הֲדֹם רַגְלָי אֵי זֶה בַיִת אֲשֶׁר תִּבְנוּ
לִי וְאֵי זֶה מָקוֹם מְנוּחָתִי. וְאוֹמֵר (תהלים קד): מָה רַבּוּ מַעֲשֶׂיךָ ה' כֻּלָּם בְּחָכְמָה עָשִׂיתָ
מָלְאָה הָאָרֶץ קִנְיָנֶךָ. אַבְרָהָם קִנְיָן אֶחָד מִנַּיִן? דִּכְתִיב (בראשית יד): וַיְבָרְכֵהוּ וַיֹּאמַר בָּרוּךְ
אַבְרָם לְאֵל עֶלְיוֹן קֹנֵה שָׁמַיִם וָאָרֶץ. יִשְׂרָאֵל קִנְיָן אֶחָד מִנַּיִן? דִּכְתִיב (שמות טו): עַד יַעֲבֹר
עַמְּךָ ה' עַד יַעֲבֹר עַם זוּ קָנִיתָ. וְאוֹמֵר (תהלים טז): לִקְדוֹשִׁים אֲשֶׁר בָּאָרֶץ הֵמָּה וְאַדִּירֵי
כָּל חֶפְצִי בָם. בֵּית הַמִּקְדָּשׁ קִנְיָן אֶחָד מִנַּיִן? דִּכְתִיב (שמות טו): מָכוֹן לְשִׁבְתְּךָ פָּעַלְתָּ ה'
מִקְדָּשׁ ה' כּוֹנְנוּ יָדֶיךָ. וְאוֹמֵר (תהלים עח): וַיְבִיאֵם אֶל גְּבוּל קָדְשׁוֹ הַר זֶה קָנְתָה יְמִינוֹ.

Five acquisitions did the Holy One, blessed be He, set aside as His own in this world, and these are they: the Torah, one acquisition; heaven and earth, another acquisition; Avraham, another acquisition; Israel, another acquisition; the Temple, another acquisition. The Torah is one acquisition. From where do we know this? Since it is written, "The Lord possessed me at the beginning of his course, at the first of His works of old" (Prov. 8:22). Heaven and earth, another acquisition. From where do we know this? Since it is said: "Thus said the Lord: The heaven is My throne and the earth is My footstool. Where could you build a house for Me, What place could serve as My abode?" (Isa. 66:1). And it says: "How many are the things You have made, O Lord, You have made them all with wisdom; the earth is full of Your acquisitions" (Ps. 104:24). Avraham is another acquisition. From where do we know this? Since it is written: "He blessed him, saying, 'Blessed by Avram of God Most High, Possessor of heaven and earth'" (Gen. 14:19). Israel is another acquisition. From where do we know this? Since it is written: "Till Your people cross over, O Lord, Till Your people whom You have possessed" (Exod. 15:16). And it says: "As to the holy and mighty ones that are in the land, my whole desire (acquisition) is in them" (Ps. 16:3). The Temple is another acquisition. From where do we know this? Since it is said: "The sanctuary, O Lord, which Your hands have established" (Exod. 15:17). And it says: "And He brought them to His holy realm, to the mountain, which His right hand had possessed" (Ps. 78:54).

Our beraita runs through five stages of history. It begins prior to creation as it lists the Torah, which was created prior to the world (*Zohar* 1:133b). It then moves onto the creation of "heaven and earth." From there, it shifts to the individual, Avraham; and then to Am Yisrael; and, finally, the Temple. These all appear in successive order and highlight key moments, culminating in the future Temple in Jerusalem.

Our beraita teaches how these momentous events are God's acquisitions. What does this mean, and how does this impact our lives? Our beraita may be alluding to a minority view in our tradition that elements in our world were created for their own divine purpose and not strictly for the sake of Israel.

The latter view, that all was created for Israel, was adopted by Rabbi Saadia Gaon and many others. It is the predominant view in our tradition. Nevertheless, our beraita shares that, in some respects, elements of creation are Hashem's own personal "acquisitions." Hashem has reasons for "acquiring" or sustaining these entities beyond the scope of Israel's mission in the world. This is how the Rambam puts it in relation to the universe: "The universe does not exist for humans' sake, but that each being exists for its own sake, and not because of some other thing" (*Guide for The Perplexed* 3:13).

What does this mean for us? This means that the world and what is in it is Hashem's and not ours. We must show honor to each and every thing, not only because it serves us but because Hashem willed it into existence and continues to care for it and upkeep it, like one would do with one's own prized acquisitions (one's home, car, etc.).

There are practical ramifications to this outlook. We must ensure our environment remains clean and healthy and do our part to upkeep it for the next generation. Additionally, we must care for the animals—which are included in the "heaven and earth" acquisition—because they, too, have their own purpose. In the words of Rabbi Samson Raphael Hirsch (from his commentary on Gen. 1:26): "This is the position humans are to have toward all other living creatures on earth. They have not been given the mission to make them all, and indeed not entirely, subservient to them. The earth and its creatures may have other relationships, of which we are ignorant, in which they serve their own purpose."

An approach like this shifts the attention outward. It teaches that we must honor and respect the universe and what is in it, not only for the sake of Am Yisrael but because Hashem has "acquired" it—showing us how important and truly valuable it is.

Ethics of the Soul

כָּל מַה שֶּׁבָּרָא הַקָּדוֹשׁ בָּרוּךְ הוּא בְּעוֹלָמוֹ, לֹא בְרָאוֹ אֶלָּא לִכְבוֹדוֹ, שֶׁנֶּאֱמַר (ישעיה מג): כֹּל הַנִּקְרָא בִשְׁמִי וְלִכְבוֹדִי בְּרָאתִיו יְצַרְתִּיו אַף עֲשִׂיתִיו. וְאוֹמֵר (שמות טו): ה' יִמְלֹךְ לְעֹלָם וָעֶד. רַבִּי חֲנַנְיָא בֶּן עֲקַשְׁיָא אוֹמֵר: רָצָה הַקָּדוֹשׁ בָּרוּךְ הוּא לְזַכּוֹת אֶת יִשְׂרָאֵל, לְפִיכָךְ הִרְבָּה לָהֶם תּוֹרָה וּמִצְוֹת, שֶׁנֶּאֱמַר (ישעיה מב): ה' חָפֵץ לְמַעַן צִדְקוֹ יַגְדִּיל תּוֹרָה וְיַאְדִּיר.

Whatever the Holy One, blessed be He, created in His world, He created only for His glory, as it is said: "All who are linked to My name, whom I have created, formed and made for My glory" (Isa. 43:7). And it says: "God will reign forever" (Exod. 15:18).

Rabbi Chananiah ben Akashiah said: The Holy One, blessed be He, wished to confer merit upon Israel; therefore, He gave them Torah and mitzvot in abundance, as it is said: "God desired, for the sake of [Israel's] righteousness, that the Torah be made great and glorious" (Isa. 42:21).

Our beraita brings two verses, one dealing with God's glory (Isa. 43:7) and the other with God's reign—"forever" (Exod. 15:18). What is the connection between these two aspects of God's providence? And what does the beraita refer to in discussing God's glory?

There was a seminar course I attended at Bar-Ilan University that left a mark on me. It was on Benedict Spinoza's *Ethics*. I remember being amazed as I methodically worked through his "mathematical" proofs and arguments at how serious he was about God. For him, everything was God! It almost sounded chassidic!

As the course progressed, I realized where he got it wrong. He was discussing the *essence* of God while traditional texts deal with how God is *revealed* to us in this world. Judaism teaches, unlike Spinoza's approach, that we can never really "know" God. However, we connect to and experience God's revelation to us, "His glory," also referred to as Hashem's garments, לבושים. There are many such garments through which we forge this connection: mitzvot, ethics, Torah learning, and more.

Notwithstanding, we do not believe that Hashem has altogether withdrawn from humanity, leaving us solely with garments! Hashem is running everything, and when we connect to these garments, we are indeed connecting to Hashem—the One "within" the garments. This is what appears at the conclusion of our beraita: "God (YHVH) will reign forever." YHVH, Hashem's ineffable name, is behind all the garments and connected to them!

This is a fitting way to conclude *Ethics of the Fathers*. What makes Jewish ethics so special is that through them, we not only become better people, but we are actively involved in God's glory. In other words, through these ethical measures, we slowly draw ourselves closer to Hashem and to the day that "God will reign forever." Being a good person is not only the right thing to do but also a way to infuse our lives with glory and draw our souls ever so closer to Hashem.

Made in the USA
Middletown, DE
05 February 2022

60578668R00156